NEW TRENDS IN INDO-RUSSIAN RELATIONS

NEW TRENDS IN INDO-RUSSIAN RELATIONS

Edited by
V.D. CHOPRA

KALPAZ PUBLICATIONS

Delhi-110052

On Behalf of
INTERNATIONAL INSTITUTE FOR ASIA-PACIFIC STUDIES
NEW DELHI

New Trends in Indo-Russian Relations
(International Relation)

Rs. 750

ISBN: 81-7835-249-4

Published in 2003 in India by
Kalpaz Publications,
C-30, Satyawati Nagar, Delhi-110052
E-mail : Kalpaz@hotmail.com

Laser Typesetting at : SKC Handle & Care, Delhi
Printed at : Mehra Offeset Press, Delhi

Contents

K. R. Narayanan
Former President of India

सत्यमेव जयते

October 21, 2002

Dear Shri Chopra,

Thank you for your letter of October 14, 2002 inviting me to deliver a keynote address at a Seminar on "New Trends in Indo-Russian Relations — a Futuristic Studies" to be held in December, 2002.

I should have liked to accept your kind invitation but regret my inability to do so due to prior-commitments. I wish the Seminar every success.

With regards.

Yours sincerely

(K.R. Narayanan)

Mr. V.D. Chopra
Vice Chairman
International Institute for Asia-Pacific Studies
K-22, Sainik Farm
NEW DELHI-110062

34, Prithvi Raj Road, New Delhi-110 011, India
Fax: 00-91-11-3016926, Email : Krnarayanan9@hotmail.com

सत्यमेव जयते

विदेश मंत्री

भारत

MINISTER OF EXTERNAL AFFAIRS

INDIA

MESSAGE

November 26, 2002

I am glad that the International Institute for Asia-Pacific Studies is organizing a two-day national seminar on "New Trends in Indo-Russian Relations - A futuristic Study".

Indo-Russian relations are time-tested. These have traditionally been based on continuity, trust and mutual understanding between the peoples and Governments of the two countries. The importance attached to them cuts across party lines in India and is not subject to political vicissitudes. There is a national consensus on the need for a strong and stable relationship with the Russian Federation. A similar consensus exists in Russia on close and friendly ties with India.

The disintegration of the USSR and the emergence of Russia as an independent State has not affected the continuity of Indo-Russian relations. The two countries have preserved the ties established during the Soviet days and at the same time have started cooperation in new areas and issues which have come up since the end of Cold War. India's relations with the Russian Federation are thus multi-faceted and encompass different sectors including political consultations, economic and commercial relations and cooperation in trade and economy, science and technology, culture, education, space science and research, peaceful uses of nuclear energy, defence, energy security, etc.

During the visit of President Putin to India in October 2000, the two countries signed a Declaration on Strategic Partnership. This established a framework of cooperation between the two countries in the new millennium. The two countries have summit level meeting every year. This year President Putin is scheduled to visit India in December. The two sides are preparing a number of documents for signature during the visit. Given the depth and expanse of cooperation, India's relation with the Russian Federation is one of our most important bilateral relationships.

I hope the national seminar will not only discuss the existing relations between India and Russia but also the prospective areas of bilateral cooperation.

I appreciate the endeavours of the International Institute for Asia-Pacific Studies in organizing the seminar and wish that it will be a grand success.

(Yashwant Sinha)

सत्यमेव जयते

D.O. 2041/ LOP/LS/OFFICE/2002

नेता प्रतिपक्ष, लोक सभा

के

सहायक निजी सचिव

Assistant Private Secretary

to

Leader of Opposition, Lok Sabha

November 7, 2002

Dear Shri Chopra,

I have been directed to acknowledge the receipt of your letter dated October 14, 2002 (No. 236/VC/02) addressed to Smt Sonia Gandhi, MP and Leader of Opposition in Lok Sabha, wherein you have invited her to address the 2 day national seminar on "New Trends in Indo-Russian Relations" being organised by your Institute in early December 2002.

Smt Gandhi thanks you for the kind invitation. She has also conveyed her appreciation for the endeavours of the International Institute for Asia-Pacific Studies for organising such seminars. She has, however, conveyed her sincere regrets for her inability to accede to it due to the Winter Session of Parliament which will be on during that period and her other important commitments. Smt Gandhi hopes that you will understand her compulsions in this matter and sends her good wishes for the success of the Seminar.

With good wishes.

Your Sincerely

(Saurendra K Gupta)

Shri VD Chopra

Vice Chairman

International Institute for Asia-Pacific Studies

K-22, Sainik Farm

New Delhi-110062

44, संसद भवन नई दिल्ली–110001 फोन : 3016705, 3034285 फैक्स : 3017470

44, Parliament House, New Delhi-110001 Tel : 3016705, 3034285 Fax : 3017470

Preface

In this book entitled '*New Trends in Indo-Russian Relations*', an attempt has been made to objectively and critically examine Indo-Russian relations after the disintegration of the Soviet Union in the new historical conditions. The book is not merely a compilation of research based articles by over two dozens outstanding Indian scholars and experts, it is something more than that. The book has been conceptualized in totality to make an assessment of the various dimensions of Indo-Russian relations within the framework of India and Russia's relations with other countries and their impact on shaping Indo-Russian relations. In this sense in this book an effort has been made to study Indo-Russian relations in the fast changing international environment and its impact on these relations. Therefore, Indo-Russian relations should not be seen in isolation. They have been examined in this book as an integral part of the current and cross-current trends of international forces.

With this objective in mind scholars and academics who specialise in their respective areas of research were identified and motivated to write articles on the specific theme allotted to them. The purpose was that the book should emerge not merely a collection of various article but should have organic inter-connection with the main theme of the book. It must be admitted that the various scholars profusely cooperated in this intellectual exercise, though this was a time consuming process. It may also be mention here that to set the tone and direction of this work, the International Institute for Asia-Pacific Studies organised a seminar on this theme in the end of 2002 with a view to have a free and frank discussion. It was in this seminar that the various scholars made their presentations, which were later transformed into well research articles in the light of the discussions. Therefore, it will not be in correct to say that all these articles reflect the collective mind of the scholars, though each one of them has looked on this subject from different dimension.

It is relevant to mention here that India and Russia have reaffirmed a long-standing friendship through the adoption of the Delhi Declaration on Further Consolidation of strategic Partnership and the other protocols signed and decisions taken in the course of the visit by the Russian President, Vladimir Putin in the beginning of December 2002. With both countries struggling to define their relations with other major players on the global stage-in a situation where the rules of international politics are in a state of flux and where the terms of the economic interaction between nations are being reset this summit between the Indian and Russian leaderships was of significance for the affirmation of continuity and mutual reassurance that it sybolised. What has added substance to it is the reinforcement of the faith that there is a real convergence of perspectives on issues as wide-ranging as the phenomenon of terrorism, ensuring the security of nuclear weapon stockpiles in a world facing a new assortment of threats and challenges, the conservation and promotion of multipolarity in global politics. Besides this it underlined the need for both the countries to make adjustments in the course of globalisation, and on issues specific to South, Central and West Asia. Russia's belief that India can and should make a substantial contribution to the evolution of a strong global consensus on these issues was revealed in its open support of the Indian campaign for a permanent seat in the United Nations Security Council.

Both Russia and India are victims of violence fuelled by fundamentalist ideology and it is natural that the two countries should strengthen their cooperation on the issue for mutual benefit. The terrorist movements in various countries are not localised problems, but feed each other through ideological and material support flowing across international borders. Russia and India have emphasized that the open societies of their countries "have been vulnerable to the threats posed by globalisation of terror, including new manifestations of linkage between terrorism and weapons of mass destruction.

There is yet another aspect of this study. It examines regional important of Indo-Russian relations. These relations from the long-term point of view will influence the developments in this entire region. If Indo-Russian relations have a special significance in the Asia-Pacific region, the emerging triangular cooperation between India and Russia, Russia and China and India and China is of far reaching importance. Above all, there is commonality of interests between India and Russia in the Central Asia. These three components of Indo-Russian relations, if they continue to develop and deepen, they will mould the course of events in this entire region. The study brings into focus the international and regional significance of Indo-Russian relations.

Finally, in the arena of bilateral relations between India and Russia, strategic cooperation between the two countries growing defence cooperation and their naval cooperation in Indian Ocean region should not be under estimated in the larger national interests of the two countries for peace and security. However, this study shows that in the sphere of economic cooperation, there is a big lag. The two countries are making an affort to address the deficiency in bilateral trade which stands in such marked contrast to the very wholesome relationship they share in almost every other sphere.

In the end, it is pertinent to mention here that scholars and academics from Jawaharlal Nehru University, Institute for Defence Studies and Analyses, Jamia Millia Islamia University, Mumbai University, Strategic Experts including retired Army Officers and Political Leaders have made rich contributions in this book. I profusely express my gratitude to them in making it possible to bring out this book which is first of its kind in the Post Soviet era but for their cooperation it would not have been possible to under take this comprehensive study. I hope this book will serve as a source of information to the scholars,, academics, researcher and policy makers. I must also compliment the senior members of the staff of the Kalpaz Publications, Delhi for their cooperation.

11 June, 2003 **V.D. Chopra**

List of Contributors

1. Mr. K.R. Narayanan	:	Former President of India.
2. Mr. Yashwant Sinha	:	Minister of External Affairs of India.
3. Mrs. Sonia Gandhi	:	Leader of Opposition in the Lok Sabha and President of Indian National Congress.
4, Prof. V.P. Dutt	:	Former Pro-Vice Chancellor of Delhi University and Former Member of Rajya Sabha.
5. Mr. R.L. Bhatia	:	Former Minister of State for External Affairs and Member of Lok Sabha.
6. Prof. B.K. Srivastava	:	Former Professor, Centre for American studies, Jawaharlal Nehru University, New Delhi and an Outstanding Expert on the United States.
7. Dr. Rakesh Gupta	:	Professor, Centre for Political Studies, School of Social Science, Jawaharlal Nehru University, New Delhi.
8. Admiral K.K. Nayyar	:	Strategic Expert.
9. Maj. Gen. (Retd.) Afsir Karim	:	Security Expert and Editor, *Aakrosh,* Journal on Terrorism.
10. Prof.Devendra Kaushhik	:	Chairman, Maulana Abul Kalam Azad Institute of Asian Studies, Kolkata, Emeritus Professor (UGC), School of International Studies, Jawaharlal Nehru University, New Delhi.
11. Dr. Anuradha Chenoy	:	Associate Professor, Centre for South European Studies, School of International Studies, Jawaharlal Nehru University, New Delhi.
12. V.D. Chopra	:	Former Head of Economics Department in D.A.V. College,

		Rawalpindi, Former Chief Editor, *Patriot* Daily and *Link* Weekly, Vice-President for International Institute for Asia-Pacific Studies, New Delhi and a well-known author.
13. Dr. P.L. Dash	:	Professor, Centre for Central Eurasian Studies, University of Mumbai.
14. Dr. R.R. Subramaniam	:	Senior Research Associate, Institute for Defence Studies and Analyses.
15. Dr. G.M. Shah	:	Lecturer, Academy of Third World Studies, Jamia Millia Islamia, New Delhi.
16. Prof. Nirmala Joshi	:	Director, Russian and Central Asian Area Studies Programme Centre for Russian, Central Asian and East European Studies, School of International Studies, Jawaharlal Nehru University, New Delhi.
17. Brig. Chandra B. Khanduri	:	AVSM, Senior Fellow ICHR, ABI and USI.
18. Dr. Meena Singh Roy	:	Research Officer, Institute for Defence Studies and Analyses, New Delhi and an Expert on Central Asia.
19. (Late) Prof. R.L. Varshney	:	Former Director, Indian Institute of Foreign Trade and an expert on International Economic Relations.
20. Dr. R.K. Wadhwa	:	Asst. Professor, Indian Institute of Foreign Trade.
21. Prof. Shri Prakash	:	Professor, Academy of Third World Studies, Jamia Millia Islamia, New Delhi.
22. Prof. Girish Mishra	:	Leading Economist.
23. Mr. Manohar Singh Batra	:	Deputy Director General (Retd.), All India Radio.

1

Putin's Russia and India : Overview

V. P. Dutt

Between Vladimir Putin's first visit to India as President of Russian Federation in October 2000 and his second visit in December 2002, the framework for India-Russia relations was firmly set. This was a framework of another special relationship of "strategic partnership", expanding cooperation, and multiplying contacts in various fields, some of them of critical importance to India. What was different and special this time to this special relationship was that it was not born out of any cold war considerations, nor was it either seemingly or even indirectly directed against any other country. It did not exclude the establishment of other special relationships provided they were not inimical to either of them. It reflected the changed and changing international situation and their mutual needs and requirements. It was also intended to provide greater balance and stability to the Asia-Pacific region. Above all it reflected the fact that not only were there no national irritants but that there was an obvious long-term complementarily of interests between the two countries.

Despite the cautionary warning of many knowledgeable analysts that Russia should not be taken for granted (of course no country should be taken for granted), Mr. Putin put his special stamp on the India-Russia "strategic partnership" even before his second visit. The Russian President had set the tone with his pointed questions to the US President during the latter's Russian trip in late November (2002) just before his visit to India. In his meeting with George W. Bush at St. Petersburg on 22 November, Putin sharply raised questions about USA's anti-terror allies, Pakistan and Saudi Arabia. "We should not forget about those who finance terrorism", he said. Turning to Pakistan, the Russian President queried the US President, "Now where has Osama bin Laden taken refuge? They say he is somewhere between Afghanistan and Pakistan". While he supported General

Musharraf, he asked, "what can happen with armies armed with weapons that exists in Pakistan, including weapons of mass destruction? We should not forget about this". Privately, Mr. Putin is reported to have referred to the Pakistani military leadership as "a junta with nukes".[1] It was not that Putin was anti-Pakistan. He was not, and there was no need for him to be so. But he showed greater awareness of the threat from extremist forces within Pakistan and Afghanistan to both India and Russia. He was bluntly critical of any form of terrorism and recognised that their resources and finances were generally the same. Russia had unequivocally condemned all terrorist attacks against India and had consistently advised Pakistan to dismantle all terrorist camps within its territory, the latest statement in this regard coming after the terrorists' onslaught on Raghunath temple in Jammu.[2]

On the eve of the Putin visit in December last year, the Russian Foreign Minister, Igor Ivanov emphasized that Russia "shares the view that Pakistan must honour its obligations to dismantle the terrorists' infrastructure on the territory under its control". Russia, he said, also faced the threat of cross-border terrorism from Chechen terrorists based in Pankiisi George in neighbouring Georgia. And therefore, he expressed "understanding for India's concerns over the infiltration of groups of militants cross the line of control in Jammu and Kashmir".[3] With this common perception of security challenges to India and Russia, the relations between two countries would necessarily be close.

Before considering the various dimensions of this relationship during Putin's recent visit and relate them to his first visit, it is highly relevant to consider something else that had happened in Russia during this time. It was a far more confident Putin who was now engaging USA, Europe, China, India and other countries. Under his stewardship Russia had recovered from the economic meltdown of 1998 and had stabilized itself. It was now on the crest of an economic revival. A Japanese analyst used the words "resurgent Russia" to describe the new situation.

A decade after the collapse of its empire, Russia appears ready for a comeback. President Vladimir Putin has revealed a deft touch at home and abroad, besting adversaries and winning new friends... In short, the foundation for a Russian resurgence is being laid... After the tumult of the Yeltsin era, Russia has stabilized under Mr. Putin. A relatively unknown quantity when he took office, the Russian President has proven to be a capable leader and politician. He has marginalized the domestic opposition, despite a number of incidents - including the Kursk submarine disaster and the Chechen hostage drama in a Moscow theater - that could have damaged his popularity. He has projected the image of a man of action and a man of the people, a marked contrast to the mostly sclerotic leaders of the Soviet era [and the ageing and sodden leadership of the Yeltsin era, he could have added].

Mr. Putin's domestic standing has been enhanced by his international stature. He has forged a special relationship with U.S. President George W. Bush and built strong ties with European leaders. During Mr. Putin's tenure, Russia has institutionalized a new relationship with the North Atlantic Treaty Organisation that turned the former enemies into partners. At the same time, Mr. Putin and Chinese President Jiang Zemin established the Shanghai Cooperation Organisation, which consolidates Russian influence in Central Asia and tightens cooperation between the two countries. Mr. Putin has also made it clear that Russia will be a player in Northeast Asian diplomacy and that any eventual framework for the region will have to take Russian interests into account.[4]

This confidence and assuredness was also discernable in Putin's comments, statements and policy approaches during his second visit which subtly contrasted with the somewhat more cautious approach that he appeared to be adopting during his first visit to India as President. The difference was only of nuances, but nuances also matter in international relations. That the India-Russia relationship was more abiding than many observers had believed was apparent even during his first visit wherein on the eve of that visit he had declared that he was the best friend of India in the international community and within Russia too. A statement endorsed by Prime Minister Vajpayee on the eve of Mr. Putin's second visit, describing the Russian leader as a "trusted friend" and noting that "our personal relations help deepen mutual understanding between our two countries".[5] The one-day Putin-Vajpayee summit produced a strong statement on terrorism. The joint statement called upon Pakistan to fulfill its obligations by preventing "infiltration of terrorists across the Line of Control" and eliminating the infrastructure of terrorism as a "pre-requisite for the renewal of peaceful dialogue". It also supported the principle of bilateralism in resolving issues between India and Pakistan. It should, however, also be noted that the Russian President kept stressing the need for improving India-Pakistan relations and for doing everything possible to settle their differences in the context of the danger from weapons of mass destruction.[6]

Significantly, on Iraq the two sides expressed complete unanimity of views, opposing unilateral use of force and supporting a comprehensive settlement of the issues only through political and diplomatic efforts under the U.N. aegies.

India and Russia signed a slew of agreements including a declaration on economic, scientific and technological cooperation, a MoU on terrorism, a MoU on telecommunications and a MoU on protection of intellectual property rights, among others. India and Russia also agreed to expand military technical cooperation, identifying for the first time national security interests of both countries as a factor.[7]

However, to properly assess and appraise these agreements and the various developments in Indo-Russian relations it is necessary to go back and relate them to Mr. Putin's first visit in October 2000 and take account of events during this period. The four-day visit boosted political, security, defence and, to a much lesser extent, economic relations between the two countries. From the political relations' point of view, President Putin's speech to members of Parliament on 4 October outlined a framework whose contours got gradually filled up in the coming two years. Addressing a joint sitting of Parliament, Mr. Putin repeatedly stressed Russia's long-standing friendship with India. He did not consider Moscow's relations with other countries to be an alternative to India, "a long-term partner and ally". He called for urgent steps, both regional and international, to counter the global sweep of "terrorist international" that had already engulfed vast regions including the Philippines, Kashmir and Kosovo. He expressed the hope that the Kashmir problem would be solved on a bilateral basis through compromise, with unconditional respect for the Line of Control and without any foreign interference. He made it clear that he was well aware of what was behind the violence in Kashmir and noted that the failure to find a solution had been feeding tension between India and Pakistan for five decades even though the peoples of the two countries had much in common.

He was categorical that there was "verified information" that the same organisations - "even the same individuals" - were responsible for terrorist acts from the Philippines to Kosovo, Kashmir, Afghanistan and the northern Caucasus. He put his weight behind the Indian initiative for a collective front against terrorism.[8] The main thrust of Mr. Putin's address was the imperative of India and Russia becoming partners in a true sense.

This pattern of relationship was further buttressed in what was called the Delhi Declaration on strategic partnership for enhanced cooperation, taking into account both political and security concerns of the two countries. The Declaration spoke of "their adherence to the common ideals of peace, democracy, rule of law, human rights and fundamental freedoms, non-violence and secularism" and went on to recognise "their special responsibility by virtue of being among the largest multi-ethnic, multi-lingual and multi-religious States in strengthening international peace and security, the democratisation of international relations and in the promotion of the establishment of a new, just and stable world order, while reaffirming their commitment to the purposes and principles of the United Nations Charter.

The two sides proclaimed "the establishment of relations of strategic partnership between them" this envisages the elevation of their multifaceted ties to an even higher and qualitatively new level, while imparting them with a specially close and dynamic character, both in the bilateral field and in the international arena". They declared that their strategic partnership was based upon the principles of sovereignty, equality and territorial integrity of States, non-interference in their internal affairs, mutual respect and mutual benefit.

They also underlined their commitment to "systematic and progressive efforts to reduce nuclear weapons globally, with the ultimate goal of eliminating these weapons". They undertook to inform each other of any planned foreign Policy initiatives in the international arena and not to participate in any military-political or other alliances or associations or armed conflict directed against the other side or to conclude any treaties, agreements or understanding that infringe upon the independence, sovereignty, territorial integrity or national security interests of the other side.[9] (emphasis added)

The defence aspect clearly enunciated with the two sides signing a $300 billion deal for the supply of military hardware, which included the acquisition by India of 310 T-90 tanks, licensed production of 140 Sukhoi-30 MK1 fighters, and the lease of 4 Tu-22 backfire bombers. The Russia also offered aircraft carrier Admiral Groshkov as a gift which had been withdrawn from the Russian northern fleet in 1996 after a major fire but the refitting of the aircraft carrier was expected to cost India about $ 700-800 million (the price has been a source of major haggling between the two countries and has not been settled as yet). India and Russia also agreed to set up an intra-governmental commission on military and technical cooperation.[10]

In a joint statement issued at the end of the visit of the Russian President, the two sides made particular mention of religious and international terrorism radiating out of Afghanistan and its impact on regional stability. They called upon the international community to impose additional sanctions against the Taliban "'unless they cease support to international terrorism, drug trafficking and conform to international norms of human rights". They also called on "the Taliban and its external patrons, specially States extending direct military support to them to return to the path of peaceful negotiations". This was an obvious reference to Pakistan. Pointing to the Taliban's destabilizing role in Central Asia, the joint statement countermand the "terrorists' activities on the territory of Central Asian States". India extended support to the steps taken by Russia to protect its territorial integrity and the constitutional order in the rebellious Chechen Republic and Russia, in turn, backed Indian efforts to restore normalcy in Jammu and Kashmir."[11]

India and Russia set up a joint working group on Afghanistan. Their lines met on this issue, as on many other issues. Together they made it possible for the Northern Alliance to keep afloat and thereby a counterforce was available when the American attack on Afghanistan took place. Their joint resistance to the proposal mooted by General Musharraf and virtually endorsed by the United States prevented the sneaking in of Taliban elements in the interim government formed subsequently in Afghanistan.

As an aside we might take note of what one newspaper analyst described as adding new sparkle to Indo-Russian ties - the agreement between one of the world's largest diamond mining nations providing small, high-quality stones to the world's largest diamond cutter and processor, reducing the global monopoly of De Beers.[12]

It needs to be underlined that President Putin particularly changed one thing for India. As was pointed out by some other analyst too at the time, he breached the international nuclear blockade against India. With Russia signing a MoU for the cooperation in the use of nuclear energy for power, India's isolation had virtually ended. Putin went one step further and visited the Tarapore nuclear plant. The Russian President certainly did not change his standpoint on the issue of nuclear weapons and Putin still wanted Indian to sign the CTBT. He told the BARC scientists and engineers in Mumbai that Russia would like to see India participate in the CTBT. Yet he significantly added that he appreciated that this should be based on India's own strategic vision, national interests and needs of the people.[13]

No discussion of India-Russia relations is possible without taking into account the defence component of it. It is one of the most critical elements in the substance of their ties. Russia cannot be substituted in this area by any other country in the foreseeable future. This paper is not designed to discuss this dimension at any great length, but its central importance needs to be kept in focus, as well as the fact that this dimension was given a decisive push by the Russian President without which the present level of defence supplier and receiver relationship might not have been achieved. On 28 December 2000 India and Russia signed in Moscow the biggest ever defence deal for the production of 140 Sukhoi-30 MK1 multi-role jets in India by HAL over a span of 17 years under Russian licence. This nearly 3-billion dollar deal, the largest ever signed by Russia with any foreign country, provided for the full production of 150 next generation combat jets in India and with this deal India and Russia had taken defence cooperation far beyond a buyer-seller relationship, as it provided for joint production in India of the state-of-the-art aircraft. The Russians also expressed their willingness to jointly develop a fifth generation fighter with India for the Russian and Indian Air Forces, whenever the political leadership of the two countries decided.[14] It was not coincidental that Mr. Putin had taken the decision to slash the prices of T-90s and Sukhoi deals with India by 320 million and $700 million respectively, according to Russian sources.[15]

The increasingly close Indo-Russian defence ties was as evident from the testing of the Russian-made OSA AK surface to air missiles from the Chandipur on-sea test sight in May. According to a newspaper report a Russian Air Force IL-76 lumbered into the old terminal area of the Bhubaneswar on 11 May. Its "sensitive" cargo was the Russian OSA missile. A second Russian aircraft landed the next day off loading more sensitive cargo and Russian scientists. The mission was to conduct "joint experiments" in missile testing so as to utilize Russian experience and expertise to test a new missile and in modernizing the missile test range facilities. The access provided to the Russian scientists was reported to be on a reciprocal basis.[16]

Two other developments were also notable in this rapid process of expansion of ties. India had signed with Russia and Iran an agreement which the Cabinet approved on 16 January (2001), to create an international "North-South transport corridor", designed to provide a shorter route for trade through Iran to Russia and beyond and was expected to save time and cost by about twenty per cent, hopefully giving Indian exports a better competitive edge in those markets.[17]

Yet another agreement signed in February 2001 between India and Russia related to a massive Indian investment ranging between $1.5 - 2 billion over five years in the Sakhalin oil and gas fields, giving ONGC-Videsh Ltd. a twenty per cent stake in the Russian far eastern offshore oil project. This was the first time that India had entered the Russian oil production market.[18] It is again significant to note that the Russian President himself took the decision to award twenty per cent equity in the Sakhalin-1 offshore oil block to ONGC-Videsh Ltd. under the Production Sharing Arrangement (PSA).[19]

A couple of important difference of approach had surfaced on issues that could not be pushed under the carpet, but were not of a nature that would seriously impact on their close relationship. These divergencies initially arose because India abandoned its traditional approach and plumped for a standpoint that surprised the world (including many Indians) - on the issue of the proposed US National Missile Defence (NMD). No sooner had the US President declared his decision to opt for the development of a nuclear shield then New Delhi announced its welcome for it. The alacrity with which New Delhi had welcomed Mr. Bush's proposal surprised and delighted Washington, but disconcerted many people in India and abroad.

The US decision on NMD had irked both Russia and China and the two had stoutly opposed the proposal as it would not only violate the ABM Treaty (which the United States in any case wished to be abrogated) but could also change the balance of power in the world. At the same time it was obvious that if the Americans went ahead as they were determined to do, there was little that Russia and China could do to prevent it. Russia had to accept the inevitable because it lacked the power to dissuade Washington from pursuing this course of action. However, neither side wanted to invest this issue with any real importance in their mutual relations and so when the Russian foreign minister Igor Ivanov came calling to Delhi in May last year, the two sides decided to push this issue to the background. Russian flexibility on this issue was helped by the then Indian foreign minister, Jaswant Singh, declaring at a joint press conference that India would back the Russian position on the 1972 ABM Treaty which, New Delhi held, should not be abrogated unilaterally. New Delhi made public its position that its support for NMD was not at the cost of Russia. The Russian foreign minister also helped matters by not directly criticizing in India the latest plans by the United States to build missile defences. He said that Russia was looking forward to consultations with the US at the expert level.[20]

The escalating close ties were also apparent from the agreement on Russia's construction of a multi-billion dollar nuclear power plant in Tamil Nadu. The agreement on the Kundakularn nuclear power plant's construction brought the Russians back into India's nuclear power programme. The project had been agreed upon more than two decades ago but was abandoned following the collapse of the Soviet Union. It had now been resurrected and was estimated to cost anywhere between $1.5 - 2 billion. Russia undertook the supply, design and ninety per cent of the equipment for the plant as well as to provide fifty-four per cent of the credit at four per cent interest with India undertaking to repay the credit in fourteen equal installments one year after the commissioning of the plant. The signing of the agreement took place when the Indian Prime Minister Mr. Atal Behari Vajpayee paid a return visit to Moscow in November 2001.

Before Mr. Vajpayee could visit Moscow, the international situation was transformed by the terrorists' attack on the United States on 11 September 2001. The visually horrifying destruction of the World Trade Centre towers in New York and the almost unbelievable attack on the Pentagon gave a new dimension to the issue of terrorism and to the fight against it. It changed history in many ways. For the first time the US territory itself became a target of the terrorists, bringing home to the people and the government in the United States the reality of the terrorist menace around the world about which both India and Russia had been warning the West. The United States now decided to build an international coalition against terrorism, and followed it up with the destruction of the Taliban regime in Afghanistan. It is not coincidental that Russia and India were among the first countries to declare their support for the United States and to offer every assistance in combating terrorism. Indeed Mr. Putin was the first foreign dignitary to call US President Bush on telephone offering both sympathy and support to the United States. Many observers have tended to believe that Mr. Putin just took the opportunity of aligning himself fully with the United States and taking whatever advantage he could take of the situation. This would amount to a distorted view of Russian policies and approaches. Russia was itself fighting terrorism on its own territory and Putin recognized that the international community had to get together and fight this menace. Whatever advantages accrued were incidental and not central to Russian understanding of the world situation.

In any case, the 9/11 attack was a defining moment and it changed many relationships, but not that of India and Russia. India and Russia were on the same side of the international coalition against terrorism. They appear to have further intensified their interaction in the wake of 9/11. The particular concern of both the countries was to ensure that the fight against terrorism would include all terrorism and not degenerate into a selective exercise. The Russian President telephoned the Indian Prime Minister to compare notes on the US-led air strikes against Afghanistan and both leaders stressed the need for consolidation of international action against terrorism and warned against "double standards" in fighting terrorism which would hamper unity in the anti-terrorist campaign.[21]

The Indian Prime Minister's return visit to Moscow beginning 5 November came in the background of this new anti-terrorist struggle. Necessarily the focus was on terrorism although their bilateral issues were not ignored.

Vajpayee and Putin signed a new Moscow Declaration on international terrorism and in addition issued a joint statement exclusively on strategic issues of global importance. The Moscow Declaration called for the "completion of negotiations under the UN auspices on the draft Comprehensive convention on international terrorism and the Convention for the suppression of acts of Nuclear Terrorism". The adoption of these conventions, they asserted, would "assist in strengthening the international legal basis for effectively combating the global menace of terrorism", even while they "reaffirmed the central role of the UN in the struggle against terrorism". They supported the adoption on the basis of international law of decisive measures against all states, individuals and entities which rendered "support, harbour, finance, instigate or train terrorists or promote terrorism". They asserted that in multi-ethnic and democratic countries like India and Russia violent actions under the slogan of self-determination in reality represented acts of terrorism which in most cases had strong international links.[22]

The joint statement was an updated declaration on "strategic partnership". They strongly condemned international terrorism and pledged to step up India-Russia cooperation in all fields, including military, in order to combat terrorism. They again warned against a policy of double standards that could result in a split in the common international position on terrorism. The joint statement noted that Russia supported India "as a strong and appropriate candidate for permanent membership in an expanded UN Security Council"[23]

Mr. Putin told newsmen that Russia-India ties were "moving ahead in all directions". He also said that he would urge President Bush to include Pakistan backed insurgents in Kashmir and the Chechen rebels in Russia on the list of terrorists to be targeted by the US-led coalition against international terrorism. "There are no good or bad terrorists", Mr. Putin said.[24]

With the attack on the home of Indian democracy when reportedly terrorists with Pakistani and Al Qaeda links tried to storm into the Parliament House of India, a tense situation had arisen between India and Pakistan. This critical situation continued to escalate in the next few months, infact almost upto a year. While Russia advised both India and Pakistan to exercise restraint, it is believed that Russia simultaneously opened a supply line of weapons and equipment for the Indian army.[25]

The Russian Foreign Minister, Igor Ivanov was the first high-level Russian visitor who came calling after the 13 December attack on Parliament. Interestingly, Ivanov raised the issue of a trilateral strategic partnership among India, Russia and China. The issue figured in the talks between External Affairs Minister, Jaswant Singh, and his Russian counterpart. Jaswant Singh told newspapermen subsequently that "the issue was discussed but it is a part of continuing exercise of deliberations on important issues among the three countries". He was cautious about the nature of the partnership saying, "it is not a formal axis". The two Ministers also emphasized the need for Pakistan to stop terrorism across the Line of Control and the international border.[26]

It would be appropriate here to consider the proposal of a trilateral strategic partnership between India, China and Russia that keeps coming up in frequent intervals. Many people not only in Russia but in India too believe that such a relationship would be of great advantage to them in meeting the international challenges. It was probably the then Russian Prime Minister, Mr. Primakov, who first mooted the idea of such a trilateral relationship during his visit to India in 1999. At that time he had said that he was "thinking aloud". While the Russians generally have remained somewhat vague about the nature of this relationship, undoubtedly many in India and Russia tend to invest this relationship with a character that would make it a counterbalancing force to the power of the United States.

It should be clarified immediately that any proposal of a formal relationship among these countries to counterbalance the Americans, in terms of an alliance, was fanciful. Firstly, neither Russia nor China nor India had accumulated enough power even jointly to be of any match to the American military power, the same should be said about their joint economic power. There was just no way they could parallel American military or economic power. Secondly, all three of them were striving for independent relationship with the United States and neither would subject this relationship to the possible demands of their trilateral relationship. China has been striving to establish reasonably stable ties with Washington that would not be submerged in divisive issues like American power, American reach around the world and even the contentious issue of Taiwan. India too has been engaged in a similar exercise of building a new level of relationship of confidence and trust between New Delhi and Washington. Russia also had neither the power nor the capacity, nor even the will to challenge US power anywhere and to subject its relations with the United States to any intolerable stresses.

Yet there is a certain relevance to the idea of a trilateral relationship if it were to be conceived in its proper perceptive. The idea could become feasible if it were intended to intensify interaction among the three countries on international issues in order to strive to expand democratic processes of international decisions, particularly the discussion on critical issues of war and peace at the United Nations, so that everyone could have more breathing space. Even to achieve that kind of and that level of understanding, India and China needed to address themselves to each other's concerns and build up a higher degree of mutual trust and confidence than exists at the moment.

Coming back to India-Russia relations, some hiccups should also be noted. Both the Indian Prime Minister and the Pakistani President participated at Almatty in June 2002 in a Conference on Cooperative Measures" that included Russia, China and the Central. Asian States. Mr. Putin tried hard but unsuccessfully to persuade Mr. Vajpayee to go to Moscow in order to meet General Musharraf so that the logjam between the two countries could be broken and a process of dialogue could be initiated between them - the shades of Tashkent were unmistakable. However, the Indian Prime Minister did not oblige Putin and refused to budge from his position that there must be some visible evidence of the secession of cross-border terrorism before any talks could begin. Nevertheless, Mr. Putin did not depart from the Russian position held all along that Pakistan needed to stop cross-border terrorism and dismantle the terrorists' infrastructure within its boundaries for talks between India and Pakistan to have any meaningful significance.

While the India-Russia relationship expanded in many areas, there was one highly important area where the results were rather insignificant. Indo-Russian economic relations had remained stagnant ever since the demise of the Soviet Union. As a Russian Minister conceded that even though the trade and economic cooperation between India and Russia had increased in recent years, it was "notably lagging behind its potential"". Indeed, the trade between the two countries was far less than just the border trade between China and Russia. The trade turnover between the two countries was a mere $1.4 billion in 2001.[27] The two sides went on exchanging ideas and taking some small steps but the overall picture remained bleak. This was a serious lacuna in Indo-Russian relations because often in the final analysis economics buttresses relations among countries far more than other considerations. We have the example of China and USA, and also of China and Japan, where no matter what the acerbity on various other issues, their hefty trade volumes obliged them to continue on a course of improvement of relations.

That brings us back to Mr. Putin's second and most recent visit in December last year. That visit sealed a new special relationship between India and Russia. The Russian President affirmed in. New Delhi that "our two countries share common views on the key issues in global politics. We are jointly fighting international terrorism which has challenged our civilization. We are ready to coordinate in promoting human rights, global and regional stability and sustainable development". He lauded India's obvious successes manifested in the achievements of its scientists and engineers, progress in education and culture and formidable economic growth rates.

The Indian President, Dr. Abdul Kalam was equally warm in his response to Mr. Putin's speech. The President noted that the Russian leader in his last visit (in 2000) had referred to the "arc of instability" stretching from the Caucasus to Southeast Asia. "The epicentre of this arc is, of course, in our common neighborhood", the President said. The world should realize that India too had stake in helping to create an international environment in which our mutually-shared interests and aspirations can be advanced"'. The President stressed that with Russia "we have a shared vision" of a multi-polar world built on consensus and accommodation of different views and interests. The hostage crisis in Moscow, the President reminded the people, and the attacks on the temples in Jammu "testify to the ruthlessness with which terrorists threatened ordinary, innocent persons in the street. We know such acts are often undertaken with foreign assistance". Dr. Kalam welcomed the joint statement (issued earlier in the day by President Putin and Prime Minister Vajpayee) which also stressed the need for international peace, security and stability, with determined action for total elimination of international terrorism and religious extremism. He warned that the struggle against terrorism would not succeed if it was not conducted in an integrated manner on a global plain.[28]

The Prime Minister reported to the two Houses of Parliament that President Putin's visit had consolidated the strategic partnership between the two countries. The Delhi Declaration had reaffirmed, the Prime Minister said, that neither country would take any action which might threaten or impair the security of the other. Both countries would be guided by these principles in their security and defence policies and military-technical cooperation with third countries. The summits were going to be annual features and he would go to Moscow in 2003, the Prime Minister told Parliament. Mr. Vajpayee also underlined that the wide-ranging defence cooperation between India and Russia transcended a buyer-seller relationship and included joint research, development and production of high-tech weapons. He mentioned as an instance "state-of the-art Brahmos missile" which was "a product of our joint research and development efforts. India and Russia are now embarking on the co-production of this missile system for its induction in the armed forces of both countries".

The Prime Minister was also obviously pleased with the fact that, as he told Members of Parliament, Russia agreed with India's position that it could resume dialogue with Pakistan only when Islamabad stopped cross-border infiltration and dismantled the terroris' infrastructure in Pakistan and Pakistanoccupied-Kashmir. Russia had also confirmed, Mr. Vajpayee said, its continued interest in cooperation with India on civil application of nuclear energy and that the Russian President had expressed the view that the international regime on these matters needed reform. "We fully agree with this", Mr. Vajpayee said.[29]

That the Russian President was clear and fully determined in carrying out in letter and spirit the agreements signed between Russia and India was evident from the way he handled the visit of the Pakistan President, General Musharraf to Moscow in February this year.[30] He telephoned Mr. Vajpayee before the arrival of General Musharraf to inform him about the nature of the visit and yet again after the departure of the Pakistani President to let Mr. Vajpayee in on the substance of the talks. Many people thought he was trying to please India. The fact of the matter is that he was abiding by the obligation that the two sides had undertaken during Mr. Putin's visit to India in October 2000. It should be recalled that the two sides had agreed that they would inform each other of any planned foreign policy initiatives in the international arena and not to participate in any military-political or other alliances or associations or armed conflict directed against the other side or to conclude any treaties, agreements or understandings that infringe upon the independence, sovereignty, territorial integrity or national security interests of the other side. Mr. Putin was carrying out the letter and spirit of the decisions taken by the two countries earlier.

Undoubtedly, both India and Russia are sovereign countries and would be looking after their own interests in the first instance. However, as I have been at pains to emphasize all along, that the understanding between Russia and India flowed from the complementarity of their interests both in historical, geopolitical and futuristic terms. Whether it was the question of terrorism, of the defence of Indian territorial integrity or that of Russia, whether it was a question of India's role in this region and the world, and on most international issues of importance to the two countries, the Russian and Indian interests generally tended to coincide. Inherent in the kind of the world we face, there is a certain empathy for each other. There is, therefore, an intrinsic value in the India-Russia ties. This does not exclude differences of approach on certain specific issues, but the general, overall parallelism of interests has been evident. Nor should this identity of interest be taken to mean the exclusion of very friendly ties with other countries, such as the United States, Europe, China, Japan or other Asian, African and Latin American countries. The two sides so far have shoft understanding of each other's concerns while retaining their autonomy of action and expanding their relations with diverse other countries.

References

1. *New York Times*, 23 November 2002.
2. *Indian Express*, 27 November 2002.
3. Statement in the Rossiiskaya Gazeta, Valdimir Rodyuhin in *The Hindu*, 2 December 2002.
4. *The Japan Times*, Editorial, 7 January 2003.
5. Interview with Intar Tass News Agency, *The Hindu*, 1 December 2002.
6. *Times of India*, 5 December 2002.
7. *Ibid.*
8. *Hindustan Times*, 5 October 2000.
9. *The Hindu*, 5 October 2000.
10. *Times of India*, 5 October 2000.
11. *The Hindu*, 6 October 2000.
12. Pramit Pal Chaudhuri, in *The Hindustan Times*, 9 October 2000.
13. *The Hindu* , 6 October 2000.

14. *Times of India,* 29 December 2000.
15. See *Hindustan times*, 26 January 2001.
16. *Ibid*, 12 and 13 May 2001.
17. Ibid, 17 January 2001.
18. *The Hindu* , 11 February 2001.
19. *Hindustan Times*, 26 January 2001.
20. *The Hindu*, 5 May and *Times of India*, 8 May 2001.
21. *The Hindu*, 10 October 2001.
22. See text in *Asian Age*, 7 November 2001.
23. *Hindustan Times*, 7 November 2001.
24. *Indian Express*, 7 November 2001.
25. *Hindustan Times*, 27 May 2002.
26. *Ibid*, 4 February 2002.
27. *The Hindu*, 22 September 2002.
28. *The Hindu*, 5 December 2002.
29. *Times of India*, 12 December 2002.
30. See the text of the joint statement issued in Moscow on 6 February 2003 in *Dawn* ,7 February 2003.

2

Indo-Russia, Sino-Russia, Sino-India Triangle

R. L. Bhatia

Recent developments have once again underlined that regional forums have begun to exercise considerable weight in the international politics. Indo-Russian, Sino-Russian and Sino-Indo relations have begun to unfold a new trend. If this trend continues and there are no reasons to believe that they will not continue, a triangular relationship between these three countries may become a reality. If this happens, it will stimulate the process of multi-polarism, which will be of far reaching significance. This shows how a wind of change has begun to blow in Asia-Pacific region. Indo-Russia, Sino-Russia and Sino-India relations are undergoing significant changes. This reflects, there is a great need to ensure the smooth management of intra-state relationship in the Asia-Pacific region, so that this region is not subjected to destabilising tendencies. It is in this context that new evolving model of relationship in the triangle needs to be objectively analysed.

Indo-Russian Relations

After the disintegration of the Soviet Union, Indo-Russia strategic relationships are once again on the upswing. Secondly, Indo-Russian cooperation in the area of defence supplies is gaining momentum. Today, Russia has become the supplier of highly sophisticated armaments to India. The export controls, non-proliferation policies and unreliability of supplies and denial of key military technology to India by the West, make it a key factor. Indo-Russian defence supplies are in the range of 70 per cent of total defence imports to India. However, India has not relied only on the Soviet/Russian weaponry, but also has looked towards the West – essentially Britain, France and Sweden for arms supply. Now India is bargaining with the United States for supply of defence technology. Despite, this strategic shift, importance of Russia in defence supplies is growing.

For instance, recent agreement on scientific collaboration between India and Russia in the area of bio-technology has begun a new phase, with the establishment of a joint centre at the Indian Institute of Information Technology (IIIT) at Allahabad confirms this trend. Again agreements have been signed for the acquisition of the aircraft carrier Admiral Gorshkov, MIG 29 K fighters, Kamov 31 helicopters, T 90 S tanks and other defence equipment. Nearly $3 billion defence contracts have been finalised. Indian Navy has acquired two submarines and three frigates from Russia, which will cost around $ 300 million each. The Navy is also acquiring three Krivak-class frigates or project 1135.6 from Russia. There are some indicators, which show that Indo-Russian cooperation in the peaceful use of nuclear technology, related particularly to nuclear energy have already taken concrete shape. One should not also ignore the Russian interest in reprocessing spent nuclear fuel for other countries, despite U.S. opposition to the idea. In the oil and gas sector, India's Gas Authority of India Ltd. and Russia's Gazprom have signed a contract in the field of oil exploration.

These cold facts show that Russia is looking towards India as lucrative customer in defence purchases in the years to come. To sum it up Indo-Russian politico-strategic defence cooperation is an important element of the strategic partnership between the two countries. There is yet another important aspect of evolving Indo-Russian relations, which is of far reaching importance.

In October 2000, the visit by Russian President Vladimir V. Putin to India gave a boost to the growing Indo-Russian relationship. India and Russia signed the strategic partnership document that the two nations would not join any military or political blocks and avoid treaties that would infringe on each other's national security interest. There was convergence of views on fighting terrorism. Again during his visit to India in the 1st week of December 2002, India and Russia reaffirmed a long-standing friendship through the adoption of the Delhi Declaration on Further Consolidation of Strategic Partnership and the other protocols signed and decisions taken in the course of the visit. Since both the countries are struggling to define their relations with other major players on the global stage - in a situation where the rules of international politics are in a state of flux and where the terms of the economic interaction between nations are being reset this specific encounter between the Indian and Russian leaderships was of significance for the affirmation of continuity and mutual reassurance that it symbolised. What has added substance to it is the reinforcement of the faith that there is a real convergence of perspectives on issues as wide-ranging as the phenomenon of terrorism, ensuring the security of nuclear weapon stockpiles in a world facing a new assortment of threats and challenges, the conservation and promotion of multi-polarity in global politics, the need for country – specific adjustments in the course of globalisation, and on issues specific to South, Central and West Asia. Russia's belief that India can and should make a substantial contribution to the evolution of a strong global consensus on these issues was revealed in its open support of the Indian campaign for a permanent seat in the United Nations Security Council.

Sino-Russian Relations

Sino-Russian relations have been improving steadily and have now taken a dramatic turn. The process of the solution of the border dispute between the two countries began in the end of 1980s when a Joint Border Commission was set up. In 1994, the two sides agreed on no first use of nuclear weapons against each other. The two countries also de-targeted the missiles directed against each other and an agreement to this effect was signed when Chinese President Jiang Zemin visited Russia in September 1994. Further, in April 1997, an accord on mutual reduction of forces was singed in Moscow by Russia, China and the three Central Asian states – Kazakhstan, Kyrghyzstan and Tajikistan. Moreover, the successful conclusion of the border agreement between the two sides, during May 1991 on the Eastern Sector and September 1994 on the Western Sector removed a major irritant. In December 1999, it was announced that the border dispute has been finally settled. Though there are some residual issues, which will be settled in future.

Economic cooperation between the two countries is undergoing basic changes. In 1999, the trade volume between the both countries was $ 5.72 billion, up 4.4. per cent from that in 1998. The trade volume of the first four months of 2001 was $ 2.5 billion, up 20.1 per cent from the same period of 2000. Russian imports from China have increased by 70 per cent, helping to balance bilateral trade. In 2000, China ranked the sixth among Russian trade partners. Trade between the Russia and China is estimated to have reached $ 10 billion in 2001.

The purpose of Putin's visit to China in July 2001 was to make plans for the long term development of bilateral relations. There is a convergence of views between the two countries to protecting their common turf. This is amply reflected in the 20 year treaty of friendship initialled in Moscow at the end of Chinese President's visit to Russia in 2001. Putin and Jiang worked together to set up a new security forum towards off Islamist threats to the Central Asian Republics.

Above all, for Moscow, Beijing has emerged as major arms destination. More than 60 per cent of Russian military exports go to China. In monetary terms, it is equal to $ 2 billion and it is no small amount for a country engaged in reconstructing its economy.

After the December 2002, Beijing visit of Russian President, Vladimir Putin the relations between the two nations have taken a new turn. It creates confidence in building a strong bilateral relationship in political, strategic, military and economic fields. Political changes in Russia and China's economic liberalisation recast the hitherto adversarial relationship into one of cooperation in search of economic development and political stability. Post September 11, the United States' rise has brought the two countries together in a bid to create a multi-polar world.

Putin's visit consolidated the gains in bilateral ties achieved over the last year. This visit laid the bases to chalk out common strategies on issues of global concerns such as North Korea, Iraq and terrorism. Nuclear proliferation and disarmament were also discussed.

The joint statement signed by Jiang Zemin and Putin provided the framework for increasing cooperation and constructing a mutually beneficial relationship.

Over the past decade, the two nations have made significant progress towards building a relationship of strategic cooperation. This is based on the principle of building a cooperative bilateral relationship while maintaining an independent foreign policy.

China and Russia are both increasingly uncomfortable with the growing U.S. power. In the joint statement issued after the visit, they agreed that the main mechanism to safeguard world peace should be United Nations and that its role in solving international disputes should be increased.

The Chinese and Russian concern arises from the growing U.S. unilateralism in global politics backed by its increasing military power.

However, Russia and China have set up multilateral fora that are not dominated by the U.S. such as the Shanghai Cooperation Organisation (SCO) that discusses regional security and economic cooperation. The two countries have also successfully renegotiated the U.S. definition of terror to include movement for self-determination under the cover of terrorism. China and Russia also have a joint working group on terrorism and have agreed to exchange intelligence on this sensitive issues. They are also keen on strengthening the ASEAN Regional Forum (ARF). China and Russia are also willing to conduct regular discussions on regional security and economic cooperation within the framework of the Asia-Pacific Economic Cooperation of which the U.S. is also member.

The carefully drafted statement welcomed the proposal for a nuclear free zone in the Korean Peninsula. The two sides also called upon the U.S. to fulfill its obligations under the 1994 Framework Agreement. Under this agreement North Korea agreed to halt its nuclear weapons programme in return for U.S. aid for energy plants including construction of nuclear plants. After the North Korean declarations the U.S. has refused to be bound by the agreement.

China and Russia are also in favour of concluding an international agreement on weapons-free outer space. Many of these concerns are also relevant to Sino-Indian relations though with different implications.

It also signalled to the U.S. that its unilateralism is breeding serious concern among big international players.

These are clear manifestation of new trends in Sino-Russian relations.

Sino-Indian Relations

Now let us examine the evolution of Sino-Indian relations in the recent years, which constitute the third side of the emerging triangle.

It has to be taken into account that China and India are the largest and the most populated countries on our planet, which is described as the Asian giants.

Sino-Indian relations remained at a low level after 1962 conflict till Indira Gandhi took the first step to upgrade the diplomatic relations between the two countries. Rajiv Gandhi's visit to Beijing in December 1988 marked a turning point in the evolution of the relations between the two countries. This was followed by the visit to India in 1991 by Chinese Premier Li Peng, and by P.V. Narasimha Rao to China in 1993. These visits brought in a large measure of political and military stability to a completely normalised pattern of India-China relationship. After that several important visits have been exchanged. President K.R. Narayanan's visits to China in June 2000 and the visit of Chinese President Jiang Zemin to India for instance are events of great significance. This reflects how the two countries have put the past aside and are now constructing their relations in mutual interests of both the nations. Let us leave this at that and examine the content of the new relationship.

Firstly, China is facing Islamic militancy, which is fuelling separatism in the Xinjiang province inhabited by Uighur Muslims. The same problems are being faced by Russia in Chechnya. A similar scenario exists in Kazakhstan, Kyrghzstan, Tajikistan and Uzbekistan. This situation has led to the formation of the "Shanghai Cooperation Organisation." The six nations have joined hands to fight the "three forces" – terrorism, separatism and extremism. This is turn has begun to influence positively Sino-Indian relations on the crucial issue of terrorism.

Secondly, China and India are engaged in economic development and modernisation. China is keen to participate in various projects for development of infrastructure in India. Indian goods and services have entered the Chinese market. There are eight Indian companies operating in the eastern part of China. It should be kept in mind that the Chinese economy is the second largest economy in the world, next only to the U.S. in terms of purchasing power parity as estimated by the world Banks's criterion.

Thirdly, serious efforts are being made by both the countries to resolve the border disputes. This is confirmed by the fact that after recording their perceptions of the Line of Actual Control (LAC) along a 345 km "middle sector" stretch, India and China are gearing up for a similar exercise along their frontier in the Ladakh area. Both sides have defined their individual perceptions of the LAC along their border in Uttar Pradesh and recorded it on maps. There is a convergence of views on the LAC alignment along large portions in this sector. However, they differ on the lay of LAC in some segments. This confirms how efforts are being made to resolve their border dispute.

This does not mean that Sino-Indian relations are developing on the same model as Indo-Russian and Sino-Russian relations. India has serious reservations about supply of nuclear capable missiles by China to Pakistan.

If Sino-Indian border dispute is resolved, it will open new vistas of economic and political cooperation. It is relevant to mention here that during the last three years Sino-Indian border has remained more or less peaceful and no major border conflict took place.

The recent visit by Defence Minister George fernandes to Beijing in the end of April 2003, bring into focus that in the new historical conditions Sino-Indian relations have begun to reveal certain positive developments.

China and India during this visit agreed to "sustain the ongoing bilateral process of clarifying the Line of Actual Control". The two countries further reaffirmed their commitment to formulate additional confidence-building measures with a military focus and expressed their determination to enhance bilateral cooperation to combat terrorism. This is how an attempt to impart dynamism in the relations between the two countries is being given. This is further confirmed by the fact that the 1993 and 1996 Sino-Indian agreements were recalled with approval on this occasion. Prime Minister A.B. Vajpayee's visit to Beijing is scheduled to take place in June 2003, which will be another milestone in improving Sino-Indian relations. This shows that step-by-step strategy of India of normalising and improving relations with China has begun to yield positive result.

The three countries have commonalty of interests in fighting global terrorism and strengthening of politico-economic cooperation in the new historic conditions.

Convergence of political and economic interests of three countries India, Russia and China is bringing them closer to each other. If this triangular relationship continues to grow and deepen, it will become a decisive factor in this part of out planet. India and China are Asian giants and Russia is a powerful Eurasian nation.

3

US -Russia Relations and Multilateralism

B.K. Srivastava

After the end of the Cold War the United States emerged as the sole surviving super power. This was the culmination of America's position on four dimensions as the sole super power, the only high-tech military power, the most advance economy in the global economy, and disseminator of popular culture throughout the world. The development was under-way by the 'eighties but was obscure because the United States was challenged by the Soviet Union in the area of security and by Japan in economy. In the Nineties the Soviet Union had collapsed, and the economy of Japan was stalled.[1] The ascendancy heightened the unilateral proclivity in American foreign policy. In the present day interdependent world countries have to take into consideration the foreign policy of other nations for realizing their own national interest. The United States in the early Nineties was in a happier position where it could achieve what it decided to be in its national interest without having to worry about others. It certainly sought the cooperation of others but if that was not forthcoming the United States was willing to follow its own course of action. After airlifting Pakistan's troops for UN operation in Somalia in 1992, an American official proudly proclaimed that while the US could not resolve all crises in the world, nothing could be done without its cooperation. An analyst in the New York Times pointed out that the Clinton Administration bombed a pharmaceutical factory in Sudan in retaliation to the al Qaeda attacks on the American embassies in Dar-e-salam and Nairobi on the basis of unproved allegation that the factory was producing chemicals for chemical weapons. Sudan strongly denied the allegation and proposed in the United Nations that a committee of experts be sent to examine the veracity of the allegation. The United States turned down the proposal. Clinton bombed Sudan without demanding international inspection, without seeking the approval of the United Nations and even without consulting the US Congress. Bombing the hideout of Al Qaeda and its leader Osama bin Laden could be defended on the ground that it was intended to prevent further attacks but for bombing of Sudan there was none. Multilateral, a columnist in the New York Times pointed out, means many sided but getting the support of many nations or forces does not change "one sided" or unilateral character of the foreign policy of a nation. It only underscores the success in attracting the multiparty support. In the Nineties the United States succeeded in marshaling the support of a large number of countries but its policies remained in essence unilateral.

Before taking a decision on intervention in a crisis during the Cold War the United States had to consider possible Soviet reaction. With the collapse of the Soviet Union and with no other power or force to restrain it, the US could easily intervene militarily without worrying about the consequences of its action either to itself or to others. Kamal Kharrazi, then the Permanent Representative of Iran at the United Nations, observed that "the international order remains secondary to and in fact, a function of the differing national interests of those who formulate international policy of the post —Cold war era."[2] Though Kharrazi did not name the United States, the latter was the main power that could be said to have formulated international policy of the post- Cold War era.

In the post-Cold War era nations sought to move closer to the United States in the hope that a favorably inclined United States would serve their economic, political and strategic interest much better. This perception gave even a sharper edge to the unilateral proclivity of the United States. The threat to American security from the Soviet Union had gone but its successor Russia was still a great continental power with the largest population and the biggest land mass in Europe, with thousands of nuclear weapons, and a permanent membership of the United Nations Security Council with veto power. Although its economy was in poor shape, it had enormous natural resources. Instead of relying on its own inherent strength to lift itself from the morass in which it had fallen, Russia expected that its foreign policy being in cooperative mode with that of the United States, it would be accepted as part of the international establishment. It was too eager to "sup at the high table". But the West saw it as a supplicant seeking favor. The G-7 countries promised a great deal of aid and delivered only a little. It announced aid package of $ 24 billion dollars and $28 billion in 1992 and 1993 respectively but delivered only about $16 billion and $8 billion in those years. The US argued that further aid could be provided only if Russia carried out economic reforms so that the aid given could be utilized better. The US exploited the economic vulnerability of Russia to the maximum. The experience of aid since 1991 gave rise not only to great disappointment but an anti western and especially anti American emotion in the Russian foreign policy elite. This trend, noted the report submitted to the Trilateral commission in 1995, "is on the rise." [3] None the less there was no immediate change in the direction of policy either of the United States or Russia.

How much Russian foreign policy was ineffective in containing the thrust of unilateral foreign policy of the United States became evident during the triangular war among the Croats, the Muslims and the Serbs in Yugoslavia from 1992 to 1995. The United States was able to get Russia on board for its policy in the Bosnia War. Russia deserted its historic ally, the Serbs, and eventually gave up the idea of political settlement of the dispute through negotiations and supported the use of force. Certainly, President Milosevic was responsible to a considerable extent for the shift in Russia's stance as he persistently refused to accept Russian advice to accept the plan for the partition of Bosnia that was being offered. Russia supported the bombing of the Serb positions that eventually forced President Milosevic to agree to the Dayton accord in 1995. In 1999, Russia again strongly opposed the use of force in Kosovo. It moved resolution in the United Nations that was defeated and the NATO bombed Serbia for seventy-seven days without any authorisation by the United Nations. The US knew very well that with both China and Russia, opposed to the use of force to resolve the Kosovo crisis there was no way it could get the authorisation for its bombing. After Belgrade capitulated and agreed to meet the demands (withdrawal of its special forces and army units from Kosovo, permitting the return of the refugees and the induction of an international force) Russia wanted to have a zone to itself for its army units serving in Kosovo. But the US saw to it that a separate zone was not given to it. Russia was willing to scale down its aspirations.

Even in its southern soft underbelly of former Soviet Central Asia, Russia was not able to prevent the Americans from moving in. Russians have large presence in the region. There are 6.2 million Russians in Kazakhstan, constituting nearly 37 per cent of its population, in Turkmenistan 36 per cent of the population is Russian, and even in Uzbekistan Russian constitute 20 per cent of its population. In all 11 million Russians live in these five republics. For Russia this is a source of strength as well weakness. The governments in these republics representing the aspirations of the non-Russian ethnic majorities would prefer the American presence in the region as a counter force to Russian influence. What attracted the United States to the region after these countries gained their independence were their vast oil and gas reserves. In Kazakhstan alone there may be as much as 35 billion barrel of oil. Turkmenistan has the world's largest deposits of natural gas estimated to be nearly 350 billion cubic feet. Russia claims that as it developed these resources, its gas giants GasProm and Lukoil should be allowed to buy in to western and local companies. In fact, the American and Russian interest in oil coincide. The US imports huge quantity of oil from Saudi Arabia. Its relations with the former has been changing and many in the United States no longer consider Saudi Arabia as a reliable and dependable strategic partner in the Middle East against the background of rising threat of international terrorism. As the energy security is one of the prime concerns of the United States, Russia can be one country that could take Saudi Arabia's place. In May 2002 in the BushPutin meeting in May 2002 discussion took place on energy. This was followed by US Russia Energy summit in Houston in the first week of October. It was attended by all major American and Russian companies to discuss potential joint projects.[4] There were large areas, particularly economic, where the interest of the two countries converged and cooperation is possible in mutual interest. Before the September 11 relations between the US and Russia was many layered relationship. Cooperation in the field of nuclear and missile regimes, and economic relations continued. It was in the strategic area that the two countries' interest diverged. While the United States surged Russia was in retreat, unable to check the American thrust in areas where earlier American presence was either non-existent or minimal.

Before George Bush was elected as the President in 2000, Bob Woodward of the Washington Post carried out extensive interview with him on August 20 for his book. Woodward quotes him as saying "We are never going to get people all in agreement about force and use of force," He favored confident action that 'will yield positive results, provides kind of a slipstream into which reluctant nations and leaders can get behind and show themselves that something positive has been- you know something positive has happened towards peace." Bush believed that the United States was "the shaping force in the world." He said, "At this moment in history, if there is a world problem, we are expected to deal with it. It is the price of power. It is the price where the United States stand. We will."[5] As the Post noted it was most direct statement on the need for unilateral action by the United States.

After the terrorist attack on September 11, the United States declared a global war against international terrorism. Bush asked other nations to join the war. Addressing the joint session of the US Congress on September 19, he declared "either you are with us or you are with the terrorists." There was an unmistakable warning "From this day forward any nation that continues to harbor or supports terrorism will be regarded as hostile regime." Russia was the first country not only to condemn the terrorist attack but also extend its full cooperation. It provided over flight facilities when the war against the Al Qaedal/Taliban controlled Afghanistan began, permitted the United States to set up air bases and station troops in the Central Asian Republics, and provided the intelligence input for operation in Afghanistan. It also extended its cooperation in the formation of a transitional government for Afghanistan by persuading the Northern Alliance over which it had considerable influence to accept the plan and join the interim government. In return for its cooperation it expected that the criticism of its war in Chechnya would cease. It wanted to make its own war in Chechnya part of the global war against international terrorism. It also believed that the United States would reschedule its debt, which were maturing and provide generous economic assistance. As the war in Afghanistan began West's criticism for human rights violations in Chechnya was toned down but only for a short -while. But there was no economic assistance, generous or otherwise. Not even Jackson -Vanik trade restrictions that were imposed in the early Seventies were relaxed.

According to a report of the Telegraph Group, London, at the European Union summit on November 12, 2002 in Brussels, President Putin stated that Islamic radicals are pursuing the systematic annihilation of non-Muslims and added that western civilization faced a mortal threat from Muslim terrorists. He alleged that they had plans to create a "world wide Caliphate." The world no longer faced isolated acts of terrorism but "a concerted effort and programe" by a global network bent on slaughter, perhaps with nuclear weapons. They talk of the need to kill all "cross bearers". If you are a Christian your life is threatened but even if you reject your beliefs in accordance with their philosophy, you will be killed."[6] By invoking the image of the "cross bearers" pitted against the radical Muslims, Putin had moved quite close to the Huntington thesis. He went on to link his diatribe against the Muslim terrorists to the problem in Chechnya and said that Chechan terrorists were religious terrorists and had links with Al Qaeda. Putin succeeded in getting a European Russian action plan to fight against terrorism but it was made clear to him that he could not have a free hand to fight against terrorism and use any means of his choice like fraction bombs.[7] There can be no doubt that the threat posed by international terrorism is real but there is also the possibility that the war against terrorism can be extended to cover up other interests.

Russia not only provided assistance to the US as part of the global effort against terrorism but yielded on two crucial issues that threatened its own security. Russia had initially opposed the inclusion of former communist countries of Eastern Europe in to NATO. But it dropped its opposition. In return the US and Western Europe made Russia a partner in NATO by creating a Russian NATO Council which provided Russia with a seat at the table where decision would be taken. This would give Russia a voice but not a veto over the decisions. Russia also would not be a party to Article 5 of the treaty which provides for a collective defense in case of an outside attack. On November 21, NATO issued invitation to seven other countries three Baltic states Lithunia, Estonia, and Latavia which were part of former Soviet Union and Bulgaria, Romania, Slovakia, and Slovenia. In 1999 NATO first expanded to include the Czech Republic. The present expansion takes it beyond the frontiers of former Soviet Union; much closer to Russia itself. The stated purpose of the expansion is consolidation of democracy and not to threaten Russia. Significantly the meeting decided to create a Rapid Reaction Force of 20,000 with a global reach. It was also agreed to appoint a US General as strategic commander for worldwide operation of NATO. Russia could not be happy with the development but it has concluded that the "future lies in cooperation with Europe and not in confrontation with it."[8]

Russia viewed the 1972 ABM treaty as a cornerstone of global security. Therefore when the US suggested that it would like to amend the treaty, Moscow warned that this might result in a renewed arms race between the two countries. The United States viewed the treaty as an obstacle for the development of National Missile defense, which it was keen to develop. In November 2001 when Putin met President Bush at his ranch in Texas ABM treaty was one of the main subject of discussion. The Russian leader reiterated that amendment of the treaty or America's withdrawal would upset the delicate nuclear balance and encourage arm race. The United States argued that as the Cold war was over the treaty was no longer necessary. And if it were not allowed to amend the treaty it would unilaterally withdraw. Condleezza Rice argued that it constrained US ability to explore NMD and anyway the treaty "was not representative of the kind of relationship that we have." There were many in the US who feared that the withdrawal would adversely affect the Russian cooperation in future when it was most needed in the war against terrorism. Professor Anna Nelson of the American University pointed out that NMD could not meet threat from unconventional weapons. Why did Putin agreed to allow the US to unilaterally withdraw from the treaty? One possible explanation was that he realized that the NMD was a low priority and would take a long time and huge amount to develop. The Russian President reassured his domestic audience that unlike other nuclear powers both the United States and Russia had prepared the defense, and the withdrawal did not threaten the national security of the Russian Federation.[9] There was no denying the fact that NMD did disturb the delicate balance between the defensive and offensive capability of nuclear weapon states. It was vehemently opposed by China because it was even more adversely affected by NMD. But the United States had its way and it was Russia that made a major concession.

Several months after the United States led the war against international terrorism and hailed in one statement after another the cooperation it was receiving from other states, Russian analysts were wondering whether their country had not been taken for a ride. In an interview on December 17, 2001 in Moscow Alexi Arbatov, a member of the Duma and its Committee on Defense wryly commented that "the relationship between the United States and Russia is between rider and a mule"[10] A few months later his negative assessment had not changed. At a conference on "US Russian Relations in the Post- September I I World" in the third week of April 2002, Arbatov stated that this was a "unique and historic period" in the US Russian relations. Not since World War 11, he said, " the two countries have been as close as they are today but it is unpredictable, fragile, vulnerable and often time shallow."[11] There were some Russian analysts who had concluded that American and Russian interests were not compatible. Gen. Leonid Ivashov, a fonner Defense Ministry director of Military cooperation and now Deputy Director of Geopolitical Problems, expressed his belief that the US and Russia could not be good partners because their economic, military and geopolitical interests differed too much. The two countries looked at the world both in terms of its present and its future in entirely different ways. Russian foreign policy was much more multipolar. It was willing to consider cooperation with countries like India and China. In contrast the US had opted for multilateral policy when it could and unilateral policy when it must. The General felt that Russia would never be able to achieve equality with the United States that has grown too powerful. Besides there was no evidence to suggest that Russia had been admitted in to the close circle of those who formulated policies in international affairs. Despite the erosion of the anti-west left, noted Leon Aaron, Director of American Enterprise for Public Policy Research, that the fact was that only a minority supports the present level of cooperation with the United States because the Russian political class believes that for all it eagerness to go along, Russia has not received reciprocal benefits for its policies.[12]

The disenchantment with the United States resulted in some shift in Russian foreign policy. It became firm in the pursuit of its interest and less willing to yield to the United States. Russia had permitted the United States to base its forces in the Central Asian Republics as part of the offensive against international terrorism. Now it felt necessary to enhance its own presence there in an effort to balance American presence. It began to deploy its military aircraft's in Kavant in Kyrgyzstan. When fully deployed the air base is expected to have an impressive array of airplanes.[13] In response to President Bush's statement on December 17, 2002 that the US would begin deploying a limited system to defend the nation against ballistic missiles by 2004, Russia reversed its plans to scrape 'Satan' and 'Scalpel' missiles. The Commander of strategic missile forces, Colonel-General Nikolai Solovtsov, stated that the nuclear tipped SS-18 missile force would remain in service till 2016-2020. Earlier Russia had announced that it would destroy all its multiple warhead missiles in the next few years. Russia indicated that it is also considering the option of installing multiple warheads on its Topol missiles. This would enable Russia to overcome any missile defense the US may set up under NMD. [14]

The prime cause of Russian retreat had been its weak economy. More recently it has been growing at a faster rate. According to one estimate the Russian economy is now *75* per cent larger than it was during the Soviet era. However, to realize its *full* potential it needs massive investment. For instance, it has the second largest energy supply in the world next only to Saudi Arabia. To develop its energy potential it needs $1 billion annually in the next few years and *$50* billion' by the year 2010. It is one of the several areas where Russia looks for foreign investment. The US is keen to Join Russia in the exploitation of Caspian Sea oil. It is the lure of such economic gains from its association with the West that has motivated Russia to take a pragmatic approach towards the unilateralism of the United States.

Russia is still extending cooperation to the United States In mutual interest, at the same time it does not want to close all its foreign policy options. It does not accept that it should not have good relations with the countries named as the "axis of evil." It has increased relations both with Iran and North Korea. Russia plans to build a nuclear reactor worth 800 million dollars for Iran. Though the Russian claim that the reactor is only for power generation and not for making nuclear weapons, the US is skeptical. It argues that Iran has so much oil. It does not need a nuclear plant for power generation and would certainly use it for making nuclear weapons. Ignoring American objections Russia is going ahead. Even a more serious matter from the American point of view was Putin's declaration on August 18 that it had entered into $40 billion economic cooperation and with trade deal with Iraq, the bugbear of the Bush Administration. Kim Ill Jong also visited Russia in August.

The Russian government wanted to dispel the impression that it is tilting too much towards the West and abandoning its former friends and allies. The Russian Foreign Minister Igor Ivanov in an interview told the KTR television in July that Russia's pro western policies do not mean that it is turning its back on the East. It would develop its relations everywhere that are in its interest. Relations with India and China "are neither small nor worse than our relations with the West, the EU and the United States."[15] What was apparent was that Russia was not required to make such turn around in its relations with India and China. With the West it was trying to break fresh ground.

The United States led global war against terrorism took an abrupt turn when the Bush Administration turned its attention from global war against international terrorism to Iraq and its weapons of mass destruction. It declared that Iraq must be disarmed and there should be a regime change in the country. It linked Iraq with Al Qaeda terrorists by asserting their presence there. Addressing the corps of the cadets on June 1, 2002 President Bush articulated his strategy of a preemptive strike rather than deterrence. He said " We cannot defend America and our friends by hoping for the best. We cannot put our faith in the words of tyrants, who solemnly sign nonproliferation treaties, and systematically break them. If we wait for threats to fully materialize, we would have waited too long."[16] In his statement on September 20, 2002 before the United Nations President Bush reiterated his doctrine of "preemptive strike"; "strike first against the terrorist threats before they are fully formed." During a press conference on November 7 last year, President Bush said "we have an obligation to lead, and I intend to assume that obligation, to make the world more peaceful."17 When confronted with the argument that if the United States claimed the right of "preemptive strike," for itself other nations could also strike against their adversaries claiming the same right India against Pakistan or South Korea against North Korea. The Bush Administration argued that each case has to be decided on its merit. And Iraq's case was different from others; it had used chemical weapons against its own citizens.

However, it was difficult to explain as to why either the United States or Western Europe did not protest against the use of chemical weapons when it took place in the eighties. The harsh reality is that it was Iran that was then the main enemy of the United States and Iraq, which was fighting a war against Iran, was seen as serving American interest. The same explanation was trotted out to explain the difference in the approach towards the WMD of Iraq and the nuclear program of North Korea. While the United States wanted to go to war against Iraq on the suspicion that it possesses WMD, it wants mediations by the countries of Asia-Pacific to dissuade North Korea to give up its declared nuclear weapons program. If the persuasion failed then the necessary action was to be discussed in the United Nations. Russia was more sympathetic towards North Korea as it was a small country and felt threatened. It favored the solution of the Korean problem through dialogue.

There was considerable opposition to Bush Administration's decision to go to war against Iraq within and outside the United States.[18] Many nations believed that all avenues must be first exhausted before going to war. And even the decision to go to war should be taken by the United Nations and not the United States. The latter repeatedly stressed, however, that if the United Nations would not act against Iraq it would only prove its irrelevance and the United States would remove its weapons of mass destruction with those countries that would follow it. At the same time the United States wanted to lead as broad a coalition as possible. And therefore the issue was taken to the United Nations. There it met with fierce resistance particularly from France, which ruled out war as an option. A majority of the members in the Security Council favored sending international inspectors to Iraq. After seven weeks of negotiations the UN Security Council passed resolution 1441 unanimously giving Iraq a last chance to prove that it had no WMD nor had an on going program for their manufacture. The resolution decided to send a UN Monitoring, Verification, and Inspection commission (UNMOVIC) to Iraq under its executive Director Hans Blix and the Director General of the International Atomic Energy Agency (IAEA) Mohamed El Baradei to look for evidence of the possession of WMD or of a program for their manufacture. Iraq admitted the UN inspection team in November 2002. As required under resolution 1441, Iraq submitted a lengthy report to the United Nations, in which it denied possessing any weapons of mass destruction. The United States declared the report to be unsatisfactory. Secretary of State, Colin Powell, stated on December 19 that "most brazenly of all, the Iraqi declaration denies the existence of any prohibited weapons programs at all." He reiterated the American position once again that "the burden remains on Iraq to cooperate fully and for Iraq to prove to the international community whether it does or does not have weapons of mass destruction. We are convinced that they do until they prove to us otherwise." While the UN inspectors carried on their work in Iraq, the United States feverishly carried on military build up in the region for attack on Iraq. It also worked out a plan for Iraq's reconstruction after the regime change.

The United States was determined to follow its predetermined unilateral course. Only a day before Hans Blix and Baradei submitted their report to the Security Council on January 27, 2003, Powell said at the World Economic Forum in Davos (Switzerland) that "the United States would not wait for ever" and went on to add "multilateralism can not become an excuse for inaction." "We will not shrink from war if that is the only way to rid Iraq of its weapons of mass destruction, we continue to reserve our sovereign right to take military action against Iraq alone or in a coalition of the willing."[19] In his report Blix said that while Baghdad was cooperating on access, it needed to do more on substance. "Iraq," he said, "appears not to have come to a genuine acceptance, not even today of the disarmament that was demanded of it." He also said that he shared "the sense of urgency" to achieve disarmament "within a reasonable period of time."[20] President Bush in his State of the Union address to the US Congress on January 28, 2003 dwelt at length on the issue of war on Iraq. He said that the greatest danger facing America and the rest of the world is "outlaw regimes that seek and possess nuclear, chemical and biological weapons," He warned that if Saddam Hussein did not fully disarm the United States would be prepared to lead a coalition to disarm him." "The world had waited for twelve years" and that "America will not accept serious and mounting threat to itself, allies and friends." Addressing the international community he made his intention absolutely clear. "We will consult but let there be no misunderstanding if Saddam Hussein does not fully disarm, for the safety of our people and for the peace of the world, we will lead a coalition to disarm him." The day after Bush's address, Blix in an interview distanced himself from the United States. He stated "whatever we say will be used by some, I did not tailor my report to the political wishes or hopes in Baghdad or Washington." He challenged Colin Powell's contention that the inspectors had found that Iraqi officials were hiding and moving illicit materials to prevent their discovery. Inspectors had reported no such incidents. He also refuted President Bush's assertion that Iraqi agents were posing as scientists. He said that he had no reasons to believe this.[21] The Security Council began discussion on the interim report of the inspectors behind the closed door. It appeared that the majority favored giving the inspectors more time. President Bush promised that Colin Powell would provide more information that it had on Iraq's WMD on February 5. In his presentation to the Security Council, Powell tried to build the case against Iraq for possessing chemical and biological weapons and trying to cheat the inspectors. He did not have much to say on nuclear weapons. But analysts noted that he did not build an "airtight" case that Baghdad " was plotting with Al Qaeda to attack the United States and its allies, a main argument for the Bush administration's contention that Iraqi threat is so urgent that a potential military campaign can not be delayed." Gary Milhallin, Director of the Wisconsin Project on Nuclear Arms Control, was quoted as saying that while Powell demonstrated that Iraq was not cooperating with the inspectors and therefore was in "material breach" of resolution 1441, but did not demonstrate that "United States is facing an imminent threat."[22] After Powell's presentation France, Russia, and China remained unconvinced of the need to wage a war. Dominique de Villepin, the Foreign Minister of France said after Powell's an hour long briefing showed that "the inspection regime must be strengthened ... Let us double, triple the number of inspectors and direct ourselves to the disarmament of Iraq in peace." And Russian Foreign Minister Igor Ivanov urged the Security Council to press Iraq "through political means."[23] The next report of the inspectors is due to be presented to the Security Council later in February but again President Bush has declared that though the United States would welcome a second resolution but Saddam Hussein's game is up, making it apparent that the world is on the verge of another destructive war.

After the United States had succeeded in ousting the Al Qaeda and Taliban forces and installed the Karzai regime in Afghanistan, it turned its attention to Iraq. It accused Iraq of possessing WMD in violation of its commitment to the United Nations to remove them. It also linked it with international terrorism without providing credible evidence to support its allegation. Russia had eagerly supported the war against terrorism for it saw itself as a victim of terrorism. For it the situation in Afghanistan was of far more serious concern than Iraq's possession of prohibited weapons. Islamic militancy was entering into Central Asian Republics from Afghanistan and threatening the stability of the region. On December 9, 2002 Russian Defence Minister Ivanov while visiting NATO Secretary General George Robertson said that Iraq was a non-proliferation problem, not a terrorism problem. A newspaper report quoted a Russian Deputy Foreign Minister as observing that the by shifting the thrust of its anti-terrorist campaign from Afghanistan to Iraq, Washington is behaving like a man who is looking for a lost purse, not where he had dropped it, but under a street lamp because he could see it better there.[24]

Russia had very cordial relations with Iraq during the Cold War era that was upset by the Gulf War. It had again started cultivating closer relations with Iraq. The latter owed Russia nearly eight billion dollars. Besides, much to the annoyance of the United States, it had signed lucrative trade and investment agreements with Iraq worth several billion dollars. It had stake in the stability of the regime. President Putin said in Moscow " the Iraq crisis must be resolved only on the basis of the United Nations charter and Security Council mechanism." He made the statement after talks with the visiting President of Yemen, Ali Abdullah Saleh. In a joint declaration the two leaders called for the settlement of the Iraqi problem through 'peaceful, political and diplomatic instruments, without resort to military force and on the basis of relevant UN resolutions." In contrast to Washington repeated assertion from the outset that Baghdad was not cooperating with the inspectors, Russia contended the opposite. A senior Russian diplomat praised "constructive" cooperation of Baghdad with international weapons inspectors. Yuri Fedorov, the Deputy foreign Minister told a Russian newspaper "we are satisfied with Iraq's constructive measured policy. Iraq is demonstrating goodwill on all issues." This reiteration of support for Iraq significantly came in the wake of the latter's decision to break off a lucrative contract with a Russian company.[25]

The Bush Administration is already thinking ahead. It has made up its mind that after the war, or after Saddam Hussein voluntarily goes in to exile, the country would need an international administration to maintain law and order atleast for two to three years. The administration would most likely be headed by the United States or it would be under its control. Iraq is the pivot of the Middle East and by controlling it the United States can hope to control the region. If nothing else this will ensure the security of Israel. After the defeat of Iraq, that has stubbornly resisted American influence in the post cold war era, the Palestinians would become weaker and would be more inclined to accept whatever peace plan is offered to them. This would eliminate most important source of tension between the United and the Muslim world. By controlling Iraq the United States would be sitting pretty on the second largest oil deposit in the . Talks are reportedly on between the United States and behind the advancing American army units and occupy northern part of Iraq. In return the US wants the use of Turkish bases for launching attack against Iraq from the north. The United States has assured Turkey that it would not support an independent

Kurdish state. Some Kurd leaders are opposed to outside intervention but Turkey would be happy if it could control the oil fields in northern Iraq.[26] After the war is over the map of the region could be redrawn. The only uncertain element in this entire calculation is the response of the people to the war on Iraq. After the United States revealed its firm commitment to the idea of a post Saddam. Hussein's Iraq, Turkey, Saudi Arabia, Kuwait, Bahrain, Jordan, Qatar have fine up behind the Bush Administration. There would be no surprise if Pakistan and Syria would also join others. Europe too is divided. If France and Germany are opposed to war, Britain, Italy and Spain, besides other European powers are willing to support the United States.

Russia is fully aware of the implications of the war that is knocking at the door of the world. Therefore, it has spoken against the United States attacking Iraq. It has agreed with France, Germany and China that if a war has to be declared against Iraq it must be done by the mechanism of the United Nations. This is as far as it would go. It is not as vocal and assertive as France has been for it still values its relations with the United States and the West Europe. France went to the extent of threatening the use of its veto in the Security Council to prevent unilateral American action. Russia would have voiced its own opposition to the unilateral policy of the United States on Iraq in very low tones that would have been almost inaudible. The United States may still decide to use force to remove weapons of mass destruction with the assistance of countries willing to join the coalition as it had declared all along that Iraq was in "material breach " of the international agreements it had signed. But it is the opposition to such unilateralism by France, Russia and China that has put the United States on the back foot and has atleast succeeded in delaying the war.

References

1. James Kurth, "Confronting the Unipolar Moment the American Empire and Islamic Terrorisn," *Current History* (Philadelphia, Penn.), Vol. 101, No 689, December 2002, p.403.

2. Keith Philip Lapor (ed.), *After the Cold War Essays On the Emerging World Order* (Austin University of Texas, *1997).*

3. Robert D. Blackwill, Rodric Braithwaite and Akhita Tanaka, Engaging Russia *A Report to Trilateral* Commission (New York Trilateral Commission, 1995), pp. 15-16 and 17.

4. Michael Lelyveld, "US Russian Officials hail Energy Partnership"

Radio Free Europe, 3 October 2002.

5. Bob Woodward," A course of Confident Action interview adopted for the book Bush at War" *Washington Post,* November 19, 2002, A 01.

6. " West In danger From Muslim Terrorists Putirf" *The Hindu,* November 13, 2002.

7. *Ibid.*

8. *The Los Angles Times,* " NATO Grows, Shifts Focus to Terrorism," On the Web, November 22, 2002. Also see "NATO invites seven Nations," *The Hindu,* November 11, 2002.

9. Radio Free Europe, December 19,2001.

10. *Ibid.*

11. Report on Russian American Nuclear Security Advisory Council Congressional Strategic Stability and Security Seminar Series Seminar 1 US Russian Relations in the Post September 11 World" prepared by Ingrid Staudemeyer, Radio Free Europe, April 19, 2002.

12. Francesca Mereu," Russia Roundtable Discusses Benefits, Drawbacks of US cooperation," Radio Free Europe, April 4, 2002.

13. "Russia deploys aircraft in C. Asia. *The Hindu,* December 2, 2002.

14. Russia to Retain 'Satan' missile *ibid.* 21 December 2002.

15. Radio Free Europe, July 14, 2002.

16. Quoted in Augustus Richard Nixon, "America In the Middle East Statesmanship versus Politics," *Current History,* January 2003, Vol. 102, No. 660, p. 5.

17. "Bush If Iraq Does Not Disarm US, Friends Will Move to Do Job," *Backgrounder,* November 8, 2002, Public Affairs Office of US embassy, New Delhi.

18. Many former American officials, who had served in the State Department, were critical of the Administration eagerness to attack Iraq without the endorsement of the UN. Some of them feared adverse fall out of the war in the Middle East. For instance, Zbigniew Brzezinski, former National Security Advisor in the Carter Administration wrote in the Washington Post" a US assault on Iraq will be perceived in the region (and probably in Europe) as part of an American Israeli effort to impose a new order in the Middle east without regard for either Iraqi or Palestinian civilian casualties." Quoted in Nixon, n., 16, p. 5.

Warren Christopher, from Secretary of State wrote in the *New York Times,* an article "Iraq Belongs On the Back Burner," on December 31, 2002. He wrote " before President Bush gives the signal to attack Iraq, he should take a new broad look at the question of whether such a policy war, at this moment is right priority for America." He went on to say that failure to raise the question would be "unwarranted and unwise. Former Republican office bearers, who had served under former President George Bush. Like James Baker also wrote advising against the US adopting a unilateral approach.

19. The New York Times, On the Web, January 27, 2003.
20. The Hindustan Times, January 28, 2003.
21. "Blix contests Bush regime's claims on Iraq," *ibid.* February 1, 2003.
22. Michael Gordon, " Powell' case Against Iraq Piling up the Evidence." The New York Times, On the Web February 6, 2003
23. Http / MSN headlines Opinions and Commentary Fred Kaplan, "Smoking Gun Colin Powell Delivers the good on Saddam," February 5, 2003. Also see ed. Ed. "Insufficient Evidence," The Hindu, February 8, 2003.
24. "Terror threat Comes From Afghanistan, not Iraq," *ibid.* December 12, 2002.
25. "Russia Reiterates support for Iraq," *ibid,* December 18, 2002.
26. Dexter Filkins with C.J. Cbivers," US in talks on allowing Turkey to Occupy a Kurdish Area in Iraq," The New York Times, On the Web, February 7, 2003.

4

Indo-Russian Relations in Global Context

Rakesh Gupta

(This paper pleads for upgrading Indo-Russian Relations away from the Icarus syndrome of unipolar US military power. This is the defining moment. A redefining moment is needed to balance the US power. The new level of relationship needs to be for joint inderdiction in various areas of mutual concerns and issues from the Middle East to Central Asia. This will be strategic partnership of futuristic vision so that only one power does not dominate the world to eternity, which is well nigh impossible, if one goes by the neorealist paradigm of Modelski's Long Cycles of Power).

Views on Indo-Russian Relations

Some Western, Russian, Pakistani and Indian scholars do not want the Indo-Russian relations to continue out of a variety of their respective positions on the 'defining moment' of the US military hegemony, or, hyper xenophobic interventionist power. Subhash Kapila suggests that the time has come to remodel the bilateral relationship since there is a change in the Russian orientation[1]. Jerome M. Cooley analyses the past Indo-Russian relations to say they were dependent on Indian needs, Russian opportunism and American ambivalence. Now in the post cold war phase the US should manage South Asian proliferation. This legacy he feels continues to dominate the Indo-US relations. This situation needs to be altered [2]. Arun Mohanty takes the position that Yeltsin downgraded the Indo-Russian relations [3]. Pakistani scholar Afzal Mehmood takes the position that Indo-Russian Defence agreement of 1999 is harmful to the delicate nuclear balance between India and Pakistan if India acquires anti missile capability. If will deprive Pakistan assured strike capability.[4] Madhavan Palat takes the position that the Indo-Russian relations are out of the cold war frame. This is a blessing in disguise since it allows us to build our relations with the US. At the same time he maintains that the

Indo-Russian relations, in the nuclear field especially, are a subset of the Indo-US relations since the latter has the capacity to punish the Russians.[5] P. R. Chari notes the unequal relationship between Russia and India by saying that they have a supplier client, relationship [6]. San jay Baru laments the fact that the Indo-Russian relations are not exploited to their full potential especially in terms of their economic relations. In fact to the Commerce ministry the trade with Russia is marginal, he says[7]. Each of them suggests that the readjustment of Indo-Russian relations should be in accorctance with the basic defining moment, that would also mean restructuring the bilateral relations and the world order in line with the US perceptions of its hegemonic world order. The thrust of the interventions is to dilute the Indo-Russian relations. For they are set in the non-history of the cold war, Indian domestic compulsions, American ambivalence, Russian opportunism and Indian need to contain China, with Russian support then, and, manage Pakistan, with the US support, now. The plea to the US is to manage the South Asian Affairs, especially the nuclearised South Asia since Kashmir makes it a most dangerous place.

Defining Moment Constrainment

The defining moment means here the period from the end of the Cold War that Gorbachev and Bush, Sr. had announced at Malta in 1989 and the collapse of the Soviet Union in December 1991 till date. The world entered in the new era of nuclear bipolarity, economic multipolarity at the base and military unipolarity at the apex. The new architecture of international relations was under the US hegemony and that is best described as the period of new globalisation. In this phase the neo-liberal economic and political agenda replaced the welfarist liberal agenda. The growth of new weak, crony, capitalist or plutocratic states replacing the socialist states. Further, unipolarity meant that the UN and the NATO, which were the Cold War constructs, were to expand themselves into world bodies as expressions of complex interdependence [8]. At the coare of it the US national interests are paramount, and, with them those of its allies. This scenario remains today since the interests of its allies are part of its national interests as 'War on Terror' indicates and treatment, with warlike fury, of Iraq underlines. The latest thinking on national security in the US regards any missile attack on its allies as a hostile act to itself. In its operative part the latest Bush doctrine aims to construct the missile defences. Still further, in the context of Bosnia-Herzegovina, Haiti and now Iraq this further means the principle of US interdiction, with or without the joint concurrence of the rest of the West/UN/NATO. The September 11 turned this doctrine into a larger implication of interdiction that may violate sovereignty of countries as the recent row between the US and Pakistan on hot pursuit shows in the wake of Huntington's clash of civilization thesis.

In view of this defining moment Indian foreign policy had in an ad hoc fashion shaped her responses. This happened especially since the Governments of V. P. Singh, who had very little knowledge and time about foreign affairs.[9] The Government of P. V. Narasimha Rao witnessed the decline of the NAM at the time of the extension of the NPT. Indian security concerns were constrained by the new unipolar reality in matters of the Earth summit at Rio de Janero, NPT, CTBT and the WTO. Either out of preference or out of perception of feeling constrained the Indian policy makers realised that they had to adjust to the US unipolarity. [10] Scholars therefore suggested that the Indian interests lay with the US. From that perspective we need to move closer to the US.

India Constrained Cooperation

The domestic elections in 1998 changed the situation as far as cooperation with the US is concerned. The BJP opted for closer cooperation with the US. India had lost already its maneouvreability. It was being made to change its position over a number of issues. Nam as a framework of policy had collapsed. This is the reflection of the new structure of international relations. Combine with this the fact of a new coalition coming to power under Vajpayee. The argument here is that even though the BJP Government chose to follow the path of cooperation it is still forced to accept things that it does not want in its overall friendliness to the USA. The friendliness is also a part of its long standing policy framework. This thrust was witnessed during the Saffronisation of Foreign policy. Vajpayee - Jaswant Singh phase (in line with the earlier Bharatiya Jan Sangh view) moved to a position of shared vision with the US. The Talbot Jaswant Singh talks gave to the Indian foreign policy a flavour unhitherto heard of. Jaswant Singh has a very poor opinion of the erstwhile Indian foreign policy. He considered that in its history of Congress rule India had suffered Himalayan blunders [11]." The focus shift amounted to ignoring them and most importantly that the domestic constituency was opposed to this Westernisation of Russia. The Yeltsin-Kozyrev phase-suffiered from the Icarus syndrome and was forced to accept what was not in their national interest. Today under Bush administration there is post post-cold war policy towards Russia.

The Western approach can be gauged from the fact of the futuristic study on Russia. There is a possibility of Russia muddling through muddling down or remaining as it is. By some accounts it is not sure what direction Russia will take. At stake is future of pluralist State, electoral democracy, fair economic competition in the market, federation on the principle of subsidiarity, due process of law and reduction of its great power status .[12] Richard Pipes the Sovietologist and now Russian expert visualises the following three futuristic scenarios for Russia. One, self-imposed isolation that will cause decline. Two, Russia playing on European sensibilities and resentment of the US power or a pro western bandwagoning.[13] There is no way in which the US or the West would like-Russia to be a significant global power. They would perhaps like to reduce it to manage the strife within the Russian Federation and just be a major power. This is the logic of the defining moment. The prescriptions for such views are that During the Putin period nothing significant has changed on issues of internal and external policies and that Putin is adjusting to the US needs.[14]

In this defining moment the national interests of the US are predominant and other interests have to be subordinated at them. This is not the criticism of the Russian and Indian foreign policies but the statement of the fact that they need to adjust to the US in the unipolar phase. If an example is needed it is their response to the declaration of 'War on terror. In terms of Neorealist analysis this could be regarded as the phase of sameness effect. The Long term Indian and the Russian interests would be to become great powers and make their region free from external powers. In the current unipolar moment the US seem to be more Bismarkian in that if they have two powers Centres win their hands and they keep the other rising, declining powers in the air and keep juggling these. US, Japan and Europe are with them as popart of the traditional strategic community.

Redefining Moment

This write up takes the case of the Indo-Russian relations in terms of looking at it as, one where a redefining moment is needed in which the real interests of the two countries can be taken into account and not the world of the defining moment. In other words the need is to 'Sight *balance of power* as an alternative to the sameness effect. The Neo-realists point to this possibility of history of internation relations. It is possible to talk about the redifining moment since long term projections stipulate the changed scenarios, in which the US may not continue to be playing the same global role that it is currently.

Modelski Thesis

At the theoretical level the Modelski thesis" [15] of the transition of powers has taken the position that so far transition of power has usually taken atleast a hundred and fifty years from the French to the British. This has happened as a result of war as a catalyst of change. He hoped that in the next round the Japanese may come to that position given their trade and technology edge. The Technology War was to involve the US, Europe and Japan. Today the US is leading in the telecommunications revolution. The competition, it was theorised, will be peaceful. This last prognostication did not happen since the US defence, cooperation with the US under Jaswant Singh. Isssues of defence relationships, involving defence exercises of the Army, Navy and Air Force, involving paratrooping exercises with the US have now become the order of the day as much as consultations on South and East Asia. The presence of the FBI operatives in the country is also now a fact. And no body minds it. A symbolic assertion of this new emerging relationship is that trade increased with the US and it decreased with Russia.

The September 11, 2001 can be-called a watershed to this relationship. The Indian who have been fighting what they call cross border terrorism at the hands of Pakistan offered to join the US effort to fight terrorism of the Al Qaida variety in Afghanistan. Vajpayee is reported to have said that Muslims all over the world are a threat. This suited the US. They were interested in not only fighting Al Qaida but also liauidating the Taliban and chose to, rely on Pakistan. Pakistan was now caught in an ambiguity. It became a front line state in the 'War on terror' as well as a sponsor of terror, as far as India is concerned. This is the beginning of what can be called the experience of Indian Foreign policy in the form of the metaphor of the Icarus syndrome. They thaught that going close to the US would lead to the realisation of the pro-active policy towards Pakistan. Twice Indians have been told that they cannot do what the US can do the first time it was when the US attacked the Al Qaida camp in Afghanistan and again now when India wanted to pursue the terrorists across the border. This was not to happen and so India kept saying that 'it would have to fight its own battle against terror. That led to operation Parakram after December 2001 attack on the Parliament. The Icarus syndrome expressed itself in the sense that the Indian foreign policy makers realised that their national interests were different from those of the US. Though the present 'Indian foreign policy is unrecognisable from the earlier one, India may have to take positions supportive of the US. Can it offend the US sensibilities in Central Asia or Kashmir, or even the issue of power projection in the Sea? It will have to reckon with the US pleasure/displeasure, Can India protest to the US about its close relationship with China, with whom the former has less than friendly relations? Can it imagine a scenario of fighting a war without the US/Western nod, as it did in 1971? Would it be able to defend its own sovereignty in case US hot pursuit brings the US troops, to Indian Territory. Since there are the US, vessels near the Pakistan shores can India navy go closer to the Pakistan shores in case need is it possible for India to reorient its foreign policy to have a more elbowh room? The elbow room will depend on what is happening; among other powers bilaterally, especially with regard to China, Russia, Japan and USA alongwith India and Pakistan.

Russia Strained

In their own foreign policy framework the Russians also came in for a rude shock. The attempt initially has been to integrate with west Europe. They were admitted to the NATO Council and the European Union, the European Bank or Reconstruction of Russia continuing to give it loans till this year, Clinton regarding the Yeltsin period as friendly. Yeltsin had introduced shock therapy that Professor Saichs of Harvard had recommended for it. And still Russians had to move away from the Yeltsin Kozyrev phase of Atlanticist foreign policy. They were faced to accept events that went against their own national interest. Given the fact that NATO was moving East, given the fact that the US and the West was not consulting them, despite the fact that the West was gained the ascendancy owing to events unimagined. This was the breakup of the Soviet Union and the end of the socialist system, Instead what-came in is the unipolar phase of global power and that in the hands of the US. , Modelski had predicted this after the Second World War, though not the manner of its coming about.

Looking at the unipolar moment theorists like Mearsheimer have argued that they were for only fifty years and not one hundred and fifty years. There were only two such moments, namely of the French unipolarity in the 17th century and that of the British in the 19th century. Currently fifteen years of the US technological hegemony are over. How long will it last; What are going to be the new elements that will make for a transition It may well be a country that controls the natural resources like oil and nuclear power. The Global 2015 report suggests that it may not be able to keep the technological edge and that it may be bogged down by the of power where lesser powers or non-government organisations may take advantage on the new military technology. Currently the US is attempting to check such a possibility. Can Japan and Germany bid to do so? This is an imponderable. By all reckoning China is not the candidate for the same. According to a global futures report China, given its political authoritarianism, even after its last Party Congress may not benefit from the process of globalisation, spite its 9 per cent economic -growth rate. It is therefore possible to see the shift away from the USA but not see the direction of its change.

Compact of the Weak

Given the Modelski theorisation what could be other indices to the movement of long cycles? These could be human resource, control or denial of natural resources that are the source of wealth and power. Therefore it is necessary that weak unite and pool in their resources much like in Plato's Theory of Justice as propounded by Glaucon, i.e. the weak agree neither to suffer nor to inflict injustice that the powerful will. In other words in case of the prėsent context it is amounting to say unite to deny and unite to build. Deny wealth, deny sphere of influence and deny badwagoning by which the US is currently benefitting. As far as the US is concerned the Bismarkian juggle could mean that today the Chinese may be in the cold to be picked up whenever necessary for the US's' own interests. If they want to deter the Chinese today they may like the Chinese to be their security partners tomorrow. This may happen from issue to issue. Or they may pick on Pakistan today and India tomorrow. They may pick up Russia today and drop China tomorrow. This depends on the predominant interests of the US and the alliance that it chooses to lead in conflict situations. Currently we notice that the US is following a two pronged aggressive policy of war against Iraq and North Korea. In both cases Russia and China have a lot at stake apart from Japan in North Korea.

Clay Feet

According to another futuristic study four scenarios have been delineated. In them three are the ones that predict turbulence. [16] In all the scenarios Sub Saharan region, Middle East, South and East Asia will not benefit from the process of globalisation. In some of these there will be distancing between the Europeans and the US. The US may be more inward looking or be unable to control regional events. How long will the present moment of unipolarity last? How far away will it be when some nation or the other will overtake the US in growth rates and start the process of multipolarity? Does the US have a soft underbelly that some small power may even exploit? A peep into this can be provided by its present military overstretch. US troops deployment in 1999 were 25 3,000 in foreign countries. Of which 46,000 were afloat in NATO countries, Japan and Korea. These were traditional places, Its further presence is marked by small-scale contingencies (SSCs) that has led to its deployment of troops in other regions. These are Haiti, Bosnia, Herzegovina, (5,800), Serbia, including Kosovo, (6,400), Macedonia, (1,100), and the Middle

East, 13,000 The number is rising with the Bush administration announcing its new deployment in the wake of impending attack on Iraq. One of the consequences is that the family life of its personnel is disturbed back home since most of these are married men. Their morale is down. Secondly the military establishment is faced with a sense of stress and fatigue. Further the realist school is opposed to this deployment since they want the US to intervene only where their vital interests are harmed. The places where there are interventions the US are not sure about the ethnic, political and social fall . ut and what all this will cummulatively hold for all of them. These are issues that will in a different constellation point' to the need of a redefining moment. There will be a window of opportunity for States, to redefine moments in terms of balance of power according to their positionality. Apart from the growth rates it will be the nuclear power that will matter. The third factor could be internal cohesion and democracy.

At the global level one does not have positive signs of the process of globalisation. If globalisation means access to more markets it has failed. This is so because disparities in prices, wages and real interest rates have persisted and this is not helpful. One conventional way of measuring globalisation is to express global exports as a proportion of the global product. As this proportion rises, the quantity of globalisation is presumed to rise similarly. However, from 1995 to 1999, a period often viewed as marked by a relentless surge of globalisation, the proportion actually fell from 17.3 to 15 per cent. In case of volume of capital flows as a sign of globalisation foreign capital flows as relative to, domestic savings were equally larger at the start of the centaury than at its end. Access by foreign business to foreign markets of Japan, China and S. Korea continue to be more restricted than access to the markets of the US and Germany. [17] In such conditions nations may challenge the US. Both India and Russia could well be on that road alongwith China and Japan. Japan is passing through a stage of continued stagnation with zero or slow growth rate. Despite its declining population growth its peoples standard of living is rising." [18] A global report for the future trends prognosticates that in case Europe and Japan are unable to manage their demographic challenge there may be dampened economic growth. [19] India and Russia have 4 or 5 per cent growth rate as of now. Both are marked by possession of nuclear weapons. In India the deployment and operative nuclear doctrine -is emerging while Russia does not seem to implement the last nuclear agreement with the US. In South Asia four future scenarios in an unstable strategic environment are stipulated from the perespective of US interests.

These are, viz., (a) major subcontinental war; (b) stagnation and state failure of Pakistan, (c) high entrophy proliferation of strategic technologies, (da high intensity Indo-Chinese arms race.[20] US Will have to bother about these in the future, especially the last contingency.

India has its own successful democracy. [21], In Russia there is atleast an electoral democracy. India has large scientific personnel and well established education system. Russia has an electoral democracy if not good party system. According to the European Commission study the Russians may muddle through, i.e. it may under clear guidance and consistency implement policies. According to the 2015 report Russia increasingly have to face the challenge of its -expectations for world leadership and its dramatically reduced resources. India says the same report will not be a power to reckon with given its lack of further liberal reforms, fractious nature of politics, uneven internal economic growth and rising gap between the poor and the rich. The same report says will the internal developments challenge the regime's legitimacy.

Future Conflicts

And yet the report suggests that India, China, Russia and possibly Iran may pose future threat to the US interests. Russia, China, North Korea and possibly Iraq are clubbed together as direct threat. Among regional threat to may negatively impact on the US are India-Pakistan conflict the report mentions, Scholars suggest that the US will contead with the possibility of limited conventional war in the future scenario, in South Asia.[22] The potential lethality will grow given the availability of WMD, longer- range missile delivery systems and other technologies. In other words, if the two conflict scenarios are merged the situation is that Russia, China, India, Iran and North Korea apart from Iraq is the potential conflict sources for the US.

Apart from this there may be warscenarios other than the ones currently developed with reference to Iraq and N. Korea. These could relate to Central Asia, Indian Ocean and Asia Pacific beyond the restricting framework of current Islamist curve of war scenarios. These may relate to conditions of more failed states, e.g., Pakistan and Pakistan having the spill over effect of the Afghan failed state that is sought to be put in place under the UN resolution. Both the role of Hikmaytyar in Afghanistan and the emerging flash of killing conflict between Pakistani forces and the US military personnel may be a prelude to larger shift of disorder. Pakistan has recently expressed its fear of a future US attack after that on Iraq. In themselves they may currently appear to be manageable but they could be serious given altered internal political change with regard to Pakistan and Afghanistan. Add to this the danger of the weak states in Central Asia just wilting under the pressure of extended accumulation that globalisation is imposing. Non of the Western counties like the kind of regimes that exist therein. In practically all of Central Asian States the regimes are unstable and not democratic. They may turn in any direction given the dynamic complexity of oil politics of the region. The US and the Russians the area already in a sort of a Cold war situation. The GUAM (Georgia, Uzbekistan, Azerbaijan and Moldova) countries are already with the US. The US presence in Kyrgistan is already causing the Russian military nightmares. In contrast there is the Shanghai group. Thirdly, Russia is keen on not allowing Kyrgistan to go out of it control. This explains the recent flying of Russian troops to Kant air base close to the Manas airbase from where the US is operating for its 'War on Terror'. Today there may be difference between Putin and his Military Chief about the US intentions. But there cannot be this difference of a permanent nature. In Central Asia Russia may succeed to deter the US.[23] Russia and China know that the presence of the US men and material is a pressure on their military security. If Central Asia becomes more like Afghanistan and focus of the great game once again it will impact on the Indian security, as much as, Russian and Chinese security.

Add to this scenario a possibility of the US developing a new policy option towards China. Its aim could be to isolate India and prevent Russia from emerging as a great power, which is in any case considered by the West as a declining power. This is not a far-fetched stipulation. Let us have a closer look. Recently US has expressed its willingness to reorient its strategic policy towards China by advising Israel to stop aid to China since the US is thinking of a new policy option for China. The China factor could be used to balance the Pakistan factor for India and Japanese factor to manage China. There is a China-North Korea-Pakistan axis .[24] That may have a wink from the US if not a direct patronage. To be more accurate there may Chinese USA understand on South Asia that may be against India".[25] Its parallel axis could be of China-US-Japan axis. Currently it is noted that there may be Japanese-Chinese confrontation. But in the future they may collaborate. (Robert satter) In this scanario both Russia and India will be left high and dry. Both want to be great powers. India could be isolated in South Asia and Russia could be isolated and needled both on Kashmir andd South Caucasia and Ukraine.

In the current US-Pakistan irritants one appears to be India's concern for cross border terrorism. Kargil, operation went without India crossing either the LOC, or the international border, The Pakistan territory is full of jihadi, Egyptian, Afghani Saudi, African and CIA operatives working independently and at cross-purpose [26] Knowledgeable people also believe that this was a restrictive presence for the Indians during their Kargil operation. Ofcourse the other side of the coin is that the US intervention did persuade the Pakistanis to withdraw their men from Kargil.

The third dimension of a possible future scenario at sea, Russian Navy is a declining one. Chinese is an expanding one. US navy is dominating one. The Indian Ocean littoral favours the US and the Chinese presence. The Chinese are present in Rangoon. They may soon be at Gwadar. The situation in Triconamalee is not yet decided with the Srilankan situation not yet sure with the LTTE. Remember the time when the Swaran Singh Bhutto round-of talks began they were made infructous by Pakistan before they could start. The Pakistanis had given to China territory from POK for the construction of Karakoram Road. [27] Let us also remember that under the current friendly relations that the US has with India it may not directly do anything at the diplomatic level at sea. It dominates the sea. There may not be room for India to manouvre at sea without the bonhomie with the Americans. It may however allow China to proceed with Pakistan as it ignored the Chinese help to Pakistan on the nuclear and the missile issue.

Common Domestic Scenarios

Both Russians and the Indians face considerable internal challenges corruption and terrorism to name the few. Russia is controlled by national crony capitalism while India has not been able to go to the second stage of economic reforms. In both cases the State continues to matter. Both have shown a consistent capacity to manage their own house.

Russia has done this in a recent case of terrorist hostage taking in the theatre in Moscow. India has conducted fair and free elections in J&K. Both confront tremendous problems with regard to internal cohesion in a segmented fashion namely in Grozny and Gujarat. Russians are putting pressure on the Chechens while India is asking Pakistan to stop cross border terror and stop calling the goings on in Kashmir as freedom struggle. Both however need to clear their stables of oligarchies and both need to galvanise their peoples to committed national goals. Both have great power ambitions. They would like to be considered as powers having interests in the land and sea. It is this identity of interests that may put them on a redefining moment in terms of looking beyond the current unipolarity. Both are concerned about Central Asia, as much as the sea.

Current Indo-Russian Relations in Fluid Strategic Environment

Let us first look at the current relations and then delineate their possible future course. Both have realised that their foreign policy has exibited the Icarus syndrome.[28] Vajpayee Government has realised that the US will not help India in J&K, as it would like it to. Pakistan will remain the US' frontline State in the latter's fight against terror in, the region. In other words it will keep Musharraf's Pakistan closer to its game plan'. [29] In case of Russia the US and the Europeans want that NATO should expand to include Ukraine and the Baltics that the Russians do not want. Both India and Russia are in diplomatic contact with China. Russia has a strategic partnership with China. This partnership may only be to deal with China since they are not opposing it in Asia. Their bilateral relations are fovcused on arms sale and, technology transfer; movement of economic relations, and pursue good neighbourlym relations. But they are doged by 'historical mutual suspicion, and respective concerns about each others long termsthreat potential' which will limit Russian-Chinese cooperation. [30] US have a nuclear understanding with China. At a future point when the Russian-Chinese schism occurs US will but in, particularly since it is so far able to keep the Japanese and the Chinse relationship in harmony. India is having diplomatic talks with China on the LOC. The strategic relationship between Russia and China has not so far altered the balance of military power that would negatively affect India Vis a Vis China. So India cannot have a ground to fear the Russian-Chinese strategic relationship.

The US has a forked policy in East Europe and East Asia. This involves' Russia and China. In Europe it wants to expand NATO to, include Poland, Czecoslovakia and Hungary but extend it to the Baltic States. The Europeans have signed an agreement with the Russians to consult each other on issues of security. This agreement is of rhetoric and symbolic value. Its validity will be seen in the future. In East Asia the US policy is strangled in a similar cleft. If it goes ahead with the Japanese American Security Allaince, it will ruffle the Chinese hairs. At the sametime it need to engage with China that the Japanese will not want. So how will it manage tight rope walking.[31] This is also the problem with South Asia. How does it handle India-Pakistan relations? It has made India its strategic friend but made Pakistan its frontline ally.[32] The balance is tilting in favour of Pakistan. It cannot afford to tilt in India's favour for a variety of reasons. One being that it will loose a significant ally in its fight against terror. Second being that the Statehood of Pakistan may itself be in jeopardy. The issue is will Pakistan be more useful to it as it is or will it be more useful to it as a failed State as Afghanistan is? Briefly putting it the limit of its unipolarity is that it cannot run with the hare and hunt with the hound. It cannot keep Russian, Indian, Chinese, Japanese, Pakistani and Indian fears in check. Not when it's own going at various levels becomes strained. As a short term option it is following a policy of containment towards China, Constrainment towards India and Strainedness towards Russia.

The current status of Indo-Russian relations is emerging from the shocks of the Yeltsin - Kozyrev phase and the ad hoc responses of the Indian foreign interventions. During that period the two had signed a Treaty of Friendship that did not have the security clause of the earlier Treaty of Peace and Friendship of 1971. In 2000 during the visit of Putin a *Joint Statement* was signed. It identified following areas of cooperation atomic energy, space, military technical cooperation and joint research and training. The statement affirmed support for strenghtening regional and international security as well as support for advancing towards general and complete disarmamnent. Its strategic partnership covered in the political field the aim of reduction of nuclear weapons, in defence area to have defence and aimed technical cooperation. In other fields it aimed at fighting terrorism, separatism, roganised crime and illegal traficking in narcotics. It refrained fron from creating a military-political alliance. Next year that is in 2001 the Russian Foreign minister paid a visit to India in the context of Bush administration announcing its plans to put in place its National Missile Defence system. The US has been, since the Reagan Administration, wanting to militarise Space and breaking out of the ABM Treaty. The world public opinion then had opposed it. The Gorbachev New Thinking disuaded the US from doing so. Now the new US Administration revived it. Both India and Russia have opposed it. So has China. It is now said that both Russia and India have made some adjustments to this deployment.

During Prime Minister Vajpayee's visit to Moscow the two countries signed an *Agreement in September in 2001 that* gave to India a nuclear plant, despite the fact that Russia had expressed negative thaughts on India's Pokharan-II. The plant at Kudamgulam will produce 2000 Mw units of power and is expected to be completed by 2006 -07. In 1997 the two sides signed a Military-Technical Cooperation Agreement and extended defence cooperation till 2010. Under the agreement covered new areas like the anti-ballistic missile systems and joint R &D of new weapon systems, like the Brahmos (Brahamputra-Moscow supersonic, 290 kg range, anti ship cruise missile, a fight generation jet fighter, advanced electronic warfare equipmet, aircraft engines and marine propulsion systems. In 2000 when defence cooperation was further deppened during Putin's visit the following defence deals were reportedly finalised, Army licensed production of T90 tanks, Air Force Licensed production of Sukhoi-30 MKI aircraft, Navy aircraft carrier Admiral Gorshikov after it was refitted as per the Indian requirements.[33] The period since Russian restructuring has witnessed the increasing accident rate of the MIGs. This according to the Russian side is owing to the Indians purchasing the spares at cheaper rates from unauthrised firms that cannot deliver authentic spares. They are advised to do so through the state agency. The military technical relationship between India and Russia are to the mutual advantage. The Russian wares need foreign market. India and China together provide it for 80 per cent of its defence equipment. India depends on the Russian supply for two reasons. First that its earlier system is based on Russian equipment ans men have been trained there. Second that the Russian innovation being slower it is easier for the India to accommodate it to the existing system. The Western systems in contrast may be more advance. The problems will be of adjusting to them and having training.

Economic ties need to, pick up to, Pharmaceuticals, tyre, hotel and steel mining have the potential to pick up. Some Indian companies have started entering the Russian markets. These are the Mahindras who are going, to export the Scorpio vehicle. The India-Russian economic ties need to he tapped .[34]

The documents signed by India and Russia during the Putin visit in December 2002 show strategic concerns with regard to Pakistan, Afghanistan, Iraq, Central Asia and International terrorism. There are two joint Working Groups on terrorism and Afghanistan. Both have agreed that they will not take action detrimental to each other' security. Both will fight the negative aspects of current globalisation and seek to contribute to, a new global order. The document also notes, the interests of the two, countries 'in putting an end to this common threat through preventive and deterrent measures nationally and bilaterally' The Delhi Declaration[35] further significantly notes in the context of global terrorism 'we have a particular interest in putting an end to this common threat through preventive and deterrent measures nationally and bilaterally.' This perspective of deterrent posturing bilaterally need to be extended given the changing scenarios in which new conflcit situations will arise.

The development of the ties between the two countries has taken place so far within the defining moment. In that sense the Indo-Russian relations are a subset of Indo-US, and US Russian Relations. Since Russia has also a Chinese dimension, and, during Putin's visit to China, preceding his visit to India in 2002, it was stated by the Chinese that there are no hurdles between the Russians and the Chinese the Indo-Russian relations also appear to be a subset of the Russo-Chinese relations. The consolidation of the strategic partnership will remain hostage to the Indo-US and Russo-Chinese relations under the defining moment. It will need to loosen in case of security and conflict scenarios in the redefining moment. The starting point of this is that the Russian and Chinese strategic partnership has not led to a change in the balance of power between China and India owing to the Russian help and military sales.

One is therefore not offering an argument for signing of the various agreements here of bilateral nature but a general argument of the need for nations to serve their national interests in long-term perspective. The current statements and declarations may be significant but have tomove beyond the ritualistic stage. Such documents have been made earlier and faded away with irony of war, e.g., Munich agreement. Documents that point to future course of action may be more relevant given the fact that current wars will be short, perhaps air and sea borne. The redifining moment will be when both countries give up the euphoria of going West and learning the logic of long-term interests that geography determine The redifining moment is to, be seen as part of the larger vision of multipolarity that they share and which will come with the reassertion of balance of power against the current sameness effect. It is currently difficult to say what are the relational position and which power will begin the onset of the reassertion of the new moment. Germany, Japan and China were at one stage suggested by those who looked at the Long cycles of history of transfer of power. We notice that the Putin Ivanov period of foreign policy is healthier for India. The Indian foreign policy is currently based on the realisation of the importance of her relations beyond -the military-technical, or the consideration of the military hardware, the cooperation in the field of fighting terrorism and being witness to the presence of the extra regional forces near their underbelly of security. India does still have to announce that its relations, with the Russian are not against any country. The US notes this statement in positive terms. However the Russian-Chinese strategic cooperation complicates the issue, India balances the China factor with its own China diplomacy and nearness to the US. Both Russian and India do not have strategic relations, with the USA, This relationship needs to be based on the interimmediate interests of managing national security in terms of self-help. All the institutionalisation since 1989 that has taken place so far is in the interest of the US. Rather the US is in no need of multilateral cooperation as the Iraq episode shows and as other post-cold war interdictions on its behalf have shown from Bosnia to Afghanistan.

The defining moment means that no one can deny the need of adjustment to the US power and its globalisation around technological capitalism. Second, no one can deny that the US is not just a sea power but is engaged in becoming a land warlord by preventing land states from becoming what Macinder had said, a land power as opposed to Sea power. Its attitude to various flash points, Russia, China and India, and, the Islamic world alongwith issues like the nuclear proliferation, terrorism, drug trafficking human rights and technology regimes need to be taken into account by each and every power. Even the 'second nuclear power', namely Russia perhaps finds it difficult to defend this status after the last arms reduction treaty as and when the treaty is implemented. The Russian have had to, accept the enlargement of NATO, the penetration of the Western capital, technology and politics in and around Central Asia for oilin the Caspian region and the US support to Guam countries. India knows of US tilt towards Pakistan.

On terrorism the War on Terror has led nations to oblige the 'war on terror' on the US terms and any, local agreements on terror as for example in Central Asia stand only second to the grand US strategy. The goings on in the UN on the issue of the impending attack Iraq shows that the US is not worried about the opposition being voiced to it. The French and the Russian coincidence on the French resolution do not seem to be deterring yet. The former Soviet Central Asia is in the grip of a new Cold War and the US has seen to it that the gains that the Russians and the Chinese made here are off. This is a feat that offset the Russian Chinese strategic partnership. The Americans are coming for them. In such a situation that obtains as of the defining moment India is advised to move out from its friendship with the Russians, Similarly it is said that since the Russians have a strategic relationship with the Chinese the Indians should be out of the Cold War mind set and recognises the new reality. For others the best way to take India out is to keep her engaged with the US in defence relationship, especially paratrooping exercises in and around the Thar.

The 'War on Terror' has also introduced the logic of US-Pakistan relationship in, this geostrategic concern of the US becoming the land overlord. India's current perceptions of the US role in the region are within the framework of the Strobe. Talbot-Jaswant Singh perspective of closer US-Indian defence ties within the strategic regional role of India in South Asia. Within this the Indians find the US role Vis-a-Vis China as an irrirant to live with. Some Indian scholars criticise us for expecting too much from the US interventions with Pakistan on our behalf We are at the sea of distance from the US on terror and Pakistan and what exactly is our perception of the US susceptibilities of China we do not have open information.

India-Chinese relations do not have a strategic relationship though both the US and Russians have. During Clinton's visit the Chinese agreed to target the US territory and this was a major breatthrough that is off set by the Chinese increasing naval presence in ports around India. The LOC has to be delineated in totality yet. That is a tortous prossess. Our concerns about China's role in Pakistan are not yet allayed despite its silences on our nuclear position and its China position.

In this brief context of fluid strategic relationships, *it would be worthwhile to redefine our foreign policy interests* with balance of power in view. We need to upstage the Indo-Russian relations so that the yearly exchange of visits are not reduced to either being as ceremonial or as adjunct to the US foreign policy interests. We are looking at the Indo-Russian relations as a subset of the defining moment and with in that as a subset of both Russo-Chinese and US-Pakistan relations. In terms of the subset of the defining moment we notice that both countries are given to give up their traditional concerns of security. This is happening out of constrainment (India under NDA), Russia under strainedness and, China under containment. Strainedness is being defined here as cooperation and helplessness. Constrainment implies inability to assert. Containment as the old dictum of Mr. X, i.e. change the internal political system- in China for its changed behaviour in the international arena. India is under pressure an space and nuclear issues and Indo-Russian relations felt that pressure of the US on cryogenic engines. China's gains I in the Central Asian States and their movement of democracy will have an impact on Sinkiang. Russia is forced to yield to issues on Iraq, NATO expansion, Central Asian Pipelines and NMD. Any assertion on the part of Russian Statehood from Chechenya to rescuing the hostages in Moscow recently in internal matters raises the carbunckled flush of Czarist fears among the western strategic community. There is the aspect of human rights to any of these acts, be they in India or the Russian regions.

We need to move to the redefining moment. The redefining moment can begin on the bilateral level. India, Putin said during his presence -in India, is having a six per cent growth. This is a welcome sign. The Russian economy is picking up from the great crash of 1998. In India there is a constant irritant of J&K and the role of Pakistan therein. Putin recognises it. In India the role of Pakistan in South Asia is a pain in the neck if not worse. The Russians know this and have not substantially altered India's conventional presence and strength. All the strategic thinking here is a silent observer to the fact of the increased US presence and collaboration in defence and intelligence networks. The Indo-US current exercises have to do with both Pakistan and perhaps its nuclear potential. The talks that India and US are having on the missile defence are at the formative stage.[36] They also have to do with the technological prowess of India and its strength. In military terms the Army, Air Force and the Navy have Russian ties for trade and aid from 75, 80 to 85 per cent respectively. The US praised the Indian Air Force. This happened when the Indian Air Forces' moved the Indian population from Iraq in 199 1. The current Indo-US exercise is in paratrooping.[37] This may have to do with Thar desert for the Pakistanis can also use it for nuclear strategic purposes. We also know that in the 1971 war India successfully negated the Pakistani naval preponderance in coastal boats with the help of the Russian boats. Currently we may understand their need. We may also understand their presence in the region. This understanding will create problems for the Russian and the Chinese. We need to keep our appreciation of our understanding as the ground for the redefining of the moment.

Our nuclear cooperation and strategic cooperation with the Russians is not against Third World countries. During Vajpayee's visit to Russia last year India signed among many other things the agreement on the Kudamgulam nuclear power project in Tamil Nadu that will produce 2000Mws units of power is expected to be completed by 2006-7. Foreign minister Ivanov said in 2001 that Indo-Russian relations today evoke optimism in their whole spectrum ranging from political to economic, from military to technological and humanitarian speheres. The Indo-Russian Agreement of 2000 visualises that by 2010 there will be cooperation on advanced weapons system worth $15 billion. Aircraft carrier, Awacs, 11-76, mid air refuellers, and Russian version of the Advanced Jet trainer were under discussion. Any change in the priority of weapons system must keep one thing on mind. The Russian redesign and innovation is slow and therefore is easily integrated. The positive conclusion of the negotiations on aircraft carrier (Goroshkov), opening of deeper cooperation in missile and space technology will boost this relationship. Our nuclear traid may find its needed help. We are committed to organise international space conference for non-miliarisation of Space. Both our diplomatic concerns and requirements of military equipment are adjusted more to the Russian attitudes and science and technology development. The Western systems are difficult to be integrated. They are costlier as well. Thirdly, we are reluctant to change from them. Fourthly our men are familiar with the Russian weapons and equipment. Indo-Russian relations during the Putin visit, viewed by some as ceremonial, need to be viewed in the long-term interest if we have to look beyond the defining moment. Let us not forget that the Yeltsin-Kozyrev period of the Atlanticists Russian orientation is over. Let us note that while the current Chinese - Russian strategic relationship may introduce current new strains on our security. The long term Russian-Chinese interests can never coalsece especially since both Russia and China will not like to play a second fiddel to each other in regional or global context. The Russian interest in its East is bound to come up against the Chinese doings in the region. One of the lessons of the Cold War is their hostility after their intitial honeymooning in the 1950s.

The US hegemony is temporary too. Look at its internal economy. Look also at the previous unipolar moments. Such moments do not last too long. Look at its internal logical contradictions. Once it starts facing competition all these will spring up as unexpected cracks in its nuclear shield and sword- The great cycle of imperial power will not be about technological Capitalism alone. It will be around -traditional sources of power- from oil, gas, nickle, gold bauxite, and geo-strategy to zero gravity benefits as well as ordinary weapons used in the unforgiveable tragedy of the twin towers in September 11, devastation of human lives and resources. It is here that the analysis of Modelski on the transfer of power will become more relevant and the technological conflicts between USA and China that he talks about will combine with other conflicts to create other power centres. Going by the current US thinking it is missile threat from the Third world, cyber terrorism and Islamic resurgence. The Indo-Russian relations as they are evolving have to be tended away from that direction. Apart from these there is the whole question of identity and Indo-Russian relations can evolve on some of the issues that are plaguing the world. Not around terrorism alone though. That is too narrow and skewed a parameter how so ever right it may be. There is enough ground in terms of views of the significant elements in Russia and India apart from the objective need that would warrant a post Icarus foreign policy reorientation and collaboration to come out of current dictation.

Scholars, are projecting four future strategic scenarios thus Russia-India-Iran, or Russia-China-India-Iran, or Russia-China -Iran, or China-Pakistan - Iran as counterpoint to the US domination.[38] .This paper suggests that another possible scenarios could be to deny to the US its foreign policy goals of unilateral or joint interdiction e.g. in Iraq and North Korea as it currently intends to do-. It is necessary to deny any such future interdictions by suggesting bilateral interdictions and move beyond the current defining moment. It is quite possible that the US may like to have failed Pakistan, Afghanistan and other Central Asian States and practice warlordism therein. These would be of direct security consequence to Iran, China and Russia. Let us not forget that during the jihad against the Soviet troops the CIA violated Pakistan sovereignty by droping equipment into Balochistan for Afghan mujahedeen .[39] The reference to Balochistan is with the intention of building up an alternative scenario to show that warlordism may help the US domination as it did in case of the Baloch tribal and Pakistan cleavage. It is traditionally known that the non Punjabi nationalisms in Pakistan have worked to Pakistan's disadvantage, especially if they have received foreign Support.[40] Such Cleavages are up in the case of the Third World countries as part of the current thrust of globalisation.[41]

India and Russia will have to develop their relations beyond the present defining moment. In a seminar on Indo-Russian relations the visiting Russian Chairman of the Duma Committee on Security Affairs said that such a possibitity of Indo-Russian collaboration could be thaught of in the future. India, alongwith Russia, has to develop a strategy of joint interdiction. If it exists for fighting terrorism, it could also be worked out for larger geostrategic long -term interests. The advantage of this would be the following. Firstly, it will show to what extent the US is prepared to go with -us-on the Pakistan issue and Central Asia. This may also draw Russia out of its parameters of the Chinese strategic partnership. Currently both Russia and the US have closer relation with China and Pakistan respectively than does India has. But there is a prediction that because of Oil the West and Russia may have conflict from Iraq to the Caspain Sea through Central Asia .[42] Since we notice that the oil interests dominate the global politics a higher level *relationship with Russia may be worth its futuristic while in geopolitical and geostrategic terms.*

References

1. Subhash Kapila 'India-Russia Strategic Cooperation, time to move Away www.Saag.org/apers2/pape4r144 .html.
2. Jerome MCooley Indo-Russian Military and Nuclear Cooperation Implication for US Security Interest

3. Yeltsin and Indo-Russian Relations, www.indiainfo.com & ISO 9001 channel INSS Occasional paper 31, February 2000

4. Afzal Mahmood, 'The Bear hugs the Cow' www.defencejournal.com/ January99/bear-hugs-cow.html

5. Madhavan Palat, Indo Russian Relations Perspectives, Report of IPCS Seminar held on November 10 , 2001, Speaker Madhavan Palat, Centre for Historical Studies, JNU,www.ipcs.org/issues/article/435 ifp.mano.html.

6. P. R Chari, 'Indo-Russian Miliatry Cooperation,. Oplim Edition -National-Newspaper Thursday, November 8, 2001www.hinduonnet.; com/2001/11/08//Stories/05082523.

7. Sanjaya Baru-'Putia Russia in Perspective', FinanciaL Express, Friday, November 29, 2002.

8. Robert Keohane & Joseph Nve, Jr. Power and Interdependence, Boston, 1978.

9. V. P. Dutt, India's Foreign Poficy in A Changing World Vikas, 1999.

10. Srimat Roy, India In World Affairs On Security Issue 1989-99, Ph.D. Dissertation, Centre for Political Studies, School of Social. Sciences, JNU, 2000.

11. Jaswant Singh National Security, An Outline of Our concerns, Lancer, New Delhi, 1996.

12. http// www.futures studies.co.uk/predictions /083 pdf. peter Rutland. Has democracy failed in Russia' Adrian Leftwitch, od Democracy and Development, polity press, 1996; The Struggle For Russia, Power and Change in the democratic revolution, Ruslan Khasbulatobv, ed. By Richard Sakwa, Routledge, London. New York. 1993; Vadim Medish, ed. My Russia .The political Autobiography of Gennady Zyuganov. M. E. Sharp Armonk, New York London, England, 1997.

13. Gordon Newspost Russia's futures, Russia's options, http//mail.1 sit. Uc 36.edu/pipemail/gordon newsport/ 2001-Nov/00 828.html.

14. Daniel Triesman- 'Russia Renewed', Foreign Affairs, November-December, 2002. pp. 58-77;

15. George Modelski and Sylvia Modelski Documenting Global Leadership, Macmillan, 1988.

16. Futuristic study 4 scenarios

17. Charles Wolf, Jr. Straaddling economics and Politics, RAND, 2002.

18. Global Trends 2015 Dialogue About The Future With Non Government Experts. NIC 2000-02 , December 2000

19. *Ibid.*

20. Ashley J. Tellis & C. C. Fair J. Jo Medby Limited Conflicts under the Nuclear Umbrella; Indian and Pakistan. Lessons from The Kargil Crisis, RAND, MR. 1450. RAND, 2001.

21. Atul Kohil, India's democracy, An Analysis of Changing State Society Relationship, Rient lonfman, 1988.

22. Ashley J.Tellis, The Changing Military - Political Environment in South Asia, RAND, 2001.

23. F. S. Larrabe, Russia and Its Neighbours, RAND, RP 958, p.14.

24. Lt. Gen. (retd) SCN Jatar, The Iraq War Strategic Implications of US Concern for Energy Security; SAPRA INDIA Monthly Bulletin, New Delhi, pp. 2-12.

25. Rajinder Puri, quoted in *Ibid.*

26 Mary Anne Weaver Pakistan. In The Shadow of Jihad, Faraar, Strau and Giroux, 2002.

27. Sumit Ganguly, Conflict Unending, Indo-Pakistan Relations since 1947, OXFORD, University Press, 2002.

28. General Andrey Nikolaev, 'Indo-Russian Cooperation in the 21st century', Indian Defence Review, New Delhi, Jan-March, 2002 Pp. 32-34.

29. Stephen Philip Cohen, 'The Nation and the State in Pakistan, 'The Washington Quarterly, Summer 2002; Antol Liven, The Pressures on Pakistan Foreign Affairs, January-February, 2002.

30. Roberty Satter, China and japan Trouble Ahead, The Washington Quarterly, Autumn, 2002.

31. Charles wolf. op. cit.

32. B. Raman, Terrorist State as a Frontline Ally, Lancer Paper 7, New Delhi, 2002.

33. Vice Admiral GM Hiranandani, 'Indo-Russian defence Cooperation, Idnian Defence Review, July- September, 2002 pp. 55-59.

34. Sanjay Baru , *op. cit.*
35. Delhi Declaration.
36. Times of India, New Delhi, 23-01-03.
37. US Ambassador, Blackwill, Asian Age New Delhi, 24 January, 2003.
38. SCN Jatar, *op. cit.*
39. Mary Anne Weaver, *op. cit.*
40. Owen Bennet Jones, Pakistan, Eye of the Storm, Viking 2002.
41. Radhika Desai, Slouching Towards Ayodhya, Three Essays, New Delhi, July, 2002, pp. 1-55.
42. Ariel Cohen, Ph.D, 'The "New Great Game", Oil Politics In the Caucasus and Central Asia,' Heritage Foundation, Backgrounder No. 1065, January 1996.

5
Indo-Russian Strategic Cooperation

K.K. Nayyar

Strategic alliances rarely survive the epoch in which they are born. But, the Indo-Soviet/Russian strategic alliance has done just that. The time-tested relations between the two nations, based traditionally on mutual trust and understanding, have survived the end of the Cold War and the post-Cold War period, and moved into the new, though yet unnamed period of global politics. Since such alliances are based on the hard facts of national interests rather than sentimental attachments, it alerts us to the simple fact that for both Russia and India, their strategic concern in Asia has not radically changed since the 1950s.

During the State visit of the Russian President Vladimir Putin in October 2000, a *declaration* on Strategic Partnership between the Republic of India and the Russian Federation was signed. This is a document of cardinal significance and marks a new step forward in the elaboration of the principles of our bilateral relations. It lays down the broad contours of bilateral relations between the Republic of India and the Russian Federation in the twenty-first century.[1]

After the disintegration of the USSR and the emergence of Russia as an independent State, Russia declared itself to be 'State-continuator' of the erstwhile USSR in the early 1990s. Nonetheless, India recognised Russia as the successor-State to the former Soviet Union. India's relations with the Russian Federation are multi-faceted and encompass varied sectors including political consultations, economic and commercial relations and cooperation in trade and economy, science and technology, culture, education and defence. It is significant that India and Russia are the world's largest democracies, India in terms of the size of the population and Russia in terms of its size.

Both countries have emphasised the importance that they attach to bilateral relations and the strategic dimension of Indo-Russian relations, and deem them not to be subject to political vicissitudes. Both countries share similar perceptions on many international issues. For instance, interactions on developments in the region lying between the borders of India and Russia have been found to be beneficial and contacts are being maintained on the evolving situation in Afghanistan.

Bilateral defence cooperation between India and Russian is limited not only to procurement but also covers areas like joint research and development and service-to-service cooperation. During the visit of President Putin to India in October 2000, an Agreement was signed on the establishment of an Inter Governmental Commission for Military Technical Cooperation (IGCMTC).

Given the constructive Indo-Russian interaction, it may not be an exaggeration to claim that post-Cold War transitional difficulties are now left well behind. On the occasion of India's Republic Day this January, the Russian President, Vladimir Putin, in his message to the President, A. P. J. Abdul Kalam, said, "Russia highly assesses and earnestly cherishes its noble ties of friendship and multifaceted cooperation with India which, in recent years, has evolved into a strategic partnership of the two nations."[2]

In a post-Cold War world of burgeoning American supremacy, even though the United States of America accounts for some 20 per cent of India's foreign trade, India has evidently neither abrogated nor curtailed its defence cooperation relations with Russia, due to the presence of large ex-Soviet inventories [3]. The latest protocol between India and Russia envisaged a package of defence sales to India worth $3 billion[4]. This included nuclear propelled submarines, strategic bombers, joint development of a fifth generation fighter aircraft and the setting up of joint ventures on the pattern of the supersonic Brahmos cruise missile. The Foreign Office spokesman said that, "The acquisitions would complete India's cherished nuclear triad. It would also aggravate the existing imbalance in conventional forces and strategic weapon delivery systems in the region."[5] The two sides also resolved to enter into new commercial tie-ups in several areas including telecom equipment and hydrocarbons, which envisage investment of over $1 billion. The issue of steady delivery of high quality spares for the existing military aircraft of Russian origin had also been the issue of discussion between Mr. Klebanov, Mr. Putin's pointman for defence ties with India, and Mr. George Fernandes, the Indian defence minister.

A concise summary of the some crucial visits of high-level dignitaries from both sides

- The landmark official visit to the Russian Federation undertaken by the Indian Prime Minister between March 24-26, 1997. The visit provided a new impetus to the traditionally close and amicable ties between India and Russia.
- The Minister of External Affairs from India visited Russia from February 9-13, 1997 to co-chair the Third Session of the Indo-Russian Inter-Governmental Commission (IGC) on Trade, Economic, Scientific, Technological and Cultural Cooperation. Besides the Protocol of the Third IGC Session, an Agreement on the Establishment of a Joint Shipping Service between India and Russia and a Memorandum of Understanding on Certification in the field of Information Technology were signed during the visit.
- The first visit by the Russian Defense Minister to India, since the break-up of the Soviet Union, was undertaken from October 21-23, 1996.
- More recently, Prime Minister Vajpayee paid a State Visit to the Russian Federation from November 4-7, 2001. This was the return visit to the State Visit to India in October 2000 by President Vladimir Putin, during which the Declaration on Strategic Partnership was signed. During President Putin's visit, the mechanism of annual Summit level interaction was reiterated. During this visit, Prime Minister Vajpayee was conferred an Honorary Doctorate by the Moscow State University.
- At the invitation of then External Affairs Minister Mr. Jaswant Singh, Russian Minister of Foreign Affairs, Igor Ivanov, visited India on February 3-4, 2002. Mr. Ivanov had detailed discussions with External Affairs Minister on bilateral matters and on regional and international issues of mutual concern. A Joint Statement was signed and issued at the end of the visit.
- Then Deputy Chairman of the Government of the Russian Federation, Ilya Klebanov, visited India from February 5-8, 2002. Mr. Klebanov, and the then Finance Minister, Mr. Yashwant Sinha, co-chaired the 8th Session of the Indo Russian Inter-Governmental Commission on Trade, Economic, Scientific and Cultural Cooperation (IRIGC) on February 7, 2002.

An Attribute of a dynamic foreign policy is the ability to respond to changing developments. The emergence of the Central Asian Republics in the aftermath of the break-up of the Soviet Union was one such recent development, and India, given the strategic and economic importance of this region, has been quick to strengthen its bilateral relations with each of these Republics.

The shift in recent years by the countries of Central and East Europe to political pluralism and market-oriented structures has also seen India trying to build upon existing business and institutional linkages so as to further strengthen the traditional ties of friendship with the countries of this region. For instance,, the Minister of Trade of the Federal Republic of Yugoslavia visited India in December 1996. This was the first such visit of a Yugoslav official after the lifting of the UN sanctions against the Federal Republic of Yugoslavia October 1, 1996. Along the same time, a Protocol on Foreign Office Consultations was concluded with Slovenia. The State Secretary in the Ministry for Foreign Affairs of Slovenia visited India from December 15-17, 1996, and signed an Agreement on Cultural Cooperation. Furthermore, Assistant Foreign Minister of Croatia visited India from 14-16 September 1996 for bilateral political consultations.

India and Russia share common interests in a stable Asia and both worry about the possibility of any single power - be it China or the United States - dominating the continent. This fundamental concern is the source of the stability of the Indo-Russian strategic alliance. Both are also, geopolitically, located in a manner that does not bring them into direct conflict with one another.

There have been periods when these ties appeared to fray, as both countries looked to satisfy other strategic needs. In the late 1960s, the Soviet Union attempted to 'balance' its relations with India by attempting to build closer ties with Pakistan. That attempt failed. In the early post-Cold War period, the Russian leadership thought that the Indo-Russian strategic relations was one of the many Cold War baggage they had to rid the new Russia of as they built a new cooperative order with the West. That attempt also failed as the Russian leadership, even before Putin, realised that despite the end of the Cold War, the principles that governed relations between nations had not changed very much, and that the West still considered Russia a potential rival.

India has had extensive cooperation in space with the former USSR. The Soviet side assisted India in the setting up of the Thumba Equatorial Rocket Launching Station and the launching of Indian experimental satellites Aryabhata, Bhaskara I and Bhaskara 2. The Indian remote sensing satellites IRS-IA/IB were launched by Soviet launch vehicles on a commercial basis. The flight of Sqdn Ldr Rakesh Sharma, the first Indian in space, was from the Salyut Space Station in the USSR. The Agreement on the supply of cryogenic engines from Russia is being satisfactorily implemented.

Over the last few years, especially under Vladimir Putin, there has been a revival of the traditional strategic comfort between Moscow and New Delhi. But, as before, strategic realities rather sentimentality will decide the fate of this relationship. And the strategic rality is that though there are significant challenges to this relationship, there is an underlying complementarity of interests between Moscow and New Delhi, which will hold these relations in good stead.

In the current scenario, Indo-Russian strategic ties confront three significant challenges. The first, and most important challenge is that both India and Russia recognise the importance of the United States in the current international order and the importance of maintaining good relations with the unipolar power. For both countries, this imperative over-rides most other strategic requirements. This affects Indo-Russian relations in a variety of ways, from the most obvious such as limitations on the extent of military ties and, particularly, research and development collaboration, to less obvious ones, such as the fact that both India and Russia have closer economic relations with the US than with each other.

For instance, Indo-Russian trade is only about one tenth of Indo-US trade, and in the last two years has actually declined, compared to the rising graph of US-India trade. Certain reports in the media have also pointed out that the present level of trade with Russia is not commensurate with the true potential, even though the total trade turnover showed an upward trend during the year 1999-2000, when it grew by 28.75 %. However, trade turnover once again declined by 6 % during the year 2000-01 to U $$ 1.4 billion compared with 1999-2000. While exports in Rupee terms fell by 1.28 % (6.36% in Dollar terms), the decline in imports was 13.18 % (17.65 % in Dollar terms). During 2001-02, trade turnover was U$$ 1.33 billion, a fall of 4.31 % compared to previous year.

The second challenge that India and Russia face is in understanding and dealing with China. There is a general reluctance in the foreign/strategic policy establishments of major capitals around the world to talk in anything more than a whisper about how to deal with China. Both India and Russia recognise the long-term threat that China poses, but are unsure of how exactly to deal with this threat. In the Russian case, this problem is compounded by Russian arms sales to China, which though necessary to maintain a Viable Russian defence industrial base, something which is in India's interest also, nevertheless impacts on the military balance in Asia and on India's security.

The third challenge that the partnership faces is that both countries are relatively weak. Unlike the Soviet-Indian partnership during the Cold War period, which was anchored by Soviet superpower capabilities and power, today neither India nor Russia has the material capabilities to back the other on significant international issues. For example, it is unlikely that Russia is today in a position to veto decisions of the UN Security council unfavourably to India, as it did during the 1971 war.

Despite these challenges, the strength of the relationship lies in the continuing complementarity of interests. Neither India nor Russia can tolerate the dominance of any single power in the global community and in the region. American power and China's potential power in Asia are realities with which both India and Russia have already come to terms. Indeed, both powers may have actually learned to use these powers to promote their own interests, as can be seen in the war on terrorism and on other issues such as on nuclear weapons and ABMs. But these are strategies of weaker powers, and both countries will be more comfortable balancing against these powers than bandwagoning with them. As both India and Russia grow stronger, their mutual interest in countering the dominance of any single power in global and Asian politics will only bring them even closer.

References

1. This paragraph has been extracted from a report that appeared in The *Hindu* on October 3, 2000.
2. Quote taken from The Hindu, January 27, 2003.
3. 'India-Us Relations Promoting Synergy' Report of an Independent core Group, published by the institute of Peace and Conflict Studies, p. 5,
4. The figure has been extracted from the report that appeared in *The Hindu* on January 23, 2003.
5. The quote has taken from the report that appeared in *The Hindu* on January 23, 2003.

6

Indo-Russian Equation : A Rapid View

Afsir Karim

Indo-Russian relations have undergone many changes since the end of Cold War. The sudden collapse of the Soviet Union initially shocked India and the impact of this event continued for quite sometime but a new policy towards the Russian Federation gradually re-emerged. Russia seemed keen to continue to base its relations with India on a strategic level but on a different footing. It consistently supported India's case for a seat in the Security Council, although it was not quite comfortable with India's nuclear tests in 1998 and it generally condemned nuclearisation of the sub-continent. Russia, however, did not support impositions of sanctions against India and did not allow the bilateral relations between the two countries to suffer. After the Kargil war the relations between the two countries improved greatly as Russia was openly critical of Pakistan's aggressive designs towards India and its policy of supporting and sponsoring insurgent-terrorism in Indian-controlled Kashmir. India was equally keen to maintain close bilateral relations with the Russian Federation, but it took time before a new equation could be established after the collapse of the Soviet Union.

A constant factor in Indo-Russian relationship has been close cultural ties and collaboration in nuclear technology for peaceful purposes. Cooperation in various international forums and supply of defence equipment critical for India's strategic needs continued through out without many changes. Some problems arose in reviving the old arrangements for supply of defence equipment in the aftermath of the break up of the Soviet Union but these were gradually overcome. Mr Putin's visit in the first week of October 2000 finally reopened the way for supply of critical defence items and weaponry to India. This visit opened many new avenues of mutual cooperation between India and Russia on use of nuclear energy for peaceful purposes. Both the countries realized the importance of mutual cooperation in reshaping their policies in the new world order and were keen to arrive at some kind strategic consensus for mutual benefit. The declaration of strategic cooperation signed in the year 2000 proposed close economic, political, cultural and scientific collaboration. The two countries pledged to share information and hold joint consultations to combat international terrorism. India and Russia agreed on the desirability of a multi-polar world order based on equality of sovereign nations.

Another significant development was the establishment of the inter-governmental commission for consultations on important defence issues and matters of security concern to both countries. Russia and India share a common view about of the necessity of total nuclear disarmament and both are concerned about increasing nuclear threats.

Incidentally, Russia is only second to the US in the arms market and is keen to further expand its arms trade. The contracts signed with India in the past for licensed production of T 90 C tanks amounted to $ 700 million and $ 1.5 billion for SU-30 MKK fighters. According to the latest reports India will lease nuclear bombers and nuclear propelled submarines, now the agreement on acquisition of Admiral Gorshkov the 44.5 thousand tones mothballed aircraft carrier by India has been finalised. The BrahMos cruise missile system fitted it Akula class submarines and the TU-22M3 strategic bomber will boost India's nuclear deterrent. India and Russia have also agreed to jointly develop a fighter aircraft based on S-37 Berkut, this would ready for use in 2010. Indian – Russian arrangement on procurement of highly sophisticated defence equipment is crucial for India in view of advanced defence equipment, and missile systems being available to Pakistan from North Korea and China, besides the armament available to it from America and diverse Western sources.

Incidentally Russia and China have agreed to keep their arms agreements under wraps but it is believed China is keen on acquiring more nuclear submarines, advanced warships and arms technologies from Russia-on hard cash payment of course Russia, has already sold S-300 PNU2 Air Defence system to China, which was worth $ 400 million. It also sold, MIGs 29 to Myanmar and Yemen and made a $ 600 million deal with South Korea in exchange for helicopters and some other items. Russia also made a $ 150 million deal with Iran for H-17 helicopters and shoulder carried IGLA anti-air craft missile system. President Putin once indicated that arms sales, which amounted to worth $ 5 billion, had hit 10 year high in 2001.

Russia is no longer a super power but there are definite indications that it is slowly re-emerging, as a major power. Russian and Indian equations should be reassessed carefully by both the countries for arriving at mutually compatible policies Developing long-term strategic relationship between India and Russia cannot, however, depend solely on arms deals, it has to encompass various political, economic, cultural and security arrangements. The necessity of forging strategic alliances against hegemonic designs of the sole super power should be considered by India though American policies may not be posing many immediate problems for India, Russia on its part has thrown hints about forging a Russia – China- India triangular alliance Russians had first propagated the idea of a strategic Russia-India-China triangular alliance in 1998. The concept could not be developed further because of the political compulsions of all the three countries at that juncture.

The security environments have lately changed drastically, because of large scale US military presence in South and Central Asian regions. Russia is still obliged to maintain strategic consensus with the United States because of its economic dependence on the West and this factor plays a restrictive role in shaping of Russian policies. Russia's nuclear status, technology and weapon systems combined with its geo-strategic importance, however, gives it an inherent potential to re-emerge as a global power in the next few decades. During recent visit of Russian President Vladimir Putin to India the topic of triangular relationship was revived according to certain media reports, although the focus of these bilateral talks between India and Russia remained on international and sponsored terrorism. The concept of the triangular relationship among Russia – India – China that originated from Russia was attributed to Yevgeny Primakov, although he denied having proposed any such arrangement. He, however, did support the idea during his visit to India in 1998, in the context of US inspired aerial attacks on Yugoslavia by NATO. Russian Prime Minister, Boris Yeltsin, former President of Russia, is also reported to have once proposed a strategic tie up among the three countries.

War on terrorism has created a new security environment in international alliances are necessary, to counter this menace Russian concept of the strategic triangle beside its other objectives can play an important role in countering international terrorism. Russia and India are already under attack by Islamic terrorist groups, China may not be facing a serious threat from that quarter now but the danger exists because of Uighar Muslim separatist movement. A concrete shape to Russian – Indian-China strategic triangle cannot be given till the current differences between

India and China remain unresolved. China would have to redefine its relationship with Pakistan to come to any strategic understanding with India. China will have to stop those policies, which are meant to encourage Pakistan to adopt a belligerent attitude towards India. This may not be easy because of China's long- term strategic aims in South Asia, besides Pakistan providing an opening to the Indian Ocean region. China gets various logistical and strategic advantages in propping up Pakistan against India in this region. In the present security environment China is not likely to be in favour of joining any alliance except for a strategic understanding with Russia. India has been silent on the possibility of the proposed triangular relationship among the three countries because of these factors.

It would be best for India to develop a lasting bi-lateral relationship with Russia based on long-term convergence of interests rather than several short-term agreements. In the current strategic environment the United States and its European allies are following the policy of marginalizing Russia, taking advantage of its current economic difficulties. The growing Chinese power and its affect on the global security has degraded Russia's standing as the second most powerful country in the world. However Russia may be out of the woods soon and new global equations may emerge. India should reassess its security requirements and re-evaluate, its political and economic ties with Russian in this light.

Russia is presently concerned with the aggressive thrust of NATO in its domain and growing propensity of the United States of America, taking unilateral military action, in West Asia and in the affairs of Eastern Europe. Russia in the circumstances would like to seek strategic support of China and India to check America's hegemonic ambitions. However, in the past three years relations between United States of America and India have greatly improved and India may not like to disturb it fruitful association with America by entering into any alliance that may appear to be basically Anti-American in nature.

Both Russia and India are facing terrorism of the Jehadi groups but they have yet to develop a strategic consensus to face this common danger. A new initiative should be taken by India to forge a relationship with Russia that can help in maintaining the regional balance both in South and Central Asia. Central Asian region is under attack by the Jehadi movement that is presently anchored in Pakistan- Afghan border areas and it will be in the interest of both Russia and India to follow a common policy to thwart its attempts to overthrow the moderate regimes of Central Asia. In a way Central Asia is a key area where the thrust of the Jehadi movement can be confronted and contained.

It will be necessary for India and Russia to engage China to join hands with them in stopping the aggressive designs of Pakistan- based Jehadi groups in their tracks. Close coordination between Russia, India and China would go a long way in overcoming the turbulence that is being created by the Jehadi groups in South and Central Asian regions. Russia may be in a position to facilitate cooperation between China and India and bring them to together on a common platform to combat Jehadi terrorism. China has already shown inclination to make a common strategic cause with Russia and presenting an alternative to the US monopoly in war against terrorism. China's problems with Uighar Muslim separatists persist in Xinjiang and Jehadi groups based in Central Asia or Afghanistan can greatly encourage Uighar separatist groups and create major problems in this mineral –rich strategic frontier area of China.

China is already a member of the five member (Russia, China, Kazakhstan, Kyrgyzstan and Tajikistan) Shanghai group, primarily this group helps China in checkmating the Jehadi forces whose aim is to foment trouble in Xinjiang.

Trade links between Russia and India should be reviewed at regular intervals since trade now has to be conducted in hard currency through private enterprises and joint stock companies. Indian companies have to learn the ways of new 'Russian bureaucracy and Mafia'. Indian goods have to be attractive and cheaper in comparison to Chinese, Southeast Asian and western goods as State trading is now restricted to certain specified items and defence purchases only.

Long-term strategic ties between Russia and India will be in the interest of both the countries and they can forge closer ties on the following lines

- A formal agreement for close cooperation in countering Jehadi movement and terrorism is necessary under the present environment as both the countries face a long –term threat from a common source. Joint training by the special forces of the two countries and combined intelligence operations will help both the countries and put the terrorists and the Jehadi groups on the defensive. Joint operations for cutting off sources of finances an arms supplies to terrorists if carried out successfully will hamper terrorist operations greatly.
- A mutual security arrangement to curb low intensity conflicts in either country, preparation of joint doctrines to combat separatist movements sponsored by external agencies such as Islamic Jehad. Sharing of intelligence to uncover insurgent's plans and movements.

- Tie up on research on weapons and armaments and exchange of information on new weapons systems and technologies. This should be managed by norms and principles laid down by the joint working groups for achieving quicker results.

  Making joint efforts to counter spreading of Islamic fundamentalism by coordinating programmes and policies on issues of common interest related to the Central Asian region.

- Special economic ties between Russia and India should be strengthened. Russia under the leadership of Vladimir Putin is moving towards economic recovery gradually and this provides a good opportunity for India to cooperate with Russia and improve economic ties with it. To achieve the required degree of mutual cooperation it will be necessary for Indian policy planners to be flexible and patient. It will be in India's interest to make serious efforts to give a push to exports to Russia. For smooth functioning of various agreements it will be necessary to develop good working relationship with Russiantrade organisations and officials dealing with trade and industry.

- Central Asia has emerged with new national identities and aspirations. They collectively form a key area of great international significance because of economic potential, rich oil resources that rival the Middle East. During the past decade this region has been the target of direct and indirect attacks of the Islamic fundamentalist regime based in Afghanistan. India has yet to make a serious effort to build appropriate economic and strategic ties with the countries of this important region. Russia remains the most important player in this region despite the efforts of the US and its allies to establish themselves here, India should develop a cooperative programme with Russia to gain influence in this area. India will also require Russia's cooperation to combat obstacles that would be created by Pakistan with the help of

- Islamic extremist groups to discourage India's access to Central Asia. The propagation of the concept of a multi -polar world is shared by Russia and India, strategic partnership between the two countries will be necessary for evolving this concept. The expansion of NATO and the latest American strategy of pre-emptive military action against those countries that do not share the American worldview have lent urgency to an integrated approach to counter hegemonic policies of the US administration.

In conclusion it can be said with certainty that Russian –Indian relations have stood the test of time and should grow further in the current global environment. The issues that have brought the countries close in the past are strategically vital for both the countries. In the foreseeable future the issues of common interest such as USA's hegemonic designs, international terrorism and sponsored Jehadi terrorist movements will remain of vital concern both to Russia and India. A long-term strategic partnership between the countries is necessary to counter these forces.

7

Changing Perspective of India-Russia Relations

Devendra Kaushik

At the beginning of the new millennium a reappraisal of the bases on which India and Russia - two powerful quasi- neighbouring states - have built their relations over a long period of more than half a century is but a timely exercise portentous for their future prospects. Ever since 1947 when India gained its independence, doubting Thomases have been cautioning time and again against close relations with Russia. It was against the backdrop of Western political and military support for Pakistan involved in dispute with India over the territory of Kashmir that India condescendingly agreed to a tactical relationship with Red Moscow. The tardiness of the West in extending assistance to India in building its heavy industrial base prolonged the honeymoon with the Soviet Union which got a new lease on account of Beijing- Islamabad - Washington axis and the SinoSoviet ideological split. The end of the Cold War following the disintegration of the U.S.S.R and the emergence of a unipolar world with the United States as the sole surviving superpower has further reduced the premium on relations with Russia – now allegedly relegated to the status of a medium-level regional power.

However, these doubting Thomases are greatly underestimating the soundness and strength of the bases of Indo-Russian relations. India and Russia are two great powers located in close proximity to each other. Their approach to various important international problems has either been convergent or quite close to each other. During the last fifty years a large number of agreements between the two countries about close cooperation in the field of industry, agriculture, science, technology and culture were concluded and successfully implemented. The people of both the countries have been benefited from the many-sided cooperation between them. Their bilateral cooperation has also contributed to the strengthening of peace and stability in Asia and the world at large. Between the Soviet Union / Russia and India there have been no hostilities ever and they have never been at war. History does not record any other example of a smooth crisis free relationship between the two big powers of the size and strength of India and the Soviet Union / Russia extending over a long period of about six decades. There is a strong historical basis for close relations between India and Russia. Their relations go back to antiquity and are rooted in geocultural traditions. It is a well-known fact that of all the Indo- European languages Sanskrit and Russian are the closest. Modern Russian language so far as grammatical rules and syntax are concerned strictly follow the great Indian grammarian, Panini, who lived in the sixth century B.C. Tilak's Arctic Home in the Vedas contains substantial evidence to show that the ancestors of the Indians and the Russians lived for a long-time in close vicinity in the northern Arctic region

Significantly American geostrategist Brzezinski's game plan as spelled out in his book The Grand Chessboard envisages Russia and India as two powers whose strategic interests converge in the Eurasian region. It is by offering Russia as a bait that America hopes to cultivate Germany, Japan and China for sustaining the unipolar world under its hegemony at least for a generation. Beijing is perceived by Brzezinski as America's "natural ally" in Eurasia. Beijing's growing interest in Central Asia is viewed by him as a move likely to prevent Central Asia's reintegration with Russia. The Chinese support for Pakistan is seen as a factor restraining India's ambition to subordinate that country as also offsetting India's inclination to cooperate with Russia in regard to Central Asia and Afghanistan.

The Perestrolka period (1985-1990) witnessed little substantial progress in relations between India and the then Soviet Union which faced a deep economic crisis towards the end of the Perestrolka reforms. The Yeltsin-Kozyrev foreign policy was only a toned down version of Gorbachev's "new political thinking". It is worthwhile remembering that Russian Deputy Foreign Minister Georgy Kunadze in the parliamentary hearings before Yeltsin's visit to India in January 1993 had opposed Russia having " special relations" with India which in his opinion might hurt Russia's relations with other South Asian countries, particularly Pakistan. The working paper on Russian Foreign Policy finalised towards the end of 1992, called for a "pragmatic renewal" of ties with India based on "realistic possibilities and legitimate interests of both sides with an emphasis on economic stimuli". But Russia's growing tilt towards pro-Atlanticism was off-set by "geopolitical pluralism" advocated by Kissinger and Brzezinski who dubbed as premature the talk of "partnership with Russia". The growing parliamentary opposition to the foreign policy course of Kozyrov also forced Yeltsin to dilute his pro-Atlanticism by putting relationship with India on a long-term basis through conclusion of a new Treaty of Friendship and Cooperation during his visit to New Delhi in January 1993. The exchange of state visits during 1994-1996 - Prime Minister Narasimha Rao's Moscow visit in 1994 followed by Deve Gowda's visit in 1996 -underscored the strategic aspect of the Indo-Russian relations. With Primakov taking over as Foreign Minister from Kozyrov, the Russian foreign policy course changed from "strategic alliance" to "equitable partnership" with America. The Indo-Russian relations started acquiring a long-term strategic perspective with the signing of Moscow Declaration in June 1994 during Prime Minister Rao's Moscow visit which was reaffirmed during Deve Gowda's visit in 1996.

President Putin's India visit in October 2000 imparted a new content to the Indo-Russian relations. It has significantly contributed to the further deepening of the strategic dimension of relations between the two countries by conclusion of ten agreements including defence deals worth 3 billion dollars. Russia agreed to transfer free of cost its aircraft carrier Admiral Gorshkov to be fitted with MIG-29 K fighters and Kamov -31 and Kamov -28 helicopters on payment basis. 140 SU-30 fighters are also to be produced in India under license for transfer of technology. Moscow also agreed to supply 300 T-90 tanks to India. The most important outcome of President Putin's visit is, however, the signing of the Declaration on Strategic Partnership between India and Russia. The Strategic Partnership Declaration takes cognisance of earlier treaties signed in 1971 and 1993, and the Moscow Declaration of 1994 but it does not contain the past formulation to consult each other to neutralise any threat to the other side. Instead of the obligation to consult which was embodied in the 1971 Indo-Soviet Treaty the new Declaration carries the provision of non-participation in any alliance directed against the other side. The Declaration proclaims the "establishment of relations of strategic partnership between them based on mutual understanding and long-term confidence in each other" and envisages the "elevation of their multifaceted ties to an even higher and qualitatively new level" while imparting them a "specially close and dynamic character both in the bilateral field and in the international arena". The preamble to the Declaration refers to the "conviction that it is necessary to build a multipolar global structure based on sovereign equality of all states and peoples" and "desire to jointly contribute to the strengthening of international peace and security as well as to the promotion of the establishment of a new, just and stable world order" in consonance with the " purpose and principles of the UN Charter." It however categorically asserts that the "strategic partnership between the sides is not directed against any other state or group of states and does not need to create a military political alliance."

The two countries as President Putin underlined in one of his statements during his New Delhi visit in 2000 held separate views on nuclear proliferation. But Russia unlike other Western powers did not sermonize India for conducting nuclear tests and impose economic sanctions. President Putin simply expressed the hope that India would continue to move towards a non-proliferation regime "taking into account its national interests". The area of disagreements between the two countries, which was never large, has further shrunk with the passage of time. Prime Minister Atal Behari Vaipayee's Moscow visit in 2001 further strengthened the bilateral ties between the two countries. The November 2001 Moscow visit of Prime Minister Vajpayee resulted in further deepening of close relations between India and Russia. The two countries signed the Declaration on International Terrorism, which condemns the double standard approach towards acts of terrorism. The two countries also signed a contract for drawing up a technological project to build the Kudankulam nuclear power station consisting of two units of 1,000 megawatt each. It reactivated the old 1988 agreement. The Indian nuclear power engineering market is estimated at $ 30 billion of which Russia is competing with the French and American company to acquire a major share. India is planning to raise its level of production of nuclear power from 2,000 to 6,000 megawatt by 2010, and subsequently to 20,000 megawatt by 2020.

The basic direction of the foreign policy course of Putin administration was outlined in the July 2000 Foreign Policy Concept. This document based on "healthy pragmatism and realism" aimed at assisting effectively the solution of internal problems by giving top priority to the protection of interests of the "Individual, society and state". While stating that Europe remained a " traditional priority", it also underlined that "Asia is acquiring great and ever -increasing significance in the foreign policy direction of the Russian Federation. It also declared, "Russia will deepen its traditional partnership with India including in the international affairs and contribute to the solution of problems persisting in South Asia and to strengthening of stability in the region".

The Foreign Policy Concept adopted in July 2000 also cautioned against "new dangers" arising from globalisation though it recognised that additional possibilities have been created by globalisation of the economic system. In his speech at the APEC summit at Brunei on 15 November 2000, President Putin referred to both positive and negative consequences of globalisation. Warning that the effects of global economic and financial crisis are felt by even small producers and shopkeepers, he demanded that "shocks do not affect the economic foundation of society". Putin insisted that the aims of business should coincide with the interests of society and also demanded that the consequences of globalisation should be the most important concern of heads of states and government.

Putin's policy of defending national interests and playing a more important role in world affairs including a more pro-active policy towards the West became known as the "Derzhavnik" course (Great Power nationalist course). It was manifested in his December 2000 visit to Cuba. However this policy showed signs of getting diluted beginning with the September 2000 speech before the German Parliament, which signalled a West-ward turn. Strategic stability now became an objective of the Russian foreign policy. Moscow favoured a permanent dialogue with the United States to achieve a changing quality of relationship with NATO. Putin declared that Russia's vital goal in foreign policy was to ensure strategic stability in the world and added, "Seeking to attain this goal we are taking part in the creation of a new general system of security, maintaining dialogue with the U.S.A. and working to change the quality of our relationship with NATO". At the conference of Russian diplomats in Moscow in July 2002 Putin spoke of Russia's relationship with the United States as "confident partnership in the interest not only of our people but for exerting positive influence on the entire system of international relations". In this conference Putin did not make any reference to the Asian aspect.

Foreign Minister Igor Ivanov, however, explained to the press that the President in his address could not outline all aspects and the Asian aspect also remained a top priority alongwith relations with Europe and struggle against terrorism. At the Moscow conference of Russian diplomats Putin also stated that "time was ripe for a serious discussion on strategic guidelines of our foreign policy". Carrying forward this discussion on strategic guidelines of Russian foreign policy Deputy Foreign Minister Alexei Meshkov published an article in the 8 August 2002 issue of the Nezavisimaya Gazeta under the title " Philosophy of Strategic Stability Foreign and Security Policy of Russia in early 21st century". He underscored the need for a new architecture of security in Europe and the world. Asia is mentioned in this article as a source of basic threats for global security and India is not at all mentioned in it. Though the significance of Asia and the Shanghai Cooperation Organisation has been highlighted by him, Meskov pleads for a fully dependable partnership with the United States which in his opinion would be not only in the interest of Russia but was likely to exercise a positive influence on the system of international relations. Besides dependable partnership with the United States, the article also mentions energy and economic cooperation with the European Union. Asia is mentioned as the second important vector of external policy of Russia because it is from there that basic threats to security emerge, in the first place from regional instability, terrorism and narco-trafficking.

However, one need not read much into the recent emphasis on dialogue with the United States in the Russian foreign policy. The Moscow summit between President Bush and the Rome summit resulting in a changed relationship of NATO with Russia have been more than off-set by the subsequent St. Petersburg summit of the Shanghai Cooperation Organisation and the elevation of the Collective Security Treaty to the level of an international regional organisation referred to as Collective Security Treaty Organisation at the CIS summit in Kishinev. The Kishinev summit revamped the structure at the Collective Security Treaty Organisation by opening it to all prospective members which could serve as a regional counterweight to NATO. That Asia remains vital for the Russian foreign policy has been once again proved by the recent December 2002 visit of President Putin to Beijing followed by a visit to Delhi directly from there. Putin's visit to China and India followed the NATO- expansion summit at Prague on 21-22 November 2002 which is indicative of Russia turning to its Eurasian neighbours.

A day before Mr. Putin started on his Asian tour Russia deployed war planes in Kyrgyzstan under a Collective Security arrangement with its Central Asian allies. Putin's visit to China and India in early December 2002 might not have resulted in a visible formal Russian-China-India Strategic Triangle, yet quiet behind the-scene diplomacy of President Putin helped advance, the idea of such a triangle first proposed by the then Russian Prime Minister Y. Primakov during his visit to India in 1998. Primakov during a T.V. interview in Moscow replied in affirmative about progress in shaping a Moscow Beijing -Delhi triangle during President Putin's trip to China and India. This emerging trilateral understanding as Primakov rightly pointed out need not be viewed as a military or political bloc. The declarations signed by President Putin in Beijing and New Delhi mirror the close identity of views held by the three nations on various international issues including terrorism, Iraq, West Asia, the role of the

United Nations and regional security. The three powers have a shared interest in security and stability in Central Asia and Afghanistan. Their proximity of views is likely to strengthen the idea of the Strategic Triangle.

There are reasons to believe that both China and India share Russia's concern over the Afghan situation, which remains volatile notwithstanding the year-long antiterror operation spearheaded by the United States. The writ of Karzai administration hardly runs outside Kabul, the Taliban and the Al-Qaida terrorist groups are regrouping again and threatening the security of the Central Asian states torn by ethnic, religious and social tensions. As Washington appears to be in a mood to leave unfinished the task of eliminating terrorism in Afghanistan and preparing to launch an attack on Iraq, the responsibility of ensuring security and stability in Central Asia and Afghanistan has devolved upon the neighbouring states of Russia, China and India. On the eve of his recent Asian trip President Putin in his interview with the Indian national daily *The Hindu* and the Star TV highlighted the great potential of the Shanghai Cooperation Organisation. Putin underscored the readiness "to hold consultations with the partners in the Shanghai Cooperation Organisation and with the Indian colleagues in order to determine Jointly in what kind of activity and in what capacity India would like to take part in the work of the organisation". "I think that India's participation in the joint work would raise the importance of this organisation, making it possible to expand the range of the problems it is solving and that would be positive" - added Vladimir Putin. Interestingly Vladimir Rushallo, Russian Security Council Secretary, recalled to journalists in New Delhi during President Putin's visit that the recent meeting of the representatives of the secret services of Russia, China and India was devoted to the struggle against terrorism and forging a joint response to this threat "at the present stage and in the future". During President Putin's visit to India two declarations were signed after the top-level talks - the Declaration on the Further Consolidation of Strategic Partnership between the Russian Federation and the Republic of India and the Joint Declaration on Strengthening and Enhancing Economic, Scientific and Technical Cooperation between the Republic of India and the Russian Federation. Besides these two declarations Russia and India signed Memorandum on Mutual Understanding and Cooperation in Combating Terrorism. During President Putin's visit in December 2002, the Russian Atomic Energy Minister Alexender Rumyantsev told the press that the work on construction of Kudankulam nuclear power plant was proceeding ahead of time and Russia would be sharing 1.5 billion dollars of the total cost of 2.5 billion dollars. It was also announced during this visit that the Indian Defence Minister George Fernandes would visit Moscow in January 2003 to discuss new projects to expand Military-Technical Cooperation. Russian Industry, Science and Technology Minister Ilya Klebanov told journalists in New Delhi that agreement had already been reached for Joint production of 100-seater military transport plane. Klebanov described Indo-Russian Military-Technical Cooperation as stable with a total turnover of 1.5 billion dollars per year. He also recalled that Russian Military- Technical Cooperation with India held the second place after China. In his interview with the PTI before leaving Moscow, Putin underscored "the need for positive development of relations between Russia and India, Russia and China, and China and India". He, added, "I think all the parties within this triangle are interested in this development". Expressing hope that China and India would resolve their border differences in the manner Russia and China are resolving, Putin dismissed the allegation that Russia's military exports to China could harm India's security by stating "Russia is not delivering weapons to conflict areas ... there is no conflict between China and India now and I hope there will be no conflict in the future".

The protocol signed in Moscow by Defence Minister Fernandes on 17 January 2003 is really an important landmark in Indo-Russian Military - Technical Cooperation. Though the details of this protocol are not known, it is believed that all major issues of procurement and related questions are covered by it. Fernandes informed that the Protocol envisages India's involvement in the Russian programme for development of a fifth -generation combat aircraft and plans to set-up Joint ventures in defence industry patterned after the Indo-Russian BrahMos Company for production and marketing of supersonic cruise missile. These joint ventures will yield benefit for both the defence and civilian sectors. The slow progress towards procuring four Tu-22M3 backfire strategic bombers and two Akula-class nuclear submarines is attributed by press reports to hard bargaining by Russia over the price for refitting the aircraft - carrier Gorshokov. There have been reports about the Indian Defence Minister and the Russian Industry, Science and Technology Minister not getting along well. The latter is reported to be not in favour of promoting factory to factory production ties between the two countries. The Russian side also felt slighted by the Indian Defence Minister not turning up for a scheduled meeting with the Russian President during his December visit to Delhi.

To sum up, in spite of petty snags and the problem in Indo-Russian relations caused by stagnating trade which is not commensurate with the level of their political relations, the bilateral relations between these two great powers have done on the whole fairly well. Both sides are dissatisfied over the inadequate development of trade and economic cooperation and are planning to take serious measures to remove the obstacles in this direction. Measures such as cooperation with third countries, formation of joint enterprises and increase in investments are being considered.

At the state banquet hosted by President A.P.J. Abdul Kalam, Putin quoted Mahatma Gandhi who said that "If we want to be a success, we are not to re-enact history but create history anew" and added, "that is what we intend to do as we make and implement future-oriented plans". The potential of these "future-oriented plans" are really great. For more than three years now Russia, Iran, Turkmenistan, India and Sri Lanka have been working on a project to establish North-South Transport Corridor by setting up a sea and surface transport link between them. This route will follow the path taken by Russian traveller Afnasy Nikitin who performed his overland and sea route from the Russian city of Tver in North Russia to India across the Caspian and the Arabian Sea. Work is underway for construction of a 250 kilometer-long railway line linking Bakdash on the Korobogozgol Bay on the Caspian Sea in Turkmenistan to Yeralievo in Kazakhstan. From Yeralievo to Russia the railway line is already functional; ships will carry the railway train across the Arabian Sea from the Persian Gulf port of Bandar Abbas. This will shorten the transportation time by 10 days in comparison to the route through the Suez and will be much cheaper.

Indo-Russian cooperation in the field of oil and energy production will help meet India's growing demand for import of oil. India has already invested 1.7 billion dollar in the Sakhalin-I offshore oil field in return for 20 percent equity in oil from Rossneft the national oil company of Russia. The Indian investment is expected to yield about 2 to 4 million metric tons of oil per year and 5 to 8 million cubic meters of gas per day from the project. Joint -ventures are being set up in India for cutting and polishing diamonds to be re-exported to third countries. Work is proceeding apace on Joint manufacture of Russian civilian aircraft in India.

The objective economic situation prevailing in the world today is also favourable to development of Indo-Russian relations. The sole super power, the United States, is also the world's most indebted nation with a current account deficit of 400 billion dollars. Forty-six of its fifty states have gone bankrupt and corporation after corporations are going into liquidation. The stock market has crashed and the derivative bubble, which is expanding at the rate of 70% annually, might burst any day. It is only India,

Russia and China who through their concerted efforts towards building large infrastructure projects in the fields of energy, transport and water management can help the world community to overcome the ongoing international economic and financial crisis and restore the missing equilibrium in the present- day international relations.

8

India-Russia Future Strategic Trends

Anuradha M. Chenoy

A projection of Russian Indian ties can be extrapolated from historical trends in the bilateral history of the two countries, as well as their ambitions in an increasingly globalized world. The political, military and economic ties as also a shared vision form the basis of Indo-Russian relations. At the same time, a trajectory of strengthening economic links with the west is a primary direction of both Russia and India since the 1990's. What is the direction of future relations between the two? Will it based on an acceptance or denial of history?

Indo-Russian relations, smooth and continuous as they may seem, have gone through distinct phases in their history and development. Interestingly, these phases relate to the national interests of these two countries as well as to the global situation. We can classify these phases as [a] 1947-1956 [b] 1956-1971 [c] 1971-1985 [d] 1985-1996 [e] 1996 onwards. In each of these phases Indo-Russian relations have grown or declined depending on the perceptions and experiences that both the countries have had with the Western powers. Indo-Soviet relations were clearly an outcome of both India and the Soviet Union's dissatisfaction and contradictions with the Western military blocs. The rough period in Russian-Indian relations after 1985 clearly arose from the felt need of both to connect more seriously with the West. The re-stabilization of relations between the two after 1996, materialized again when both Russia and India experienced that the West, especially the United States did not live up to their expectations and deliver its promises to both these countries.

Each of these phases has some distinct characteristics in terms of trade and political relations. For instance, in phase b and c trade between the two was state dominated. This ended after phase d. During phase trade is dominated by military hardware and joint military production between the two sides. There is a fundamental base line in the relation between these two countries that has built up over the years. This base involves India's dependence on military hardware imports from Russia, political support on its position on Kashmir, and other economic, cultural and political links as also no real antagonism on any major issue. It would appear then, as several analysts have noted, a military-political sub-system of bilateral relations between the two has been created.[1] Currently both countries find themselves on similar platforms on issues ranging from terrorism, impact of globalisation, Iraq, etc. There is thus a common vision between the two countries that seems to be re-emerging.

Political Relations

When official documents use terminology like "Indo-Russian- relations are civilisational and time-tested," and that "importance attached to them cuts across party lines in India and is not subject to political vicissitudes, ,[2] the future of bilateral relations stand firm. The test of bilateral ties lies in the commonality of approach to problems and conflicts. And here too there appears a convergence of interest.

To take one example. International terrorism is perceived as the main threat in the Russian National Security Doctrine and was evident during President Putin's visit here and the important Indo-Russian Treaty signed at that time. In this, Russia and India saw eye to eye on the issue and resolved to exchange information and set up foreign policy working groups. Russia and India both keep to this position, and their interest in this has only increased. The Russians have complained that the US understanding of terrorism has been different than that of theirs. This is because US and EU have for the past few years focused on human rights abuses as their primary concern in the civil war in Russia, where Russia has used military means against the Chechen secessionist movements that had established linkages with the Taliban. The Indian government has felt let down by the US coalition against terrorism. This is because instead of taking up issues of cross border terrorism, or completing the agenda against the Al Qaeda, they turned instead to Iraq, which in no way appears to be a threat of any kind to much of the world.

On Kashmir, it is the Russians that have stood squarely with the Indian position, and have provided support and their good offices for any discussion with Pakistan if the need should arise. The gradual thawing of relations between Pakistan and Russia should not be seen with a paranoia by India. It will serve Indian interests if Pakistan can be approached by powers other than the United States and China.

On issues of foreign policy like the US position of unilateral military action against Iraq, both India and Russia have opposed this and looked for peaceful solutions. The contradiction between the US and Russia have sharpened on this issue since Russia will not support them in the Security Council, Russia's search for a counter balance in international affairs like alternate relations has increased.

India -China Russia triangle

Russia has pushed the former prime minister Evgeny Primakov's proposal for a Russia-China-India informal strategic alliance. This proposal fits in with Primakov's hypothesis that though there is one super power that is trying to assert itself. It is possible to have multiple poles. Countries like India, Russia and China need a multi-polar world, in order to get their national interest across and have autonomy of decision making. To construct a multi-polar world, the Russia-India-China triangle would be indispensable. Though there are unresolved issues between India and China, movement between the two towards a better understanding is evident. The new Chinese national security document specifies strategic partnership with Russia and normalization with India and all round contacts with Central Asian Republics so as to stabilize and neutralize the separatist trends. Though currently the Chinese and Indian response to this alliance is hedged with their own bilateral problems; the China-Pak relation; the China-US relation. These three countries are bound to find this useful in the future, even if it is used for negotiating a better position for themselves vis-a-vis the US. I

India and Russia have 80 bilateral documents since 1992 which gives the necessary politico-legal basis to this relation. The belief that Russia will grow closer to Pakistan, as predicted by some because of President Mushiarraf 's recent visit is unlikely. While Russia is constantly looking for countries for new defence contracts, India's relation with Russia is far more than that. Russia at most will offer to provide their good offices to facilitate talks between the two. Anything more is unlikely.

Economic Relations

While Indo- Russian trade has been at a low of $ 1.5 billion annually, many Russian imports are sourced through international suppliers, and do not come from the traditional channels. There exist 11 working groups on different areas and there is work on joint infrastructure projects. The Indian government has made the largest ever foreign investment in the Sakhalin 11 gas pipeline. A system for trade, foreign investment between the two countries needs to be evolved and trade is likely to grow and increase. The private sector will go where the profits are. This will be the mantra for future Indo-Russian economic relations.

In Russia the new national security doctrine of January 2000, shows Putin's confident hold over the power apparatus and incorporates a review of the past. This doctrine combines the assessment of internal and external security. Radical shifts from the earlier doctrine are evident because at this juncture the authors believe 'Russia's foreign economic interests do not lie with the West; instead Russia must seek markets in the Third World countries'. [3] This clearly establishes that Russia's economic relations with the West have not been up to Russian expectations. The FDI expected has been inadequate. Further, the West has become the agency even between Russian- East Central European trade. On the other hand, trade and economic relations between Russia and its eastern partners, especially India, China, Iran, Malaysia etc. have grown with every passing year. The stabilization of the Russian economy and the recovery of the manufacturing sector augur well for Indian ventures here.

Military Relations

The Indian defence budget that was around a steady 3.0% of the GDP in the 1980's increased in 1998 to 3.2 % and in 1999 to 3.4% of the GDP. India's defence budget in 2000 rose by nearly 30% in nominal terms or 20% in real terms and and was Rs.709 billion (US $ 15.9 billion). This was perhaps the biggest ever increase.[4] India thus remains one of the worlds most lucrative arms market. In 2000 it ranked the 2nd largest arms market with imports of $4.8 billion cornered by Russia.

In 1987 Soviet Union had supplied 44% of global arms export while the US had 29%. By 1997 Russian share of the global market had fallen to just 4%. In 2000, Russia has revived its arms sales and is third after US and Great Britain. The finalization of the sale of the aircraft carrier Admiral Goroshkov and nuclear submarines, only indicate that defence cooperation between the two will continue into the future.

As part of this expansion of military exports, the Russians agreed to sell 16 Mi-17 helicopters to Pakistan, on the basis that this would in no way hamper Indian security mterests.

Popular Perceptions/ People to People Links

Russian-Indian relations are interestingly matched by popular and elite perceptions of Russia's foreign policy. In a survey by Russian Institute of Nationalities and Freidrich Ebert Foundation, of all kinds of experts involved in shaping foreign policy in government, academic, private institutions, news papers, NGO's political parties etc. Experts held views that reflected the views of society as a whole. In answering the key question whether Russia follow the Western path, seek alternatives -or Russian uniqueness, ordinary people supported uniqueness. Most believed that Foreign Policy should be more balanced between the East and West now and this accords with Russian national interest. (64%) For the first time, the pursuit of strategic partnership with the leading Asian powers (India and China) occupied first place at 67%. Partnership with Europe and then CIS came second and third. America has lost ground to Europe in popular perception. [Izvestia, May 25, 2001, CDSP, Vol. 53, No. 21, 2001, p. 6.]

Conclusion

It is perhaps easier to make a prediction of the strategic compulsions and continuation of Indo-Russian partnership than that of any other bilateral relation. Whether or not the India-China-Russia triangle takes of or not, the strategic course of these two countries seems fairly set and regular. This is based on past history, current politics and future trends of the international political system.

References

1. Lounev, Russia and India Political Cooperation in the sphere of Global, Regional and Bilateral Relations. China Report 381 (2002) pp. 109-111.
2. "Bilatela Relations Between India and the Russian Federation" Ministry of External affairs (Central and East European Division) 28 November, 2002.
3. Russian national Security Doctrine, Jan 10, 2000, CDSP Vol. 52, No.4, pp. 19-20.
4. The International Institute for Strategic Studies, The Military Blance 2000-2001, p. 298-299.

9

Significance of Indo-Russian Relations in Asia-Pacific Region

V.D. Chopra

Asia-Pacific region is a one of the most important segments of the globe. On account of its geo-political, geo-strategic and economic significance. It is passing through a critical phase in the 21st century. It is inextricably interwoven to twin dimensions, the role of external powers in the region which is not always benign and the multitude of national and regional problems of change and development. These are posing grave challenges to the managers of national and international affairs.

Statistics are indicators of processes taking place in social development. If one goes by statistics, Asia-Pacific is indeed emerging as a region of the future, a region which in the 21st century will become a decisive factor in international relations. In this sense in the current epoch, which is marked by increasingly close interdependence among states and regions, social and political changes that are taking place in this region have become key factors in shaping the course of history on our planet in the beginning of the 21st century. If till recently Japan was described as a super economic power, the pace of economic development in China, its rate of growth within what Chinese call 'socialist oriented market economy' has baffled many economic experts.

Significantly the recent first summit (November 5, 2002) between India and the Association of South East Asian Nations registered a take-off which may turn out to be of far reaching significance. This strategic vision of this new linkage at the highest level would be translated into a reality through "concrete programmes of cooperation", that would "comprehensively" combat "non-traditional security threats", inclusive of terrorism, within the framework of the existing ASEAN Regional Forum.

The anti-terror cooperation, in the present context of the "threat" to South East Asia from the Jemaah Islamiyah might be channelled, at this stage along bilateral lines between India and the countries concerned.

Above all the concept of creation an ASEAN-India free trade area has come on the immediate agenda.

However, what is relevant to mention here is that this development shows that stern measures should be taken against terrorism on an international scale on the basis of multilateralism and not unilateralism. Though China and Russia have not distanced themselves from the U.S.-led anti-terror war, they have certainly made a joint effort to compete with the U.S. for the common strategic policy in this global campaign.

China and Russia have portrayed the Shanghai Cooperation Organisation, which binds them with some Central Asian Republics. It lays down that anti-terror strikes should be undertaken only on the basis of international law and in observance of the U.N. Charter and its resolutions. They should not have double standards. They have taken the stand that the U.N. and its Security Council should take the lead and play a "core role" in so far as international anti-terrorist operations are concerned. India by and large shares this perception. It has gone on record again and again that in dealing with terrorism there should not be double standards. India has advised the sole superpowers without naming the United States to avoid war with Iraq and resolve the issues of alleged its stock piles of weapons of mass destruction (W.M.D.) and its programme of making a nuclear bombs. Prime Minister Atal Behari Vajpayee has emphasised that a war in the Persian Gulf would disturb the balance there. He has advocated that all efforts should be made to avoid a conflict and solve the dispute through negotiation with the mediation of the United Nations. Identical has been the stand of Russia and China. France and Germany too have taken the same positions. It is relevant to mention here that in the report to the Security Council of the United Nations on February 14, 2003, U.N. chief weapons inspector, Hans Blix said that conditions had improved for weapons inspector in Iraq and that inspections had *found no weapons of mass destruction*. However, he maintained that many prohibited weapons had not been accounted for. In his finding the International Atomic Energy Agency chief, Mohammed ElBaradei to told the Security Council in his report that inspectors had found no evidence that Iraq has restarted its nuclear weapons programme.

This trend needs to be seen in the new trilateral relations between India and Russia, Russia and China and India and China which have begun to take a concrete shape. This brings into focus how resistance to unipolarity has begun to manifest itself through assertion of multilateralism. This also illustrates how Indo-Russian relations have begun to mould the course of events on issues which threaten peace and stability in various parts of the world. The stand of the various nations in the U.N. Security Council on Iraq is a clear manifestation that multilateralism has begun to influence the international events. Let us look at the problem from another angle.

This development should be seen in the background of other significant changes. That moment of confidence of unipolarism is wearing out though slowly and steadily. As the 21st century begin the world is in the midst of a profound geopolitical shift. Moving to the fore today is a nation that just over 50 years ago was extricated from the wreckage of war by its conquerors, now Japan has become arguably a powerful economic factor. What is equally significant is that China is emerging as an Asian economic giant, the most populated country in the world.

In era of rising Asian powers a period that experts have already described Asia-Pacific century, "if things continue as they are now", predict some experts "it won't be much beyond 2020 before China becomes the leading power in world politics". The Asia-Pacific's rising economic influence in the end of last century were the so-called 'four tiger' – the newly industrialised countries (NIC's) of South Korea, Taiwan, Singapore and Hong Kong. Now China is growing as a major economic power. Stirring ever more energetically after decades of economic idleness, China is on the verge of becoming a superpower. India too is struggling to evolve its model of industrialisation. With Asia coming on so strong says William Overholt, a Bankers Trust economist in Hong Kong, the United States in the next hundred years could "become a giant Australia".

While the Asia-Pacific region is rapidly expanding its global economic influence, the United States has gradually shifted its global interests from Western Europe to the East. The readjustment of U.S. economic strategy has far reaching influence.

After World War II, the United States, emboldened by its greatly increased economic and military strength, declared that its interests spread over the whole globe. It then began to consolidate these interests by expanding its economic influence. U.S. economic interest was focused on Latin America and Canada from the early postwar years to the 1950s. In the 1960s Western Europe became the focus of U.S. economic activities. And since the mid-1970s, the United States has gradually shifted its emphasis to Asia and the Pacific. Since then also great changes have taken place in U.S. foreign trade pattern. For capital export and sources of important raw materials, Asia-Pacific region seems to have replaced Western Europe as the centre of U.S. global economic interests.

Asia and the Pacific have become the largest market for U.S. foreign trade. From the end of World War II to 1975, Western Europe had held that position. In 1970, for example, 31.5 per cent of U.S. foreign trade was with Western Europe, and 26.1 per cent with Asia and the Pacific. But by 1982, 25.7 per cent of U.S. trade was with Western Europe, while its Asian and Pacific trade rose to 34.8 per cent.

The United States has expanded its trade and investment enormously in Asia-Pacific region. The rate of U.S. investment is growing much faster in the Asia-Pacific region than in Europe. From, 1975 to 1982 the gross volume of U.S. Direct private investment in the Asia-Pacific region rose from US $5.95 billion to U.S. $28.5 billion. In 1982, the net volume of US investment in the Asia-Pacific region reached U.S. $1.32 billion, almost equal to the net investment in Western Europe, and that is not including China. U.S. investors are clearly looking to the East. This is confirmed by the fact that according to American experts U.S. investments in India was estimated at $4.5 billion in 2000 as against $41 billion in China. This underlines the depth of U.S. economic interests both in India and China, in China in particular. This is a major geo-economic development, which should not be underestimated.

One reason is that Asian and Pacific countries have much of the raw materials and highly skilled labour and technicians, which the United States must import to feed its electronics computer and aeronautics industries. The picture becomes clear if one bears in mind American dependence for crude-oil on Middle East, its penetration in Central Asia an the new ties, it is building with Russia for crude-oil supplies. Of the 11 minerals the United States imports in large quantities eight come from Asia and the Pacific. Titanium from the East accounts for 97 per cent of the gross volume of U.S. titanium imports, along-with 82 per cent of tin, 80 per cent of mica, 42 per cent of tantalum and 27 per cent of aluminum. The Asian-Pacific region also supplies the United States with 88 per cent of its imported natural rubber, 99 per cent of its palm oil and 95 per cent of its coconut oil.

Oil Factor :

It is relevant to analyse the importance of oil factor in the global economy to understand strategic importance of the Asia-Pacific region, where a large number of oil producing countries are located, including the

Gulf countries. The terrorist assault on US business and military centre on 11 September 2001 and concentration of American armed forces with its allies around Iraq in mid February 2003 highlight geo-political importance of oil factor. This is confirmed by the fact that both these developments led to a steep rise in the oil prices in the world market. Significantly some of the major oil producing countries Iran, Iraq and Libya are hostile to the American administration.

According to the both, the International Energy Agency (IEA) and the US Department of Energy's Energy Information Administration (EIA) world proven oil reserves are around one trillion barrels, enough to meet demand well beyond 2020, at current rates of production. That being the position the American policy makers are looking beyond the next two decades. The reason is obvious. The United States is the biggest oil consumer in the world today. The American Gulf policy has another dimension. There is no doubt that the majority of the world's future supplies will be sourced in the Gulf region, which holds 66 per cent of the world's oil reserves. The current production capacity of the major Persian Gulf countries is around 23 mbd, with potential capacity additions to the tune of 3-6 mbd in the near future. This brings out how the American policy makers have already begun to look at other oil resources in this region such as Central Asian Republics and Far Eastern region of Russia.

Another important development is that since the late 1980s, Gulf oil exports to Asia-Pacific countries including India, have overtaken those to European OECD countries. For instance, in 2000, almost 60 per cent of Gulf oil exports went to Asia, as compared to 21 per cent to Europe, and 14 per cent to the U.S. While Europe has increasingly been substituting coal and oil with natural gas, mainly for power generation, the U.S. has been increasing oil imports from neighbouring countries like Canada and Mexico at the cost of Gulf imports leaving Asia-Pacific countries as the chief importers of Gulf crude. This in itself brings out how peace and stability in the Gulf region has a direct bearing on oil importing countries of the Asia-Pacific region.

There is yet another factor which has to be taken into account. Russia is today the second largest oil exporter and third largest producer after the US and Saudi Arabia. Its production is 7.25 mbd. Oil production is crucial for the country's economic revival. Its proven oil reserves is 49 billion barrels (bb) though according to some estimate proven reserves are closer to around 60-70 bb. Russia is in a position to be one of the world's major oil suppliers. It provides 16 per cent of Europe's oil requirement. It is trying to establish an energy corridor along-with other Central Asian countries to East Asia. This in itself shows how another area of cooperation between India and Russia make expand. It may be mention here that former Soviet Union provided technology to India for oil exploration and oil refineries, which laid the basis for the development of the oil industry. According to some experts Russian technocrats were the first to come to the conclusion that India has wast sources of crude oil and gas.

New Economic Power Centres in Asia-Pacific

Japan has long been the United State's biggest trade partner in its growing business with East, while Australia takes the lion's share of direct U.S. private investment. But in recent years, the United States has also been strengthening its economic ties with members of the Association of South East Asian Nations (ASEAN) and rapidly expanding its business with South Korea, Taiwan and Hong Kong. In fact, the shifting emphasis of U.S. economic interest is far more economically, politically, and strategically complex than just the presence of raw materials. And now there is a shift in its investments towards China and India.

The Asia-Pacific region's economic development is an enormous attraction to American monopoly corporations. Since the 1970s, the unprecedented economic development of Asia-Pacific has increased its influence in the world economy. Japan led the way in 1971, when it emerged as the third economic power after the United States and the Soviet Union. From 1970 to 1980, the average annual increase of Japan's Gross National Product (GNP) was 4.9 per cent, compared with 3.3 per cent in other developed countries. The proportion of its GNP in the world rose form 4.8 per cent in 1960 to 10.2 per cent in 1980.

South Korea, Hong Kong and Singapore had already become important regional economic powers when they emerged on the world scene in the 1970s. Their average annual economic growth was over 8 per cent. And now China is emerging almost the second biggest economic power in the world. Though the Western economic crises of 70s had slowed the pace of development of South Korea, Hong Kong and Singapore, it remained high when compared with Western countries. The year of 1983 marked the beginning of their economic recovery South Korea's economy grew by 9.7 per cent, Hong Kong's 5.7 per cent and Singapore's by 7.5 per cent.

China, with its successful modernisation programme and its open door policies, is also exerting a growing economic influence in the world. Its gross industrial and agricultural output value grew at a rate of more than 7 per cent from 1981 to 1983, and now it has registered the highest growth rate in the world.

The Asia-Pacific region enjoys the advantages of rapid economic development, its economic position is bound to improve still further. It has been estimated that from 1970 to 2000 the Asian economy grew at a rate of 6.3 per cent, while that of the whole world grew on an average of only 4.8 per cent. For the same period, Asia's proportion of the global GNP grew from 16 per cent to 23 per cent. Western experts have estimated that by the end of the 20th century, the Asia-Pacific region's economic growth exceeded the world's average increased level, and the focus of international trade had shifted from the Atlantic to the Asia-Pacific.

The United States is experiencing its own shift in economic focus, from the East to the South-West. From 1950 to 2000 the population in the East increased just 1.25 times, as against 1.6 times in the South and 2.14 times in the West. For the same period, the income of the North-East grew only 7.4 times, in sharp contrast to the south's 12.8 times and the West's 13.27 times. The income of the South and West was only 49 per cent of the national income in 1975, but it climbed to more than 50 per cent in 2000.

The relatively stagnant economies of all the Western European countries have also speeded up the eastward shift of U.S. economic interests. Between the 50s and the 60s, Western Europe was the fastest – growing region in the world. But its growth has slowed in the recent years.

From 1960 to 1973, the GNP of the European Economic Community (EEC) increased by an average of 4.7 per cent a year while from 1974 to 1981, it went up by just 1.9 per cent annually. In 1981 it went up by just 1.9 per cent annually, and the year actually saw a decline of 0.4 per cent. Economists have predicted that by the year 2000. The EEC's share of the global GNP, which was 20 per cent in 1970, has dropped to 15 per cent.

In the early 80s Japan seized the first place in competitiveness among the industrialised countries in the non-socialist world. This is evident from a study conducted by an organisation called the European Management Forum. Japan's high competitive ability assessed by numerous criteria (284 were used all in all) shows that the Japanese have managed considerably to push back their rivals in much tougher competition. This is confirmed by changes in the geographic distribution of exports from the Organisation for Economic Cooperation and Development (OECD) countries. Between 1975 and 1982 Japan's share in the total export costs of the countries belonging to this group has increased from 12.8 to 16.1 per cent while the share of the member-countries of the European Economic Community (EEC) has fallen from 57.7 to 53.2 per cent, with the U.S. share remaining unchanged (17.5 per cent).

The present-day Japanese expansionism is backed by that country's growing economic might. According to the estimate of Japanese economists, their country's share in the world economy rose to 9.9 per cent by the year 2000 from 9.3 per cent in 1980 while that of the USA decline from 23.4 per cent to 22.6 per cent.

In the beginning of the 21st century, China has become a major economic player in the world economy. Chinese consumer goods are carving out an enviable position in the world, in Asia-Pacific region in particular both for their quality and prices. This shows China is becoming a major competitor in the world economy, notwithstanding the fact that purchasing power of the Chinese people is also increasing.

Another indicator of changes in the international economy of Asia and Pacific region in particular is a marked shift in the Purchasing Power Parity (PPP). India is now the world's fourth largest economy after the U.S., China and Japan in PPP measured in U.S. prices according to the latest development indicators. India's PPP gross national income in 1999 was $2.23 trillion against $8.88 trillion of the U.S., $4.45 trillion of China and $3.19 trillion of Japan, the indicators issued by the World Bank said.

India's per capita in PPP increased from $2,06 in 1988 to $2,23 in 1999 and PPP gross national income from $2.02 trillion to $2.23 trillion in 1999, the 396 page publication said. Other countries in the trillion dollar league in PPP in 1999 were : Germany ($1.93 trillion), France ($1.32 trillion), United Kingdom ($1.32 trillion), Italy ($1.27 trillion), Brazil ($1.15 trillion), and the Russian Federation ($1.02 trillion).

These cold facts speak for themselves and underline how China and India are becoming important economic players in the world economy. This however, does not mean that in the new pyramid of economic structure of India, the weakness of its base with millions of people living below the poverty line should be minimised. This stands as a complete contrast to the Chinese model of industrialisation and modernisation of economy, where the purchasing power of the people at the lowest rung too is increasing. In India, we have created a middle and upper middle class with highest purchasing power which constitutes only 7 to 10 per cent of the population.

This analysis however doesn't take into account the recent recession in the economies of both the United States and Japan, where unemployment rate is increasing.

It may further be mentioned that International trade in services is now estimated to be around $1,500 billion and it is expected that this would increase to $4,000 billion by the end of 2005. In the case of India, the services sector accounts for 42 per cent of the country's GDP as against 30 per cent contributed by the industry. Since the country's service export has bright potential for software exports, a big thrust to this sector is considered necessary. A large number of Indian professionals are already working abroad and bright potential exists for widening the scope in view of the country's strength of cheap labour.

In the U.S. the services sector accounts for 89 per cent of GDP. Information technology has emerged as the fastest growing sector. Among its two vital constituents, software and telecommunications, India enjoys most favourable cost-quality rating in software in the world. A World Bank survey has ranked India as the number one preference for offshore software development with abundant opportunities for Indian software exports at $5.0 billion per annum by the end of 2001. Notwithstanding the new politico economic relationship, which is developing between India and the United States, "prohibitions will remain on transfers of technology related to India's nuclear weapon and missile programmes. But access to a full range of other technologies of interest to India might be easier. Bilateral defence cooperation too is likely to get a boost" as American Ambassador to India Robert Blackwill put it on September 27, 2002 in New Delhi.

This shift in America's India policy has to be seen in the background of the fact that India is now the world's fourth largest economy after the U.S., China and Japan in Purchasing Power Parity (PPP) measured in U.S. prices according to the latest world development indicators as mentioned earlier.

In totality of the situation if economic indicators are taken into account Indo-American relations have yet to be elevated from the present level of political and strategic relations to a higher level of economic relationship. This is confirmed by the fact that in 2000 business agreements between India and U.S. companies totaled $3 billion over $2 billion in commercial ventures and $1 billion in U.S. export-import bank financing. This underlines how Indo-U.S. economic relations need to be restructured in the new period.

As far as Sino-Indian relations are concerned they have begun to take a new turn and a process upswing has begun. This is confirmed by a number of recent developments.

Firstly, India and China agree that they have face a common enemy in terrorism. They are keen to expand cooperation on countering terrorism, they have decided to hold a regular dialogue in this field. It is relevant to mention here that while Pakistan seems to have blocked the movement of the terrorist to China, Beijing continues to remain concerned about cross-border terrorism from some of the neighbouring Central Asian Republics. It is also of significance to mention that during the recent Indo-Pak conflict, China followed a policy of neutrality.

Secondly, keen to remove irritants in the relationship, India and China have decided to accelerate the clarification of their disputed boundary. Both sides have already arrived at an understanding of the alignment of the LAC in Himachal Pradesh and Uttaranchal. They are now gearing up for similar exercise along the Sino-Indian boundary in Ladakh and Arunachal Pradesh. India and China differ on the LAC alignment at eight spots in the western sector and six in the east.

Thirdly, commercial relations between India and China have begun to shape rapidly. Indian goods will now have access into the Chinese market under the WTO guidelines. According to reports from Beijing, India-China trade in 2001 has crossed the three billion marks. It is expected that during the year 2002 this figure will touch $5 billion.

It is relevant to mention here that China today is a major power in computer hardware, and India has emerged as a big force in information technology's software segment. This makes an ideal meeting ground for the two to complement each other.

Indian experts are keen to assimilate Chinese experience of modernisation and industrialisation in a short span of time, which has entitled it to be described as an Asian-Economic giant. It may be mentioned here that Chinese economy grew by 7.9 per cent in the first half of 2001 and recorded value of industry 24.7 per cent in government revenue, 18.9 per cent in investment in fixed assets, 10 per cent in retail of consumption commodities and 9.6 per cent in import-export trade, which amounted to 330 billion, an increase of 209.4 per cent. China's foreign exchange reserves had reached $194 billion in 2002.

In the development sphere, emphasis is being laid infrastructure, science and technology and environment protection in China. To ensure uniform spread of high living standards, the income of both urban and rural population is sought to be raised through a series of measures. Agriculture still remains the backbone of the economy, which has diversified into consumer goods, as well as machinery and electronics.

Conclusion

This shows that normalisation of relations between India and China on one hand and further deepening Indo-Russian relations on the other will lay a new economic basis for multilateralism. This conclusion has to be seen in the context of a new phase of consolidation of politico-economic relations between China and Russia. We have dealt with in other articles the trends in Indo-Russian economic cooperation and their future prospects.

The inevitable conclusion from this study is that, the Asia-Pacific region is now the place where civilisation is stepping up its pace. The Russian economy though still in the process of reconstructing itself has already evolved a policy of harnessing it natural resources to boost its economic growth. The Russian economy is moving to Siberia and Far East. Russia today is the third largest oil producing country in the world, after the United States and Saudi Arabia. Perhaps it has more oil resources than even Saudi Arabia.

Nothwithstanding, the complexities of this region and conflicting perceptions, the problems of economic cooperation among the countries of the Asia-Pacific region have become living issues. As a matter of fact, it will not be incorrect to say that some structures and forums have already begun to surface themselves for economic cooperation among the countries of this area, though they are still in their elementary stage. The experience of SAARC, ASEAN and the Indonesian concept of ZOFPAN (Zone of Peace, Freedom and Neutrality) graphically illustrate that the urge to evolve some viable structures for economic cooperation among the countries of this region has begun to assert itself. In this sense multilateral economic cooperation in a period of globalisation of economy has begun to reveal new trends. In this context Indo-Russian political, strategic and economic cooperation will play a vital role in the processes of change which are shipping themselves in the Asia-Pacific region that being the position it will be native to look at the Indo-Russian relations from a narrow angle. It has the potentiality of becoming a key factor in the Asia-Pacific region.

It will be relevant for instance to mention here that India's connections with Pacific region date back to the pre-historic period. There are racial and cultural affinities between India and the Pacific region, as is evident from the presence of a large proto-Australoid element in the Indian population and trails of South-East Asian culture in India. This proves a very ancient connexion between India and those regions. Indian cultural influences spread through Central Asia into the Far East as well as directly into South-East Asia. In the colonial period India held crucial position in the west's links with the Far East and the Pacific region. This resulted in a two-way migration over the centuries.

Normalisation and improvement of relations between Russia and China is in India's interests. It is therefore, watched with keen interest by New Delhi. On the other hand deepening of Indo-Russian relations is welcomed by all section of Indian political opinion. There is a broad national consensus on it.

Above all the Indian Ocean enjoys a vital place in the security framework of Asia and the Pacific. This linkage between the Indian Ocean and the Pacific is a post-World War II phenomenon, and more particularly, after the decline of the traditional powers, like Britain and France and the rise of new Great Powers like the USA and Russia. Traditional powers, that had dominated the Indian Ocean for centuries, were European powers and hence their line of communication passed through the Mediterranean and the Atlantic. The new entrants were Pacific Powers and their force projection in the Indian Ocean was directed from the Pacific. That was true not only of Russia but also of the USA.

Two more Pacific powers, China and Japan are also seeking to enhance their role in the Indian Ocean region. Thus, in the years to come, the politics of Indian Ocean will be increasingly linked up with that of the Pacific. Since the balance of power is fairly static in the Atlantic, Great Powers are bound to concentrate more on the Asia and the Pacific regions. Hence, there are chances that the Indian Ocean would get further sucked into the vortex of Great Power rivalry in the Asia-Pacific region. India is bound to be affected by these developments.

Security of the Indian Ocean is affected by the geostrategic environment at the global level; the Indian Ocean commands vital sea and air routes connecting the Atlantic and the Mediterranean with the Pacific. Of course, the Panama Canal also does so but it has serious limitations for countries of Europe. Thus, there is no alternative to the Indian Ocean routes even for a land power like Russia which has over land access from Europe to the Pacific. Russia also depends to a great deal, upon the Indian Ocean for East-West movement of its goods.

These air and sea routes are important not only for trade and commerce but also for military purposes. Hence, these powers have tried to control directly, or to have access to strategically located ports, bases and base facilities. Some of them like the Subic Bay base and the Clark air base in the Philippines have been with USA for decades. Others, like the Diego Garcia, have been acquired recently. There are also other bases and base facilities to which these Great Powers have access. They are the visible symbols of the strategic importance of the Indian Ocean for these extra-regional powers.

Besides the air and the sea routes, the Indian Ocean is also important to these powers because of the availability of strategic materials there, such as the fossil fuel or tin, copper and rubber. Control over these resources and their exclusive use has been one of the cardinal principles of these powers. Of them, oil has assumed increasing importance because of energy needs. The dependence of the West for energy upon the Gulf oil and also the huge petro-dollars generated by the hike in oil prices made the Gulf a prime target of the Western strategy in the Indian Ocean. This shows commonality of interests both geostrategic and geoeconomic of India and Russia.

In this situation, India is likely to face greater challenges in the coming year. India needs to restructure its South Asian policy and build political and economic relations with all these countries. It also needs to further strength its relations with ASEAN states. It is unfortunate though the maritime strength of India is growing, it is far less than other Great Powers such as China.

India needs to meet these challenges by a new political drive. India is the natural kingpin in any regional arrangement for maritime cooperation in the Indian Ocean Area. This highlights the importance of Indian-Russian cooperation in building India's maritime strength. This maritime cooperation needs to be on a wider framework of Southern Asia which should seek to interlink the maritime developmental processes and cooperation between the Indian Ocean states of South-East Asia, South Asia and of the Arabian Sea and its natural extensions. India's deal with Russia on Gorshkov aircraft carrier and nuclear capable long-range bombers and submarines are significant developments, if seen in this context.

10

Indo-Russian Defence Cooperation and India's Independence and Sovereignty

V.D. Chopra

Introduction

In the beginning of the 21st century, national defence of a country has assumed a new dimension, particularly after the American theory of "liberating" other countries as in case of Iraq. This raises a fundamental question as to who will decide the internal, political and economic structures of a country, the people of that country themselves or some foreign power with its most sophisticated military might. It is in this new context that India's defence relations with other countries with Russia in particular need to be objectively examined.

It is important to go into details of what precisely is the essential content of this aspect. Unless this is grasped, one may miss the turning point in the evolution of India's relations with Russia on the one hand and with the Western countries, on the other in the sphere of defence cooperation.

The basic factors in evaluating India's defence are important constituents, the growing threat to its sovereignty and freedom from internal subversion and cross border terrorism from outside. Above all its territorial disputes with Pakistan and China further compound the situation. If in the fifties, the PAK-U.S. pact was a threat to Indian freedom and together with SEATO, it was also a threat to peace in the whole of Asia, in the early eighties, the security environment of our country and of the entire region underwent a basic shift because of Pakistan becoming the Kingpin of American strategic policies for this part of the world. Now that Pakistan has become a nuclear power with overt and covert support of Western countries, the security environment of India has undergone another basic change.

The policy of strengthening defence cooperation with Russia is linked with the consolidation of India's freedom. The genuine freedom of a country has of necessity to be a synthesis of political freedom and economic freedom. This is, however, not a static concept.

Dynamics of socio-economic change goes a long way in strengthening and consolidating political freedom of a country. It is precisely this change which has made and continues to make India more and more independent. To put it in other words, the socio-economic changes in India which have taken place since independence have made India genuinely sovereign. This among other things is due to the fact of existence of the Soviet Union and now of Russia, which opened for India other channels of economic and military cooperation. India is an outstanding example of cooperation with all the countries. She can now exercise her independence and sovereignty without any constraints because she can rely on the moral and material support of both East and West. This is a new international phenomenon. Even small countries are now in a position to maintain their sovereignty without any coercion from those countries which till recently were dominating their economy. However, the tragedy of Iraq has put a major break on this trend.

By and large, major political forces in the country agree that India should preserve her independence and that India should keep her channels of cooperation open with all the countries. To say that does not mean that there are no differences in the various political parties over the policies of America as a super power.[1]

Jawaharlal Nehru will go down in the history of contemporary world as an outstanding politician, one of the top leaders of the national liberation movement, fighter for peace, architect of modern India and above all one who made a major contribution to the realisation of the noble concepts of peaceful co-existence and friendly relations between the countries of the world in general and with the former Soviet Union in particular. It was during the period of his leadership that the edifices of enduring friendly relations with erstwhile Soviet Union were laid.

There is an important aspect of the friendly Indo-Soviet relations which has a direct bearing on our country's defence and security. India, for years after independence, was forced by historical circumstances to lean on industrialised nations of the West for purchase of arms, including sophisticated weapons. But the Western Powers and the USA in supplying highly strategic weapons to India formulated its policy by what it called "balance of power in the region". This is confirmed by the fact that during the Chinese aggression on India in 1962 and thereafter up to 1965 when the USA placed an arms embargo the total U.S. military assistance received by India constituted only a negligible per cent of the defence budget of any year. On the other hand, Pakistan which had joined the CENTO and SEATO, in the first year of its military partnership with the USA, received from Washington 30 B-57 bombers, 20 F-104 Star Fighters, 120 F-86 Sabre jets and a large number of C-130 giant transport aircraft and other types of military hardware.

By, 1959, the indications started coming to New Delhi that China was likely to create problems on Indo-China border. Though it was a period of euphoria of "Hindi-Chini Bhai Bhai", India's defence experts had started paying attention to the strengthening of country's defence on Indo-China border. It was in this situation that India made an approach to Washington for supply of C-130 transport planes and helicopters to enable its men and material to be carried to high altitude areas. The USA summarily turned down this request.

Seen in this context, Soviet Union's decision to help India for building industries in public sector, particularly in the field of precision instruments, oil, aircraft etc. had a direct bearing on India's defence preparedness. But even more significant is the fact that Soviet assistance to increase India's defence preparedness dates back to 1955 when the Soviet Union gifted two IL-14 transport planes to the Indian air force. Again in 1960, when India asked for more such planes, the Soviet Union complied with the request by readily giving 24 transport planes.

During this period, the Soviet Union offered to India, not only to provide MIG-21 supersonic fighter-interceptor planes on rupee credit, but also to give all assistance, including the technical know-how, for enabling their manufacture in the country itself. 1962 agreement provided for the sale of MIGs and for the setting up of a MIG factory in India.

As was expected, this agreement angered the Western countries, particularly Washington and London. Pressure was mounted on India to annul the agreement. But Jawaharlal Nehru in unmistakable terms made it clear that it was for India to decide from where to buy its defence requirements.

Within two years, the area of cooperation between the Soviet Union and India in the field of defence was enlarged and given a new dimension. In 1964, India signed another agreement with the Soviet Union. Under this agreement, India received four squadrons of MIG-21, helicopters, light tanks, missiles and other sophisticated weapons. But what is equally important to note is that India was to pay for these supplies in rupees or in goods produced in the country and that too over a period of ten years. This undoubtedly eased India's efforts to strengthen her defences.

Again in the Middle of the 50s, India approached several countries for assistance in the construction of three metallurgical plants at Bhilai with the participation of the USSR, at Rourkela with the help of Federal Republic of Germany and at Durgapur with British assistance. For Soviet Union, the 50s were not free from difficulties. The country had just started healing its wounds inflicted by the Second World War. Another war-cold war was also being imposed on it by the West. Despite this, the Soviet Union came forward to help India realise its goal of building an independent economy. The agreement to build the Bhilai Steel Plant was signed on February 2, 1955. The two steel plants built with the assistance of the Soviet Union-Bhilai and Bokaro accounted for more than one-third of steel production of the country till the late seventies, according to official figures.

In December 1953, the first Indo-Soviet Trade Agreement was signed. It was this agreement which laid the basis for rapid expansion of trade between the two countries. In 1951-52, India's exports to the Soviet Union amounted to just Rs. 6.92 crores and imports figured up to Rs. 1.39 crores. In a short span of 12 years, this trade had enormously expanded. In 1963-64, India's exports to the Soviet Union increased to Rs. 52.10 crores and the imports to Rs. 68.46 crores. Indeed, it was a phenomenal progress. But what is more important than this is that India's trade with the Soviet Union during the Nehru era, by and large, was favourable to it, while its balance of payment with the rest of the world was obviously unfavourable[2].

In area of oil exploration and development of petroleum industry, the Soviet Union and now Russia have made a rich contribution.

This shows how Indo-Soviet and now Indo-Russian cooperation is helping our ancient nation to strengthen its economy and defence potential.

Defence Cooperation

Armed forces, adequate in size, suitably equipped, well trained competently led and held in readiness to aggression are but one, though essential, element required for safeguarding national security. A sound economy and dependable sources of effective defence equipment are essential elements of a national defence policy. The proverbial man behind the gun is often the decisive factor in combat, but the gun, thanks to advances in technology, is becoming increasingly more powerful and it is the man-weapon combination that would ultimately prevail. The recent developments in Iraq have broad into focus how sophisticated arms have become a key factor in winning the war. India has acquired a fair measure of industrial competence and established a number of defence production and research units. Yet dependence on imports, particularly of high technology items such as aircraft, certain types of naval craft, combat vehicles and electronic and other instruments, continues. It is in this context that new contours of Indo-Russian defence cooperation should be objectively assessed.

In his book, entitled "Self-Reliance and Security" Col. R. Rama Rao has made out a cogent case that by developing competence to design and produce these items indigenously, the country would not only free itself from undue dependence on others for critical defence items would also save valuable foreign exchange besides strengthening important sectors of industry. There is a good deal of commonalty between civil and military sectors of industry manufacturing high technology products. Thus, units producing civil aircraft and associated materials and instruments could provide and in turn receive immense support from units producing military aircraft. In the case of electronic, computer and similar instruments, commonalty between civil and military equipment could be even greater. This underlines the real significance of Indo-Russian defence cooperation in the sense that Russia not only supplies defence equipment but also gives technology to our industrial units engaged in defence equipment production.

The environment of South Asia with sustained military build up by neighbours, the strengthening of bases in the Indian Ocean region by foreign powers and the positioning of their forces in the various parts of the region gives a totally new dimension to the nature of security threats to which the country may be exposed in the near future. Indian defence planners thus will have to take measures to ensure national security over the long as well as short term periods. This implies that in the foreseeable future, Indo-Russian defence cooperation will grow. Prudence and statesmanship lie in reconciling the imperatives of maintaining national sovereignty by avoiding dependence on external sources with the need to cooperate with other in promoting matters of common interests. But considering our present state of development and security needs, self-reliance in the production of defence equipment is essential and the sooner the country achieves it the better[3].

Throughout the Cold War, the Soviet Union was a major exporter of arms and military technology to the developing countries. After the end of the Cold War, a new Russia has found itself competing with the United States, United Kingdom and France. There has been a consensus to maintain Russia's weapons export to the world market, which will ensure the survival of the Russian defence enterprises by facilitating their revival[4].

Russian arms export policies, norms and institutions have been in flux since 1991, though in the recent years a well defined mechanism for export of arms has been evolved. In March 1992, a working group on Military-Technical Cooperation (MTC) was set up within the Committee for Industry and Power Economy headed by Deputy Chairman V. Ya. Vitebsky. This working group was composed of representatives of the Committee for International Affairs; Foreign Trade; Industry and Energy; Defence and Security; Budget Planning, Taxes and Prices. The state foreign economic companies Oboronexport and Spetsvneshtechnika (formerly the main engineering and the departments) were responsible for issuing licenses for arms transfers. These were autonomous agencies under the Ministry of Foreign Economic Relations (MFER). Through presidential decree, the licensing system for export of military equipment was introduced. In April 1992, then President Yeltsin signed a decree on the measure to create export controls in the Russian Federation. In May 1992, the presidential decree on MTC of the Russian Federation with foreign countries was signed. This agency was charged with coordinating bilateral and multilateral inter-governmental commissions on MTC, licensing of sales to third countries sales of arms and military equipment manufactured by foreign states with Russian assistance and endorsing documents on procedures for MTC. Regulatory functions were also vested in the Ministry of Foreign Affairs (MFA). This ministry supervises Russia's compliance with international obligations and ensures that all participants in MTC respect the political interests of the Russian Federation[5].

To prevent further damage, a single specialised state agency, Rosvoorouzhenie (State Corporation for Export and Import of Armaments and Military Equipment) was set up in November 1993. Rosvoorouzhenie works under the direct supervision of the Russian government and is accountable to the president of the Russian Federation[6].

The restructuring of arms export and MTC has gone through three phases in post-Soviet Russia characterised by a separate model in each phase[7].

Indo-Russian defence cooperation in the post-Soviet era has undergone a radical change. President Yeltsin's visit to New Delhi in January 1993, saw a marked shift in the relationship between the two countries. Yeltsin and Prime Minister P.V. Narasimha Rao signed a 20 years Treaty of Friendship and Cooperation replacing the similar 1971 Soviet –Indian Treaty. The two leaders also signed on sale and production of Russian weapons and the supply of Russian spare parts. June 1994 saw this reiteration once again when Prime Minister Narsimha Rao visited Moscow. In October 1996, Russian defence Minister Igor Rodionov visited New Delhi and signed a military technology cooperation agreement with his Indian counterpart, Mulayam Singh Yadav. In early October 1997, Indian Defence Minister Mulayam Singh Yadav visited Moscow and the Russian president agreed to extend bilateral defence cooperation till the year 2010. Initially, the period was from 1994 to 2000. India was the only country with which Russia signed this type of bilateral defence cooperation programme in 1994. This extension by a decade has added a new dimension to Indo-Russian relations. During Prime Minister Primakov's visit to New Delhi in December 1998, out of the seven agreements signed between India and Russia, the document on long-term military technical cooperation till the year 2010 is the key document. On a visit to New Delhi in March 1999, Russian defence Minister Igor D. Sergeyev and his Indian counterpart, George Fernandes signed a military cooperation agreement to train Indian defence personnel in key Russian military academies[8]. The long-term bilateral defence cooperation programme will cover such new areas naval nuclear technologies and anti-ballistic missile defence systems. This long-term MTC will enhance the joint R&D capabilities of the two countries in the production of new weapon systems. On December 27, 2000, India and Russia finally signed the single largest arms deal the Su-30 MKI will be manufactured in India with Russian assistance. This means complete transfer of technology to India. This Indo-Russian Sukhoi deal is the single largest defence deal ever signed by Russia with any foreign country. Under this deal, 150 Su-30 MKIs will be manufactured in India, including indigenous production of all the components over a period of the next two decades. The Su-30 MKI will have onboard avionics and other support systems developing by India and also equipment from countries like France, Israel, South Africa, and the United Kingdom[9].

China also has MTC with Russia. Both China and India account for almost three-fourths of Russia's armament exports[10].

Russia remains India's biggest supplier of defence products but as the Prime Minister, Atal Bihari Vajpayee, stressed during the Putin's visit in December 2002, the India-Russia defence relationship goes beyond that of merely buyer and seller as it now encompasses a wide range of activity including joint research, design, development and co-production.

The Admiral Gorshkov purchases itself is far from over and the Russians remain both keen and hopeful that the price negotiations for the purchase of the retrofitted carrier, a package which including about 40 aircraft, the naval variant of the MIG-29. Besides the negotiations on the aircraft carrier, what is keenly watched is whether licensed production of the Sukhoi (SU-30 MKI) will be speeded up. India is keen that it should be given a top priority. The first squadron of these multi-role aircraft is already operational. But as many as 140 of them are scheduled to be made under license by HAL within a couple of years from now, after the Russians transfer technologys, supply raw material and provide support technicians. Speeding up the deliveries of two Krivac stealth frigates and the progress on the Smerch multi-barrel rocket delivery system are among the other things that will count towards forging closer defence relationship. India has broached the subject about the possibility of leasing two Russians nuclear submarines but is evident that any progress on this will have to be within the parameters of Moscow's commitment to the various non-proliferation mechanisms it is a party to[11].

Moreover, the deal for purchasing a berthed Russian aircraft carrier has been stuck on the price for refurbishing it, according to Indian specifications. The pace gathered momentum 3 December 2002, after the Russian Minister Ilya Klebanov, met the Defence Minister, George Fernandes and told him about the final offer from the Russian side. In order to ensure that both sides do not violate the missile control regime, Russia plans to replace the submarines 3,000 km rang cruise missiles with 300 km range ones[12].

One of the major irritants about supply of Russian defence equipment is regular and timely flow of spare parts. The problem is complex because there is no single supply source as a large number of Russian companies are engaged in manufacturing of different spare parts. So far spare parts have been supplied to India through intermediaries and now Russia is evolving a system under which the original manufacturers will directly supply the spare parts to India. Indian anxiety is that the spare parts should be supplied well in time.

Under an agreement reached recently, India's defence acquisitions from Russia will now be negotiated on the basis of a model contract which will have a sub clause dealing with the life-long supply of spares or setting up facilities for their production in India. Russia has also agreed to provide unified price lists for spares and components and give Indian specialists access to technical documentation of the hardware sold to India.

The new rules have come just in time to cover the all time biggest defence deal the purchase and license production of the multi-purpose long-range fighter jet, Su-30MKI. India is to manufacture about 140 Su-30MKI fighters and AL-31FP engines for them. The first batch of SU-30MKI, assembled at an Indian aircraft building plant will take off in approximately 2004.

In a recently published article, Russian expert has claimed that the MIG-21 is the most popular aircraft in the world today and about 6000 aircraft of this type are there in different countries. The Nizhni Novogorod aviation plant Sokol, has modernised its avionics, replacing them with French ones, installing the latest Kopyo (Spear) radar and arming it with modern R-73 close combat missiles. Consequently, the MIG-21 has been converted into an absolutely new aircraft, MIG-21 BIS, which fires missiles at air targets and drops remote control bombs on ground targets with precision.

Significantly, about 85 per cent of the military hardware the Indian Navy has, 80 per cent of hardware the Indian Air Force and 65 per cent of hardware of the Indian Army are Russian made. India is the only country with which Russia has long-term military technical cooperation which is worth more than eight billion.

It is pertinent to mention here that Russia sees the proposed privatisation of the Indian defence industry as a welcome chance for its arms manufacturers to consolidate their foothold in the Indian market.

"The Russian weapons industry is ready to look into opportunities for investment in the Indian defence sector," said Viktor Komardin, deputy chief of the Russian arms exporting monopoly, Rosoboronexport on 17 February 2002. This shows that integration of the Indian and Russian defence industries would be in line with the current shift from the buyer-seller relationship to joint development and production of new weapon system.

"We have joint R&D projects with India in almost all types of military hardware," Mr. Komardin said, citing as examples the Brahmos cruise missile, built last year, and a medium-haul transport aircraft, to be developed jointly on the lines of the Russian built Il-214 plane.

Top defence factory managers of Russian have been visiting India, to examine strategic partnership with India.

"We take interest in the privatisation of India's defence plants," said Mr. Vladimir Korenkov, General Director of the Bazalt factory, Russia's leading manufacturer of unguided munitions. "If Russia and India are strategic partners, it would be logical to integrate out defence industries".

Bazalt, which has been supplying air bombs and artillery shells to India, is now proposing joint developments of new-generations munitions, such as winged air bombs that enable the pilot to hit targets 6 km to 15 km away while staying out of range of enemy air defences.

"We are prepared to consider setting up a joint venture with an Indian entity and manufacture new munitions for out two countries as well as for export to third countries," the Bazalt manager said.

Participation in India's defence sector disinvestments programme can also help Russia face up to mounting competition from Western arms manufacturers.

"We propose to increase the share of high technologies in our defence exports to India, to move from licenced assembly of Russian made weapons to joint development and production and to promote factory-to-factory ties," said Mr. Komardin.

Experts said the Russian defence Industry, which is wholly state-owned could invest both cash and technologies in the Indian defecne sector. "The Russian defence industry is capable of investing in India $ 600 to $700 million over the next three to four years," said Alexander Vaskin of the Indo-Russian Security Forum. "As for technologies, the Russian contribution could be far more weighty, if, for example, the two countries go for the joint development of a fifth-generation jet fighter or a fourth generation tank on the basis of the Russian T-95 MBI"[13].

This shows that Indo-Russian defence cooperation is not only expanding but has begun to take a multi-dimensional character. This leads to the conclusion that Indo-Russian defence cooperation has already entered a new phase.

Conclusion

Weapons trade is a unique type of business in the international market. Leading industrial powers as well as a few developing countries focus on their defence industries by actively promoting R&D in order to modernise, upgrade and consolidate their defence industrial base for national security and economic returns as well.

In the era of intense competition in the international arms market-which has been dominated by the United States-Russian defence companies are seeking to supply any armaments from basic to the highly sophisticated ones and many developing countries see Russia as a source for their military equipment. The stress on arms exports is taking place in conditions where the macroeconomic situation is grim. Russia requires hard economic reforms for its growth. The government is committed to radical economic reforms aimed at integrating Russia to the global economy. Developing new armaments through joint collaboration with other countries is a salient feature of the present day corporate policy.

Russian armaments and military hardware are the most competitive in today's world market. The combat characteristic are in no way inferior to the armaments and military hardware being sold by the West. The combat aircraft of Su and MIG family, are known in the world for their unique flight characteristics. Diesel electric submarines of the 877EKM and 636 models are in great demand. 'Smerch' multi-launch fire systems, 'BMP-3' infantry combat vehicles, 'T-80U' and'T-90S' tanks, air-defence systems 'S-300-PMU-1', 'S-300-V' 'Buk-M-I', 'Tunguska self-propelled SAMs' and 'Igla' are in good demand in the international arms market.

Russian arms export in the Asia-Pacific region has increased. Malaysia, Philippines, Singapore and Indonesia have shown great interest in Russian weaponry. Russia has supplied (and modernised) an entire squadron of MIG-29 fighter-bombers to Malaysia. The Philippines had embarked on Air Force modernisation and intends to procure from Russia. Singapore has bought Igla (Needle) Man-protable Air-defence system (MAN-PADS) and the relevant production license from Russia for 120 million dollars. Indonesia's ambitious plan to procure MIL-MI-17 military cargo helicopters and 8 Su-30 fighter aircraft from Russia.

Russian key export to India during 1995-1998 has been the Su-30 MKI multi-role fighter aircraft. India and Russia signed an agreement on November 1996 for 40 aircraft. Ten more were ordered in September 1998. India has received 18 Su-30 MKI and is due to take delivery of 32 Su-30 MKI. The Indian contract is being fulfilled by the Sukhoi design bureau and the Irkutsk Aircraft Production Organisation (IAPO). India would start licence production of Su-30MKI multi-role fighter aircraft. India has also selected MIG-29K Fulcrum to equip the aircraft Admiral Gorshkov, which it plans to buy from Russia. To support MIG-29K operations MIG-MAPO will develop a two-seater naval trainer, the MIG-29KUB. On the bilateral MTC between Russia and India, Klebanov concluded "big contracts, joint work and joint production of arms are waiting for us in the future."

The achievements of the Rusian defence industries are impressive. After the break up of the Soviet Union, the steady recovery of the defence industries in noteworthy. Full cooperation and joint control has created a solution for the defence enterprises to present the latest equipment and technology in time to its customers in a competitive future.

More attention is to be given to conversion, modification and maintenance. Engineering support services are to be offered in a responsible way to the customers. Russian defence industries are meeting the challenge of the 21st century by delivering the latest combat hardware to their customers[14].

References

1. V.D. Chopra, India and the Socialist World, pp. 150, 154, 156.
2. V.D. Chopra, India and the Socialist World, pp. 40-42.
3. Col. R. Rama Rao, Self-Reliance and Security, pp. XI, XII, XIII.
4. Baidya Bikash Basu, Strategic Analysis, June 2001, pp. 437.
5. Yevgeni M. Kozhokin, "Arms Exprort Controls What Role for Parliament?" in Andrew J. Pierre and Dmitri V. Trenin eds., *Russia In The World Arms Trade* (Washington D.C., Carnegie Endowment for International Peace, The Brookings Institution Press. 1997) pp. 50-54.
6. Baidya Bikash Basu, Strategic Analysis, June 2001, p. 438.
7. *Ibid*, p. 440.
8. Vinay Shukla, "Russia in South Asia A view From India" in Gennady Chufrin, ed., Russia and Asia The Emerging Security Agenda (Sweden SIPRI, OUP, 1999) pp. 247-269. Also see in this, Shanon Kile, Appendix 2, pp. 500-505.
9. See, "India, Russia Sign Deal for 140 Sukhoi-30 in Jasjit Singh, ed., jets" The Hindustan Times, December 29, 2000.
10. Baidya Bikash Basu, Strategic Analysis, June 2001, pp. 445.
11. The Hindu dated 7 December 2002.
12. The Hindu dated 4 December 2002.
13. The Hindu dated 18 February 2002.
14. Baidya Bikash Basu, Strategic Analysis, February 2000, Trend in Russian Arms Export, pp. 1919, 1922, 1923, 1927, 1928, 1929.

11

Strategic Importance of Indian Ocean and Indo-Russian Naval Cooperation

V.D. Chopra

Introduction

The Indian Ocean occupies a strategic place in the security framework of Asia and the Pacific. The linkage between the Indian Ocean and the Pacific is a post-world war II phenomenon. This has assumed a new important in the recent decades after a series of developments such as decline in the influence of Great Powers like Britain and France disintegration of the Soviet Union and rise of the United States as a major actor in the world politics. Traditional powers, that had dominated the Indian Ocean for centuries were European powers and hence their line of communication passed through the Mediterranean and the Atlantic. The new entrants were Pacific Powers and their force projection in the Indian Ocean was directed from the Pacific. That was true of the USSR before its disintegration and of the USA in particular. To say this does not mean that Russia as a major naval power has lost its strategic interests in the sea-lanes of the Asia and Pacific region. In the Nineties, two more Pacific powers, China and Japan, had also begun to increase their role in the Indian Ocean region. This shows that in the beginning of the 21st century, the politics of the Indian Ocean will be increasingly linked up with that of the Pacific. This brings into sharp focus the strategic importance of the Asia-Pacific region and thereof of the Indian Ocean. The growing American interests in the Indian Ocean countries, the network it has set up and expanding its military presence in the Indian Ocean region should be seen in this context.

Indian security expert cannot ignore this new development, particularly the manner in which the United States is acquiring land base for itself in the region, the recent examples being Afghanistan and Iraq. Its special military relationship with Pakistan should not be ignored.

Security of the Indian Ocean is affected by the geo-strategic environment at the global level; the Indian Ocean commands vital sea and air routes connecting the Atlantic and the Mediterranean with the Pacific. Of course, the Panama Canal also does so but it has serious limitations for countries of Europe. There is no alternative to the Indian ocean routes even for Russia which has over land access from Europe to the Pacific. Russia also depends to a great deal, upon the Indian Ocean for East-West movement of its goods.

Besides the air and the sea routes, the Indian Ocean is also important to the Great Powers because of the availability of strategic materials there, such as oil and gas fossil fuel or tin, cooper and rubber. Control over these resources and their exclusive use has been one of the cardinal principles of these powers. Of them, oil has assumed increasingly importance in recent years. The dependence of the West for energy upon the Gulf oil and also the huge petro-dollars generated by the hike in oil price has further enhanced the Gulf a prime target of the Western strategy in the Indian Ocean[1]. Notwithstanding the depletion in the oil resources of the Gulf region, it will continue to be of strategic importance at least for the next three decades.

Yet another factor that influenced the strategic importance of the Indian Ocean was the new nuclear strategy based upon submarine launched ballistic missile fired from a nuclear powered submarine. This system, commonly known as the SLBM, was introduced around 1963 and became an important component of the strategic nuclear triad: the manned bomber, the ICBM and the SLBM. The SLBM was especially important as a second strike weapon and hence a crucial factor in the Great Power strategy. The USA pioneered it. The former Soviet Union also perfected it soon after. The U.K. and France followed suit. The Chinese have recently perfected it[2]. Above all, American base in Diego Garcia has given a new dimension to this trend.

This shows that the Indian Ocean will continue to be important to the Great Powers in the coming decades, both in terms of nuclear strategy and also for its natural resources. The focus of Great Power activity has gradually increased in the Indian Ocean. In that context South-East Asia and the area around South China Sea have acquired increased importance as the connecting link between the two oceans, the Indian Ocean and the Pacific Ocean. China and Japan, therefore, are increasingly getting involved in the politics of the Indian Ocean..

The Indian Ocean will continue to be relevant to the West, especially to the USA, in its global strategic nuclear war-fighting doctrines and their-interaction with weapon systems like the air and sea-launched cruise missile, strategic nuclear weapons that form an important constituent of the CENTCOM strength and the SDI related anti-satellite and anti-ballistic missile defence system[3].

This brings us to the conclusion that in the post Cold War era, the strategic economic and political dynamics are slowly drifting towards the Asia-Pacific region and simultaneously the oceanic focus has been shifting from the Atlantic-Pacific to the Pacific-Indian Ocean region. The Indian Ocean is likely to be the "ocean of destiny in the 21st Century"[4].

It is relevant to mention here that although smaller than the Pacific and Atlantic Ocean, the Indian Ocean is of special significance because of its geo-strategic and geo-economic position. It covers an area of 74 million sq. kilometers, comprising some 20 per cent of the total oceanic area of the world. It touches the shores of three continents – Asia, Africa and Australia, and its southern end reaches up to Antarctica. The Indian Ocean provides shorter and more economical routes for transportation and communication between the two major seas.

Above all, its littoral states as well as the Ocean itself are tremendously rich in natural resources as mentioned earlier. Significantly, more than half of the world's known oil reserves are in the Indian Ocean region. Other valuable minerals such as gold, diamonds and uranium are also found in abundance in this region. The possibility of discovering other types of minerals from its seabed are immense[5].

There is yet another aspect to it. Due to its important geo-economic position, the Indian Ocean has become all the more important in the world economy as the new silk route from the Persian Gulf to the Sea of Japan passes through it[6].

As seen earlier, the Indian Ocean littoral states have been putting pressure on the USA, both within and outside the UN, to remove its strategic nuclear presence from the area. These pressures have proved futile so far. Now, there are chances that a new power might also seek to introduce, in the near future, its strategic-nuclear weapon systems in the Indian Ocean.

China's Policy :

China has been experimenting with its own SLBM since the late seventies and gained success in the early eighties. It first tested its SLBM (CSS-NX-3), with 1800 nautical range, in April 1982 from a sea based platform.

The first successful firing from a submarine was conducted in the Pacific on September 28, 1985. The first XIA-class nuclear powered submarine, with 12 tubes for the CSS-NX-3 missiles, became operational in 1985. China operates four of these submarines and more are being planned in the near future[7]. The Chinese are planning to increase the range of their SLBM. The American also started with 1,200 nautical mile range for their Polaris A-1 and ended with 2,500 nautical miles range for the final Polaris A-3 version. There is little doubt that in the coming years, the Chinese will also increase the range of their SLBM, that will enable them to operate it from the Indian Ocean also[8]. China has already emerged as a world power.

Since 1992, China has intensified its activities in the Indian Ocean region. The July 1992 report of the General Logistic Department of the People's Liberation Army outlined the plans for the expansion of Chinese naval capabilities through construction of three large bases by 1998, and called for stepped up naval visits in the Indian Ocean and more frequent port calls to foreign countries in the region. Myanmar, which faces Indian across the Bay of Bengal, is undergoing a naval infrastructure modernisation programme with Chinese assistance. The construction of a new naval base at Hanggyi Island in the Bassein river at the mouth of the Irrawady; development of existing facilities at Sittwe near the Bangladesh border and development of radar facilities in the Coco Islands at a distance of only 30 nautical miles from the Andaman chain of islands of India are all significant Chinese moves. The facility could monitor Indian naval communications and even India's ballistic missiles tests off its eastern coast. India naturally is concerned about Chinese military activities on the western sea coast of Myanmar.

A U.S. study report points to the possibility that China may deploy its nuclear submarines in the Indian Ocean. According to an article written in 1993 by Marcus B. Ziner, a naval attaché in the U.S. Embassy in Bangladesh, "China is both a land and sea power, Pakistan's most powerful ally"[9].

Pakistan's Role

Pakistan has improved its military facilities at Karachi, Gwadar, Jiwani, Ormara, Pasni, Peshawar and Lahore with U.S. aid. The supply of F-16, and other weapons from the U.S. to Pakistan was handled through the U.S. Central Command in coordination with its Rapid Deployment Force. Reports on the possibility of the U.S. getting listening posts in Pakistan were also significant.

The U.S-Pak strategy of having an undeclared military alliance at that stage perhaps was based on the assumption that this would not evoke popular criticism in Pakistan. However, in the late eighties, particularly, after the movement for restoration of democracy and finally the establishment of democracy with its own limitations, people of Pakistan began to assert their independence.

An important point to note is that the Reagan Administration had recast the security role for Pakistan in the U.S. strategy in South-West Asia. In the pre-Reagan era, the main direction of the American policy was to provide military aid to Pakistan to keep the Afghan problem alive; and as such it was a limited role. But under the Reagan Administration a sea-change took place. Pakistan was transformed into a 'frontline' state, both literally and metaphorically. It was assigned the role of a bulwark of defence south of Afghanistan. At the same time, Pakistan also became a key link in the geopolitical strategy of Washington in the Gulf and the Indian Ocean regions. Pakistan through its military strength now was required to provide 'stability' to Iran, Saudi Arabia and other Gulf countries, on the one hand, and influence the course of development in the South Asian countries on the other[10]. Let us leave this analysis of that period at that, though it is in all essential is relevant even today. This is proved by concrete evidence of recent years.

In the 1990s, Pakistan increased its naval capabilities considerably. Between 1992 and 1995, it was the second largest recipient of warships in the Indian Ocean region and the fifth largest in the world. Britain, the Netherlands and France were the major sources of supply during this period. The arms package provided by the U.S. through the Brown Amendment further augmented its strike capabilities. Rahul Roychaudhury in his article of February 1996, titled "The Brown Amendment: Implications for the Indian Navy", dwelt in detail about the impact on the Indian Navy of the U.S. arms package worth $368 billion to Pakistan. It was predominantly a naval package as 70 per cent of it, in terms of value, was maritime equipment.

Pakistan purchased French-made Agosta submarines in 1999. It has developed Jinnah Naval Port at Ormara in the Arabian Sea and since August, 2001 is developing a strategically important port at Gwadar with economic and technical aid and assistance from China.

Indian Option

In the context of these new developments, India is likely to face greater challenges in the coming years. Because of various factors including Indo-Pak conflict on cross border terrorism. It still has deepened its relations with ASEAN states. These political constraints will have to be overcome. It is unfortunate that the growing maritime capability of India, which is far less than that of China, its main competitor, is being projected as a source of threat to other countries. The massive interventionist capabilities of Great Powers and the newly developed strength of China vis-à-vis South-East Asia are projected as forces of stability.

India needs to meet these challenges by a new political drive. India is the natural kingpin in any regional arrangement for maritime cooperation in the Indian Ocean area. This maritime cooperation needs to be on a wider framework of Southern Asia which should seek to inter link the maritime development processes and cooperation between the Indian Ocean littoral states of South-East Asia, South Asia and of the Arabian Sea and its natural extensions. Regional consciousness can best be fostered through the process of regional integration within the framework of South-South cooperation.

It will be relevant to recall here that during the last phase of the Bangladesh liberation war, a big U.S. task force entered the Bay of Bengal on December 14, 1971, through the Straits of Malacca. The presence of *USS Enterprise* in the Bay of Bengal was seen as coercive diplomacy to restrain India. After their 'benign belligerent' demonstration the *USS Enterprise* sailed out of the Indian Ocean through the Straits of Malacca on January 10, 1972. The U.S. role during the war radically changed India's security perceptions and induced it to expand its naval build-up in the Indian Ocean. Indian efforts towards a naval build-up were charged by littoral countries as 'hegemonistic and as an attempt to convert the Indian Ocean into 'Indian' Ocean.

The Indian Navy, though the fifth largest Navy in the World and the largest indigenous Navy in the Indian Ocean, could not increase its naval capabilities in the 1990s due to a financial crunch. It only acquired and old leader class frigate from Britain for training purposes.

The Indian Ocean was the only ocean not having an economic grouping like NAFTA and APEC at a time when the world scenario is swiftly becoming ocean-centric. Only in March 1997, fourteen countries of the region signed the charter of Indian Ocean Rim Association for Regional Cooperation (IORARC). The formation of IORARC has provided the countries of the Indian Ocean rim a collective oceanic identity and a platform for cooperation. The membership of IORARC should remain open for all littoral countries of Indian Ocean and efforts should be made for developing regional amity and cooperation. The convergence of economic and security interests would help them emerge as a global force with global impact[11].

Indo-Russian Naval Cooperation

It is in this background that Indo-Russian naval cooperation; its strategic importance for the security of the country should be objectively assessed. If India have to play role as a Great Power commensurate with its size and geographical location it has no other option but to strengthen its naval strength. India needs to consolidate its strength and influence. Admiral Sushil Kumar has emphasised the up-gradation of naval security in the Indian Ocean. Admiral Madhvendra Singh has underlined the necessity of further strengthening the Indian Navy. India urgently requires an aircraft carrier. *INS Viraat* is due to be de-commissioned in 2003. It is reported that negotiations for acquisition on a Russian aircraft carrier are in the final stage and the project to build submarines based on the French 'Scorpene' at the Mazagaon Docks in Mumbai and indigenous construction of warship is going well.

It may be mentioned here that although the U.S. had begun reducing its military forces worldwide, it has not done so in Diego Garcia. The Indo-American naval relations are slowly taking roots but they are still uncertain. The U.S. government has proposed to have Indian naval escorts for U.S. Navy vessels at the straits of Malacca. When approved by the Indian Cabinet, it will advance Indo-U.S. naval cooperation over the Malabar-type exercise that was cocoordinated in 1995-1998. In the September 2002, India and the U.S. had their week-long naval exercise 'Malabar-4' which was tactical in nature and warfare-oriented, in the Indian Ocean. India may be keen to cooperate with the U.S. troops and provide escort to U.S. naval vessels in the Indian Ocean. But the crux of the problem is that despite this trend in Indo-U.S. cooperation, the American administration still considers Pakistan as its strategic partner. The Indian defenc experts cannot minimize this aspect. But it needs to make sure what it is going to gain from such cooperation. As despite Indian's gesture of cooperation in fighting terrorism, the United States relies more on Pakistan and it remained the main player in America's retaliatory attack on Afghanistan.

That being the position in the foreseeable future Indo-Russian naval cooperation will be a key factor in strengthening India's maritime strength. It is in this setting that the importance of India's negotiation with Russia for acquiring Gorshkov aircraft carrier should be seen. The long awaited package deal for the acquisition of the Gorshkov aircraft carrier, as well as nuclear capable long-range bombers and submarines may be finalised in the near future. Defence Minister George Fernandes had indicated that "we have agreed that all efforts will be made to complete the three contracts by the end of March 2003".

It may be mentioned here that the 44,500 tonne Kiev-class Admiral Gorshkov aircraft carrier is tied to the supply of four Tu-22M3 Backfire strategic bombers and two Akula-class nuclear powered submarines[12].

Indian Navy has already acquired the capability of operating nuclear submarines on the earlier Russian leased out INS Chakra Class nuclear submarines in the eighties. The submarines were decommissioned in 1991.

The Indian Navy has even subsequently been keeping alive its skill in operating a nuclear submarine. "Training of personnel is an on-going process".

The Indian Navy also wants two Tu-22 (black Jack) nuclear bombers on lease while its Tu-124 long-range maritime reconnaissance aircraft are being overhauled.

Russia has also made a formal after to India for jointly developing a fifth generation fighter, which is expected to roll out-simultaneously with the U.S. Joint Strike Fighter (JSF).

Regarding the delivery schedule of three Krivak-III Class stealth frigates under construction in St. Petersburg the Defence Ministry hopes that all the three warships Talwar, Trishul and Tabar would be handed over to the Indian Navy within 2003[13].

These facts show that within the framework of naval cooperation with all the countries, at the present face Indo-Russian naval cooperation continues to be a key factor.

References

1. Prof. K.R. Singh, Indian Ocean, Asia-Pacific Region : Conflicting Security Concepts, p. 94.

2. *Ibid.*, p. 95.

3. *Ibid.*, p. 100.

4. Anand Mathur, Growing Importance of the Indian Ocean in Post-Cold War era and its implication for India, Strategic Analysis, October-December 2002, pp. 551.

5. *Ibid.*, p. 550.

6. *Ibid.*, p. 556.
7. Prof. K.R. Singh, Indian Ocean, Asia-Pacific Region : Conflicting Security Concepts, pp 100.
8. *Ibid.*, p. 100.
9. Anand Mathur, Growing Importance of the Indian Ocean in Post-Cold War era and its implication for India, Strategic Analysis, October-December 2002, p. 552.
10. V.D. Chopra, Asian Peace and Indo-Soviet Friendship, Indo-Soviet Relations : Prospects and Problems, p. 167.
11. Anand Mathur, Growing Importance of the Indian Ocean in Post-Cold War era and its implication for India, Strategic Analysis, October-December 2002, p. 553, 556, 557.
12. The Hindu dated 18 January 2003.
13. National Herald dated 19 January 2003.

12

India and Russia : Too Much Done; So Much to Do

P. L. Dash

Russian president, Vladimir Putin's second official visit to India on 3-5 December, 2002 was as hectic as his maiden one a couple years ago. One still remembers 3 October, 2000 as a day like none other in the annals of Indo-Russian relations. Autumn aura had added an eerie feeling to the advent of an unknown winter. The day was impeccably bright in New Delhi. Inside Hall No.6 of the sprightly decorated Vigyan Bhavan, a special convocation was being held by the Jawaharlal Nehru University to confer Honoris Causa the degree of Doctor of Laws on his excellency, the Russian President, Vladimir Putin. The audience, mostly professors and invitees along with media men, were all agog to greet a friend of India, Vladimir Putin, with applause.

The function began as usual. Human Resources Development Minister, Murli Manohar Joshi, spoke for about ten minutes on Russia under Putin with somewhat stale statistics. After conferment of the degree, by the Chancellor, Professor M.S.Gore, when Putin's turn came to speak, he politely thanked for the honour bestowed on him. However, behind that politeness lay the thundering voice of a president, who suddenly corrected Joshi by throwing most recent developmental figures on Russia. He lauded the strong foundation on which Indo-Russian ties were built and ended his speech with optimism for a millennium of progress. This author, sitting in the audience, was amazed at the thorough preparedness of the president, who gave extempore, off the cuff data to which he alone perhaps was privy as President of Russia. Young and ebullient, strong yet mild, chary but charming, Putin was abreast of and confident about his country's affairs with crimson hopes for an optimistic future. This was a president Russia has had never seen. He carried his day and swayed his audience the way he liked.

Little over two -years have passed since then - indeed too small a time to redeem a tattered relationship that had suffered the blows of Soviet disintegration. Yet Putin's focused attempt to further age-old Indo-Russian ties is indeed commendable. The forward march of bilateral relationship between October 2000, when Putin first visited India and his second official visit in December, 2002 alongwith an interloping visit by the Indian Prime Minister Atal Behari Vajpayee to Moscow in November, 2001, is suggestive as much of the new closeness emerging as the shape of things to come. Five and half decades of close diplomatic ties beginning 13 April, 1947, over four decades of mutual economic cooperation beginning mid 1950s, almost four decades of close military collaboration starting early 1960s, and all along these years, an equal stretch of affable political relationship are all in the backdrop to back up a palmy future. The petals of the flower called Indo-Russian relations are once again beginning to blossom to rejuvenate a limitless future with their fragrance.

Both countries are marketizing and globalizing in their own ways, both are reforming their economies in a unique fashion, both have common approach to vital issues of international concern, both have an incredible blend of understanding on destabilizing issues such as international and cross border terrorism, narcotic trafficking, Islamic extremism, arms smuggling and a host of other issues facing their neighbourhood. They may be taking baby steps in resolving what seems gargantuan, but these steps and their resolve are certainly in the desired direction.

The Millennium Agenda

The visit that set the tone for a new beginning in relationship was the one that witnessed the signing of eleven agreements on a wide range of issues. India and Russia had signed in October, 2000 eleven elaborate agreements that covered

- Integrated long term programme on cooperation in the field of science and technology up to 2010.
- Intergovernmental agreement in the field of agriculture
- Cooperation in postal communication services
- Treaty on mutual legal assistance and legal relations concerning civil and commercial matters

- Memorandum of understanding on cooperation between Ministries of Law, Justice and Company affairs of both countries
- Signing of Cultural, scientific and educational exchange agreement between India and Russia for 2000-2001
- Agreement on mutual protection of confidential material
- Protocol of intentions between MMTC Limited, India and Gokhran of Russia under the Russian Finance Ministry on cooperation in the field of Processing and trade of raw diamond and precious metals.
- Product sharing contract between Government of India and Public Joint .Stock Company 'Gazprom' and Gas Authority of India with respect to contract area identified as Block NEC-OSN-97/1.
- Agreement between India and Russia on principles of cooperation between governments of the states and union territories of India and the bodies of Executive Authority of the constituent entities of Russia; and finally,
- A Declaration of Strategic Partnership that mandated to hold annual summit level meetings and make efforts to reduce nuclear arms globally with the ultimate goal to eliminate these weapons.[1]

A cursory look at all the eleven agreements enumerated above suggested a substantive improvement in mutual understanding, It implied that both countries have resolved to expand ties in the fields of economic cooperation including oil and gas exploration, scientific and technological cooperation including educational exchanges, contacts between law enforcing bodies of both countries to oversee implementation of the accords reached including close collaboration between their ministries and establishment of contacts in a decentralized manner between Indian states and Union territories and Russian territorial entities. Besides, the Declaration on strategic partnership bound the two countries to non-participation in any military political or other alliances or associations or armed conflict directed against the other side ...[2] Thus, defence, legal, scientific, trade and economic, political, cultural and technological cooperation made the cornerstone of the agreements and their wider implications are the matter of future course of interactions that would stud this century with renewed vigour and strength. [3]

Partnership in Perspective

The concept of a strategic partnership, embracing India, China and

Russia in a trilateral security arrangement was not a new one in bilateral relationship. Although the idea was sounded in the Brezhnev years in the form of collective Asian security, it was never vigorously pursued. In the last week of December, 1998, the idea was, however, revived when it was mooted by the then visiting Russian Prime Minister, Yevgeny Primakov in New Delhi.[4] This may be an axis of error or an ephemeral eddy of Russian overtures in Asia. But it is certainly born out of the conviction of having a viable regional security arrangement that would simultaneously countervail the growing American influence in the region. Therefore, Moscow-Beijing-New Delhi axis continues to receive overwhelming support in the subcontinent from a section of its population for a variety of reasons. First, it purports to legitimize bilateral relations from the strategic view point, a point that has been refrained in several agreements in the past few years as much between Russia and China as between Russia and India. Secondly, it would align in a block three of the world's most populous countries, whose economic weight is nonetheless significant. Besides, their own populous weight, the surrounding areas abound for half of the world population living in South, Central, West and East Asia, where their strategic depth is obvious. Thirdly, a factor that cannot be hectored is the nuclear capability of all three partners, straddled in an area pregnant with possibilities of impending conflicts of all sorts. Finally, it is widely felt in all three economically reforming countries that close cooperation would accrue greater mutual benefits, particularly in the economic field, than at present.

However, the idea has been receiving gingerly response from certain academic quarters on the ground that the whole perception remains ill conceived, loosely defined, its long term and short term objectives unclear, its structure vague, its content ambiguous and its membership uncertain.[5] It does not receive overwhelming alacrity because of the conservative mind-set prevailing over mutual distrust among its proponents, particularly relative to border disputes between Russia and China and China and India. Supporters of the idea, however, say that the changing, post Cold War international context has precipitated the imperatives to put disputes and differences in the back burner and focus on economic character of an increasingly borderless world in order to exploit the benefits of globalisation to mutual advantage. Ever since the thaw in international conduct began through Gorbachev years, successive leaders of all three countries have endeavored in all their powwows to iron out differences to the advantage of their economic progress.

Russia's emphasis on mutually beneficial cooperation under the

Shanghai Five and Putin's stop-over in Beijing on the first leg of his Asian tour before he landed in New Delhi on 3 December, 2002 underscore these efforts. At the same time, Putin's strong and unambiguous condemnation of Pakistan's role in the American led war against terror and his apprehensions and worrying reaction about nuclear weapons materials falling into the wrong hands of Islamic extremists/ terrorists, and its subsequent endorsement by the Indian Prime Minister,[6] further elucidating its dangers, is once again a polarizing signal on the face of it that pits Moscow, Beijing and New Delhi clearly against US-Pakistani alliance. This message is elementally primal and its implications are implicit for the future.

Coming as it is from a veteran of Putin's vintage, the statements are apparently premonitions of shape of things to come in the region. The regional scenario, complicated by the American military entanglement in Afghanistan, has given each country its own compulsions vis-A-vis the USA. China is already a regional power that aspires to equal the US in world standing. Its covert help to Pakistan, first to go nuclear and then behave truant, can run counter to its forming an axis with Russia and India against Pakistan-US allies. Similarly, Russia's present economic status does not mandate upon itself to substantially oppose the USA and its partnership with Pakistan. India would not also like to wash away the warmth of relationship it has built with the USA in recent years. In three major Central Asian countries - Kazakhstan, Uzbekistan and Kirgyzstan - all contiguous to the proposed partnership countries of Russia, China and India, American soldiers are stationed as operational force in Afghanistan. With all these nuances in mind, what Putin said is what really exists, and what India really wants is to put pressure on the USA to bridle Musharaff on the issue of cross-border infiltration along the Line of Control and stop exporting terrorism to Kashmir.

Events after events after events, India's pleas about containing the breeding ground of terror have fallen on deaf years. Musharaff continues to talk Kashmir, Kashmir and more Kashmir, thus overshadowing the core issue of terrorism with rhetoric. The torrents of terror is gradually flowing into the lives of innocent people. From the explosion of J&K assembly to bombardment of Parliament to bomb blast in Akshardham temple, the imprints of terror are explicit. The terrorists of today were trainees of yesteryears from the special training centers based in Pakistan. For over two decades, it has been done through the overt US support to Pakistan to fight the Soviets through trained Afghan Mujaheedins, a naked truth that the world has enough evidence to believe. Whether America believes it or not is a matter of time. Calling a spade a spade is the way of direct diplomacy that Putin has chosen now to address.

And it has resonance all over. For the first time, a permanent member of the UN Security Council has drawn attention to the dangers of a nuclear Pakistan. For the first time, it is from one of America's closest allies in the war against terror that such warning has emanated. For the first time, one of the three original signatories of nuclear non-proliferation is talking with candor about Pakistan's weapons proliferating elsewhere. Whether all these persuade the USA to adopt a tougher line against Musharaff is an open question to the Bush administration to judge. However, the joint message stemming out of Putin's India visit is clear and loud enough to suggest what is essentially required to bridle a nuclear bully to save the region from an impending catastrophe. Not Iraq, but Pakistan ought to be in the priority list of the US to deal with.

Two Years in Review

A composite review of Indo-Russian relations in the interloping period between Putin's two visits to India highlights more continuity and less change. Rather a check on the precipitously sliding trade and revival of the past glory is what Russia opts for. After a total downswing in bilateral trade following the Soviet break-up, by 2001-2002, it was visible that the annual volume of Indo-Russian trade turnover had stabilized around $ 1.4 billion. Bulk of the trade is transacted through three known routes 1. Normal commercial route of import-export through hard currency, 2. Debt repayment route, and 3. ESCROW account channel. All the three paths are, however, riddled with bureaucratic bottlenecks which both sides are trying hard to overcome. For a comparison, one could take Sino-Russian trade turnover as an example. Currently, the Sino-Russian trade turnover staggers at $ 3 billion annually, while that of Indo-Russian trade is a lowly volume of just half of that - $ 1.5 billion. Equally disquieting is the Chinese share in the Russian arms market. As much as 40 per cent of the Russian arms are bought by China. India, as the second biggest buyer, gets some 25 per cent.[7]

As could be seen from the table, the trade volume is not that great; it is also not the most important thing. Trade is just one aspect of bilateral ties. Unless corrective measures are taken right now, bilateral trade is likely to suffer setbacks in 2005, when debt repayment channel dries up. Since India's trade with Russia through the debt repayment channel constitutes nearly 80 per cent of the total volume, an end to annual debt repayment of Rupees 3000 crores would severely affect the fledgling

VOLUME OF INDO-RUSSIA TRADE (2000-2002)

(million US $)

	Export	Import
2000		
First Half	142.311	171.607
Second Half	133.098	220.932
2001		
First Half	126.357	248.172
Second Half	126.225	328.428
2002		
Total Volume	$ 1.5 billion	

Source. Newsletter, India-CIS Chamber of Commerce and Industry, Vol. XV, No.7, October-November, 2001, p. 23.

Indo-Russian trade, albeit its upswing through Putin years. Adventurous forays by Indian entrepreneurs and businessmen into Russia's virgin markets in the distant regions and investment by private companies without any protection umbrella of the government would presumably facilitate a sustainable trade in the years to come.

However, the sprawling tree of Indo-Russian Relations has branched out variously to affect lives in many fields. There are two significant aspects to bilateral contacts in the past two years. First, Russia's west centric euphoria has evaporated, paving way to a balanced East-West approach-a scheme of things in which India's importance is tangible. The two successive visits by President Putin within a span of just two years underscore this. Secondly, both sides have realized the mutual potential of furthering bilateral relations to the advantage of their overall progress. All discussions and efforts are revolving around the second pivot, and both countries are once again eager to revive and expand age-old ties. A peculiar combination of nuclear weapons, Islamic fundamentalism, narcotic trafficking and terrorism sweeping the peripheries of both countries provides a further challenge to close bilateral interactions now as never before.

Notable among the hallmarks of achievements in the past two years are the cooperation in the conventional and nuclear energy sectors, identification of potential areas for future ties, the North South corridor for speedy transportation of goods, joint cooperation in the international arena on issues of vital, bilateral concern, arms deals and agreements on scientific and cultural cooperation including information technology.

In the nuclear energy sector, Kudankulam joint venture along a 25 kilometer strip from Kanyakumari across the Gulf of Mannar, is by far the biggest one in recent years. Initially signed between the former USSR and India in November,1988, the project was hanging fire for ten years, when it was further amended through a supplement in June 1998. India is to finance 46 per cent of the construction cost, while Russia provides a credit for the rest of the 54 per cent at 4 per cent interest to be repaid after commissioning of the power plant in 2007. Designed to be built at a cost of 140 billion rupees, this nuclear power plant was projected to provide India 2000 Mwe nuclear power from two reactors. However, subsequent induction of a new Light Water Reactor, based on latest technology could provide a fillip to the proposed facility, enabling the project to produce another 6000 Mwe of nuclear power by 2020.[8] Thus, when India will receive an additional 8000 Mwe of power from Kudankulam, the project would be a salutary addition to Indo-Russian joint ventures. It would immensely benefit the state of Tamil Nadu, and its neighbouring states and boost India's energy security system. But for now, the work is in full swing, while everyone is looking forward to the target year of power production production -2007 for the first reactor and 2008 for the second one.

With a view to bolster India's energy security, 18 thermal and Hydro power projects have already been built with Soviet/Russian collaboration. Some of them are already working, while others are in pipeline. They include such names as the Vindhyachal, Hardwaganj, Korba, Tehri, Bhakra and Balimela. In recent years, joint collaboration has assumed a new meaning in the energy sector. Indian companies are venturing aggressively in to the Russian energy market. ONGC Videsh, the foreign investment subsidiary of the ONGC, signed a deal with Russian oil company Rosneft on 10 February, 2001 to invest $ 1.75 billion on a 20 per cent stake on Sakhalin-I project alongwith Japan's Sodeco and Exxon Mobil Corporation, who have 30 per cent stake each. Russia itself has just 20 per cent share. The target year for start of production is 2005 and India expects to get 2.5 to 5 million tons of crude oil per year as its equity share.[9] The Sakhalin is an ongoing programme with at least five different projects of oil exploration conceived at present in different stages that will keep India engaged with Rosneft for many years to come. Negotiations are on for Sakhalin 11 project and Bharat Petroliurn would participate with Rosneft at a later stage for full-fledged exploitation of Sakhalin oil and natural gas.

While these are major developments in the energy sector, for a long time transportation of goods has posed a nagging problem in bilateral trade transaction. Both sides have been exploring ways of making transportation sustainable and cost effective. With this in view, there were trilateral negotiations between Russia, India and Iran on a North South corridor. The outcome of these negotiations was an intergovernmental agreement signed in September, 2000 in St. Petersburg on creation of a North-South transit transport corridor.[10] The agreement was ratified by president Putin on 13 March, 2002. The corridor, once fully operational, would facilitate sea and land links across three countries - India, Iran and Russia - and shorten transit time between India and Russia by nearly ten days that would reduce transportation cost by about 20-25 per cent.[11]

Defence Deals

One area that has never escaped attention of all Indo-Russian summits, past or present alike, is bilateral defence cooperation. There are many gray areas here to be addressed. India's near total dependence on Russian weaponry and military hardware is as much a native concern as Moscow's willingness to keep India engaged in bilateral defence deals. The Indian Army requires a fleet of modern tanks. Air Force's MIG -21 fighters have apparently outlived their utility and need modernisation or replacement. The Navy also requires subs and frigates. Therefore, the past two years were full of hectic activities, mutual exchange of visits by defence delegations that have brought incredible results by setting into motion encouraging trends in mutual military technological cooperation.

In February,2001 India's Defence Minister, George Fernandes and Russian Deputy Prime Minister, Ilya Khlebanov had signed a defence deal that made provision for the purchase of 310 sophisticated T-90 battle tanks at a cost of $ 600 million. The T-90 battle tanks have superior mobility, better fire power and communication system and night vision capability. These tanks could fire missiles at enemy targets. In the first phase of delivery, India has got 124 tanks assembled at Uralvagonzavod in the Russian city of Nizhny Tagil and the remaining 186 in semi and completely knocked-down conditions will be assembled in India at the heavy vehicle factory in Avadi in Tamilnadu.[12] For this purpose, 40 Indian experts will be trained in Nizhny Tagil in the art of assembling T-90 components. The same visit finalized two other agreements one involved technology transfer and manufacturing of Main Battle Tanks in India, and the other envisaged production of weapon systems of these tanks. The missiles of the tanks will be procured in knocked down condition to be assembled by Bharat Dynamics in India.

The Indian Air Force has also procured the first batch of a fleet of multifunctional Sukhoi-30MKI fighter aircrafts. The official ceremony for induction of these aircrafts was held on 27 September, 2000 at Lohagaon air base near Pune. Considered to be the most advanced fighter plane in the world, Sukhoi-30MKI is armed with newest air-to-air missiles, air surface missile system, state of the art avionics and phased array radar. Its A 1 -3 1 FP engine, featuring thrust vector control capability, makes it a formidable aircraft, provides the fighter in it with unbeatable manoeuvrability and substantial combat efficiency. Negotiations are going on with Illyushin Aviation Complex, Irkutsk Aviation association, Hindustan Aeronautics Limited and Rosoboron export for making multi-role transport aircraft. It was reported in the Russian press that India had signed a deal worth $ 3.3 billion for procuring six IL-78 tanker aircraft and 140 fighter of Sukhoi modifications in 2003.

Just before coming to India, Putin had visited a suburban city, Reutovo, near Moscow, where a supersonic anti-ship Brahmos cruise missile is being jointly developed at a mechanical engineering research and production association. This is the most modern naval cruise missile. The second successful test launch of it had taken place in Chandipur in April, 2002[13] and the missile would now be ready for induction to the Indian Navy. In August, 2002, Chief of the Indian Navy, Admiral Madhavendra Singh visited the Baltic wharf in St. Petersburg and supervised the manufacture of 'Talwar' and 'Tabar" frigates, specially made for the Indian Navy. Admiral Singh also met the crew of the Trishul frigate, who are undergoing shop performance trial in the Baltic wharf.[14] Thrishul will be tested in the Gulf of Finland. In addition to Sindhuvir and Sindhughos submarines, currently operational in the Indian Navy, India will be provided with another Submarine called Sindhuratna. This will be a diesel-electric submarine with upgraded features. Negotiations are also finalized about the procurement of Admiral Gorshkov for the Indian Navy. In a nutshell, there has been close defence collaboration in the past two years and trends are encouraging for the future.

Defence cooperation is incomplete without collaboration in the field of informatics and information technology because any modem gadget is electronically controlled. In order to expand bilateral relationship in this area, a member Telecom and IT delegation headed by Minister, Promod Mahajan visited Moscow and St. Petersburg on 10-14 September,2002. The focus of the visit was to explore potential areas of cooperation in telecom spheres. The participation of many private telecom equipment manufacturers is suggestive of the interests India has for joint collaboration in this area. Defence and Information Technology are two potential, interrelated areas for joint ventures and collaborations between India and Russia.

Present Concerns

Putin's three-day state visit to India took place at a complicated time accentuated by the post 9/11 scenario and American military entanglement in Afghanistan. It's a time when, both India and Russia, have joined hands with the USA in its global fight against terror. The visit also took place in the backdrop of many terrorist acts perpetrated by Islamic extremists such as attack on Indian parliament in New Delhi and Chechen rebels taking hostage of theatre goers in Moscow. Far too long has India pleaded with the USA to curb terrorism abetted by Pakistan and far too long it has received lukewarm response. Therefore, bilateral trade and military negotiations this time were in the sidelines; terrorism and regional issues dominated Putin-Vajpayee talks and overshadowed all other problems. No wonder there were joint vituperations of Pakistan in a loud voice for the international community to hear. The joint declaration also echoed the selfsame criticism of Pakistan and her role in the fight against terror.

The visit was a discernible demonstration of continuing commitments and abiding faith in holding annual, summit level talks on a regular basis with a view to taking stock of developments, and charting out future action plans. However, this time it seemed as if terrorism and Pakistan were in the top of the agenda. Putin was categorical about his remarks, that Pakistan is not a reliable nuclear power, that its titubation in the American led war against terror is raising doubts, that Osama Bin Laden continues to live in Pakistan and operates his terror network with covert political support of Pakistan, that Al Quaeda and Taliban elements have relocated themselves along the Line of Control from where export of terrorists to Kashmir continues. And all these are not desirable developments in the direction of combating terrorism from the earth; nor they are likely to bring about any tangible or sustainable solution to the Indo-Pakistani dispute over Kashmir.

What remains incredible was Putin's appreciation of India's diplomatic endeavour to convince the international community about the true nature and source of terrorism in the Indian sub-continent. Putin's candor was explicit apparently because his country was as much at the receiving end of terrorist attacks on the civilian targets as was India, and a teaming up was essential. Rather a political support to India at this stage was crucial on this pressing issue of common concern that does convey a clear message that being on the right side of each other, India and Russia are not in the wrong side of the USA. The objectives to eradicate the menace of terror remains as much unchanged as the total commitment to fight it out. But with dubious credentials, a country like Pakistan is unlikely to evince its total commitment. The volatility of the political situation within a nuclear Pakistan under Musharaff after the October elections in that country may precipitate a situation, when Islamic extremists will be in control of the nukes, and in that case, Pakistan's participation in the war against terror would be a whimper. The unending spiral of breeding conventional and nuclear terrorism would not only endanger regional peace and security, but be a direct threat even to the USA. The common concerns were, therefore, terrorism with focus on Pakistan's role to combat it, besides nuclear security issues and bilateral cooperation.

The outcomes of Putin's recent visit to India were 8 bilateral agreements, including a Delhi declaration with an overall objective to enhance cooperation between the two countries. The visit was reassurance of mutual commitment, reaffirmation of yesteryear's promises, reiteration of commonalities of interests and revelation of a strong desire to expand bilateral contacts. The canvas of Indo-Russian cooperation is broad enough to cover such diverse fields as diamond cutting, cultural exchange, film festivals, technology transfer in the military sector, international cooperation within the UN framework, space expeditions, exchange of scientists and scholars, trade and commerce, ship building, oil exploration, manufacturing of pharmaceuticals, exchange of parliamentary delegations and numerous other things. From trader Afanasy Nikitin to grammarian Lebedev to Indologist Minayev to artist Roerich, the breadth of Indo-Russian ties is longer than centuries and it continues to expand boundless with time and space. It is an immortal contribution, an anthology of footprints left over the sands of time by innumerable sons and daughters of both India and Russia. Like Tennyson's Brook, it goes on forever to witness the twists and turns of time with welter of events taking new shapes. Putin's visit was a step in that direction.

References

1. The Statesman, 4 October, 2000.

2. *Ibid.*

3. For full text of the Declaration on Strategic Partnership, Please see Hindu, 4 October, 2000, p. 8.

4. Hindu, 23 December, 1998

5. Mohd. Moazzam Ali, Russia's foreign policy and Strategic Partnership Moves since 1991 Implications for India, in the book "Amidst Turbulence and HopeTransition in Russia and Eastern Europe, Edited by Shashikant Jha and Bhaswati Sarkar, Lancers

Books, New Delhi, 2002, p.233.

6. Putin's exclusive interviews to the Star News Channel on the eve of his visit to India on I December, 2002 also see the Times of India, Mumbai, 3 December,2002.

7. The Indian Express, 4 December, 2002.

8. International Times, An Economic Times Report, 4 December, 2000.

9. Newsletter, India-CIS Chamber of Commerce and Industry, Vol. XV, No.8. November-December, 2001, p. 20.

10. Ibid, No.7, October, 2001, p. 11.

11. Newsletter, India-CIS Chamber of Commerce and Industry, VoI. XVT, No. 3, March, 2002, p. 22.

12. Newsletter, India-CIS Chamber of Commerce and Industry, Vol. XV, Nos. 2-3, February-March, 2001, p. 9.

13. News from Russia, Vol. V, No. 47, November 22, 2002, p. 22.

14. News from Russia, Vol.V, No. 35, August 30, 2002, p. 23.

13

Indo-Russian Collaboration in Space and Nuclear Technology

Dr. R.R. Subramanian

Indian and Russia have collaborated in space and nuclear technology in a major way. Even before the late Kalpana Chawla ventured into space aboard the American space shuttle the 'Challenger' Sqdr leader Rakesh Sharma of the Indian Air Force went into a manned mission in space on the 'Cosmos' rocket and docked with the space station 'Mir' in 1984. In April 1993 the Russian space company GLAVKOSMOS tied to supply four cryogenic liquid fuelled engines for the Geosynchronous Satellite Launch Vehicle (GSLV) of the Indian Space Research Organisation (ISRO).

Washington at that time wanted India to buy the expensive ($800,000) engines from the company General Dynamics. When ISRO opted for the cheaper ($300,000) engines the US sought to impose sanctions on both ISRO and GLAVKOSMOS. These sanctions were imposed under the US domestic law the Missile Technology Control Act (MTCA) Washington and Moscow are members of the Missile Technology Control Regime (MTCR) created in 1987. Today this regime has thirty odd members that impose punitive sanctions depending on their domestic laws.

However, the Russia of Boris Yeltsin did not yield to the US sanctions and subsequently supplied the four cryogenic engines to ISRO and also transferred the technology of these engines to India. Indo-Russian relations in space technology have thus withstood the constraints of iniquitous MTCR regime that seeks deny technology to countries outside the industrialized west. Russia unlike the predecessor Soviet Union charges India with hard currency yet it does not deny to India its trusted friend the essence of major technologies be it in space or nuclear.

Russian space technology may not be as sophisticated as its American counterpart but there can be no denying that its Space Scientists are second to none. In fact according to some documents captured by the American Central Intelligence. Agency (CTA) several years ago Russia had considered a 'Space Shuttle' for launch earlier. But for some reason Moscow had abandoned the idea. In view of the tragedies that have bedweld the US Space Shuttle programmers it seems to have been a wise decision.

The Soviet space station 'MIR' with which Sqdr Leader Rakesh Sharma and other cosmonauts had docked has continued to function in spite of the financial squeeze caused by the collapse of the Soviet Union. Several of the vehicles in the COSMOS series have docked in space with 'MIR'.

Washington's obsession with missile proliferation has thawrted Moscow's attempts to collaborate in Space with India. China had entered space since the 1970s; it is today contemplating putting a man or woman on the Moon. India's ISRO too is contemplating the same.

China was aided in the development of ballistic missiles by -the USSR in the early sixties. Subsequently, the collaboration collapsed. China modified the Soviet missile SS -4 to produce the 'Dong Feng' services (DF -1/2/3/4) of liquid and solid fuelled missiles. This was done under the able leadership of Qian Xuesen who defected from the US in 1954. India's Dr. Abdul Kalam now President of India also helped ISRO and DRPO to achieve great strides through the development of the Agni and Prithvi serves of missiles.

These missiles like those of China have been developed indigenously. However, the latest cruise missile variant. The Indian BRAHMOS travels at Supersonic speed and has been test fired into the waters of the Bays of Bengal. This then is the status of Indo-Russian collaboration in space and missile arena. Let us now turn to nuclear technology.

Indo - Russian Nuclear Co- operation

It was during the visit of India's Human Resource Development Minister Shri. Murali Manohar Joshi to Moscow on July 5, 2000 an important agreement was signed for cooperation in nuclear physics [1]. A memorandum of understanding (MOU) was signed between the Government of India and Russia's leading nuclear research institute - the Kurchatov Center. Russia has also eased restrictions on export of nuclear material and technologies for India and Russia to exchange visits of nuclear scientists and experts [2].

A major step has been taken with the signing of an agreement for protecting the safety of the nuclear plants very recently. President Vladimir Putin's visit to New Delhi in November 2000 led to further vistas in Indo-Russian cooperation in the peaceful uses of atomic energy.

Indo-Russian Nuclear Cooperation

Vladimir Putin's visit to New Delhi led to an agreement on Indo-Russian cooperation in the peaceful uses of atomic energy. The earlier agreement with the Soviet Union for the supply of giant atomic power plants with a capacity of 1000 Mw. at Koodankulam, Tamilnadu had been signed in May 1988[3]. It was the then Prime Minister Rajiv Gandhi and General Secretary Milkhail Gorbachev who had initiated the agreement.

However, the collapse of Soviet Union in 1991 had delayed the implementation of the agreement. Also wrangles over costs to be paid in foreign exchange and American objections raised in 1992 greatly delayed implementation of the agreement. The Indo-Soviet cooperation for the peaceful uses of atomic energy came to the fore in September 1976 when Soviet heavy water was supplied to the second unit of the Rajasthan Atomic Power Station (RAPS II) in lieu of Canada stopping all supplies of heavy water because India had conducted a peaceful nuclear explosive in May 1974. The agreement with the Soviet Union took two years to negotiate as Moscow was insisting on stringent safeguards to ensure that there was no clandestine diversion to non-peaceful activity. This inspite of Moscow endorsing in May 1974 the conduct of a peaceful nuclear explosion by India.

The successor state of Soviet Union-The Russian Federation has continued this cooperation and as a result four units are now in place at RAPS and the last of them has attained criticality only recently in October 2001.

On September 29th 2001 prior to the visit of President Putin, Mr. Reshenikov the Russian Deputy Minister for Atomic Energy pushed a nuclear fuel bundle of natural minimum into the fuel vault of the fourth reactor at RAPS.[4+2] In the third week of October the reactor was expected to reach 'criticality' and generate electrical power.

The Russian Delegation with Mr. Reshenikov included some of the world's best nuclear scientists and technologists. Their arrival ahead of President Putin was significant. Nuclear cooperation in the peaceful use of atomic energy was firmed up. After the visit to RAPS Reshenikov made it clear that four more units of the VVER type reactors of 1000 Mw .capacity would be set up at Koodankulam. He remarked that from the economic point of view it is viable to have four units at the same site if not six. [3+2=5]

Mr. Reshenikov's contemporary Dr. V.K. Chaturvedi Chairman and Managing Director of the Nuclear Power corporation of India Ltd. (NPC) are respectively co-chairman of the co-ordination committee at Koodankulam. At their meeting in New Delhi on Sept. 28 it was decided to prepare a Detailed Project Report (DPR) on Koodankulam. This would be ready by April 2000.

According to Dr. Chaturvedi work started at Koodankulam from 2002 Earthwork for the first unit would began in March 2001. One year later a similar cycle of work began for the second units. Reshenikov said that in December 2001 Russia submit the technical and commercial offer write the cost of the project.

The Inter-Governmental Agreement on the project was signed on Nov. 20 1988 by Prime Minister Rajiv Gandhi and Soviet President Mikhail Gorbachev. The project remained in limits for 10 year. On June 21, 1998 Russian Minister for atomic energy Yevgeney Adamov and India's Atomic Energy commission Chairman Dr. R. Chidambram signed a supplementary agreement.

Under the first agreement Koodankulam was to be a turnkey project with the NPC providing the site. The then USSR was to provide the design of the VVER 1000 type Pressurized Water Reactor (PWR). It would also bring the fuel, equipments, components and spares and build the reactors. Under the supplementary agreement that is a technical one Russia will give the NPC the design and bring most of the equipment whilst the NPC will build the two reactors. Russian will also supply the enriched uranium fuel for the life of the reactors. Unlike the RAPS, light water will be the moderator.

India and Russia have thus entered a new phase of nuclear cooperation. The construction of the Koodankulam reactors with the help of the Russian Federation would improve electricity generation and availability. The Russian delegation that accompanied Reshenikov included the Director general ZAO Atomstroy export, dr. V.V. Koziov, Deputy Director General Dr. G. O. Kumani, director VVER Center, RSC Kurchatov Institute, Dr. G. 1. Lunin, director Atomenergo project and Dr. A. B. Malyshev Atomstroy export handles the export of Russian reactors, components and fuel. Dr. Lunin, a nuclear scientist has worked on the core physics of every type of reactor, dr. Malyshev was in charge of the overall design of 1000 Mv reactors.

Dr. Malyshev has opined that the VVER 1000 type reactors planned for Koodankulam would have additional safety features compared to the prototype made in Bulgaria. Russian nuclear power stations rank third in terms of safety after Japan and Germany, Russia was building two VVER type reactors in Iran and China also.

A major feature of President Putin's visit to India was his trip to the Bhabha Atomic Research Center (BARC) at Trombay, Mumbai on Oct. 5. This was indeed a significant development. It signals the support of a major head of state towards the strengthening of Indo-Russian relations. However, there were some points of divergence between New Delhi and Moscow of today on the politics of nuclear non-proliferation.

The Russian federation, the successor state of the Soviet Union continues to be a member of the NPT regime as also a member of the nuclear suppliers group (NSG). The NSG is concerned with nations that export nuclear technology to countries outside the NPT framework also. At the April 3, 1992 meeting of the 35 nations that constituted the NSG, it was decided that as a consequence of Iraq attempting to develop nuclear weapons at was necessary to strengthen the safeguards system so as to prevent any more new nuclear states from engaging in clandestine non-peaceful activity. They decided to adopt full scope safeguards that would be "triggered" on all nuclear facilities of a country that wished to import nuclear technology from a sate that is a member of the NSG.

Russia at that time refused to comply with the comprehensive safeguards system proposed by the a NSG members-even though its predecessor the Soviet Union may have been a party to it at the Hague meeting in 1991.[4+2=6]

India as a non-signatory to the NPT has resisted all attempts to impose "full scope" safeguards on its nuclear activities. Russia was able to pursue the Koodankulam agreement without insisting on full scope safeguards since the NSG guidelines allowed for limited safeguards that applied to the plant transferred alone.[5+2=7]

The relevant paragraph in the NSG guidelines dealing with safeguards {(para (a) INFCIRC/254}Rev {Part 11} states "Suppliers' should transfer trigger list items or related technology to a non-nuclear weapon state only when the receiving state has brought into force an agreement with the IAEA requiring the application of safeguards on all source and special fissionable material in its current and future peaceful activities".

It is important to bear in mind that the NSG guidelines are to be implemented by each NSG member in accordance with its national laws and practices. Decision on export applications is taken at the national level in accordance with national export licensing requirements. Also the NSG guidelines do not mention anywhere the NPT and hence do not define what is meant by a nuclear weapon or non-nuclear weapon state.

The Russian laws do not define any where in their national legislation what is meant by a nuclear weapons state in fact it is the US alone where the domestic legislation the nuclear Non-proliferation Act of 1978 and 1994 defines states according to the NPT regime.

Russian President Putin urged India to sign the Comprehensive Test Ban Treaty (CTBT) during his visit to India. India has in any case stopped further nuclear resting since May 1998. Putin made his plea on the CTBT in a meeting with scientists of the Bhabha Atomic Research Center in Trombay near Mumbai. He did however; appreciate the Indian stand that its natural interests and the needs of its people should also be considered. Yet Putin felt it would be better for India if it were to sign the CTBT. [6+2=8]

There is in the present era- division between Moscow and New Delhi on Nuclear non-proliferation and arms control issues. Russia and China are two major powers who are both members of the UN Security Council as also a member of the NPT regime. Their strategic cooperation on military and nuclear issues is necessitated by the need to reduce tensions and concentrate on economic development, Russia would also favour the emergence of a Russia-India-China triangulation of cooperation. The idea has as yet to take shape because neither India nor China would like to be freed from the bilateral arrangements that presently exists with the lone superpower the united states.

It is unrealistic to expect the triad of these countries to discuss the sensitive nuclear issues. In any case Russia was party to the Resolution 1172 passed by a committee of the UN Security council, which called on India to desist from further nuclear testing and immediately sing the CTBT.

Also China favors India's adversary Pakistan as a strategic partner and New Delhi has often enough cited China as a "threat" At another level, it must be pointed that the United States as a unipolar power has sought to object before the nuclear suppliers group to any further Indo-Russian nuclear cooperation in the peaceful uses of atomic energy. [7+2=9] In March 2001, the Russian Minister of Atomic Energy (Minatom) Mr. Yevgeny Adamov announced that Russia planned to export five more nuclear rectors to India. In 1992 the NSG had changed its rule in response to the 1991 Gulf War and had decreed that no member state including Russia could supply any nuclear equipment on NSG's list to any non-nuclear weapon state unless all its activities are subject to IAEA's full scope safeguards. This meant that the US in talks with Russia in Moscow held that Russia was barred from selling nuclear reactors to India, which was not a party to the NPT.

When the Russian Federation resuscitated the original May 1988 deal with India after the collapse of the Soviet Union, it had argued that Minato's arrangement to sell two VVER reactors to India was covered by an indo-Soviet bilateral cooperation pact which predated the NSG decision. The US objected to that position in bilateral talks but finally accepted the Russian position before the NSG.

But a senior US official, had said on 6 April Washington will not accept any new claims by Moscow that the indo-soviet nuclear accord sanctions sales of additional reactors to India. The official said that if Adamov goes ahead with plans to build more VVERs in India, the US would raise the issue in talks with Russian ministry of Foreign Affairs and also protest before the NSG that Russian plans violate NSG units. The US is categorically that the NSG would allow more VVERs to be sold to India only if it puts its entire nuclear programme under IAEA safeguards.

In short, then, the indo- Russian nuclear cooperation agreement in the future would be greatly determined by how Moscow resists the US as a unipolar power in fastening its brand of western hegemony in the feud of nuclear arms control. It is also in this regard that space collaboration must be seen.

References

1. *The Hindu* July 06, 2000.
2. Toc at.
3. IAEA, Vienna 1976.
4. T.S. Subramaniam, "Koodankulam Calling" Frontline, October 27, 2000.
5. SIPRI year Book 1993, Taylor and Francsis London.
6. SIPRI year Book 1992 Taylvor and Francsis, London.
7. C. Balachandran, "Indo-Russian nuclear Cooperation", The Hindu, October 18, 2000
8. Newl Parti, "Nucleonics week" Washington D.C. USA October 19, 2000.
9. Mark Hibbs "US will protest before, NSG Fresh Indo-Russian VVER deal", *Nucleonics Week,* April 13, 2000.

14

Indo Russian Cooperation in Economy, Science and Technology

V. D. Chopra

Any study of new trends in Indo-Russian relations that too after the disintegration of the Soviet Union and growing tendency of unipolarism, both in politics and economy has to take into accounts certain basic factors in the relationship of these two countries what was once described as 'Natural Partners'.

Firstly, Indo-Russian relations have a unique character in the sense that there is no basic geo-political conflict of interests. There are no border disputes and no irritants inherited from history. On the other hand even after the disintegration of the Soviet Union, slowly though steadily convergence of political and economic interests between the two countries have once again come to the forefront. Though Russian is still in the process of evolving its own model of modernisation and industrialisation, Russian nationalism has come to assert itself, the under current being primacy to the national interests of this erstwhile super power. Through a zig-zag processes the pro-American and pro-West tilt in Russia's foreign policy is coming back to the even keel. Therefore the dominant Russian political elite has evolved a worldview, which is moulded primarily by its national interests and not influenced by extraneous factors such as American Western aid to restructure its economy. To say this however does not mean that Russia is not striving to build its economic relations with the United States and other Western countries. Nevertheless the driving force behind Russia's new foreign policy orientation is its national interests in the context of globalisation of economy and emergence of an interdependent world. Seen in this context, Indo-Russian relations have begun to reveal new tendencies, keeping in view the commonality of interests of the two countries.

India in the beginning of 21st century has become a focus of international attention more than ever before. Over five decades, since India became politically independent, have witnessed tremendous changes in the socio-economic base of the country and there upon in its political structure-political system and political parties. In fact, the 50 years will go down in the history of India as an era of change-change hitherto unprecedented in scale and depth. This has altered the entire course of the history of the Indian people because they have not only become masters of their destiny but have already begun to play a significant role, influencing world events and moulding world-situation. It is, therefore, but natural that every major power in the world should have started watching India from close quarters.

India is the seventh largest country, in the world and next to China has the highest population on our planet. It is well marked off from the mountains and seas which give the country a distinct geographical identity. Bounded by the great Himalayas in the north, it stretches southwards and at the Tropic of Cancer, shrinks off into the Indian Ocean.

Such a vast country and that too being so densely populated and lying entirely in the northern hemisphere, obviously has a strategic position in the geopolity of the present day world. All the great powers of the world have begun to recognise this reality, the leaders of the erstwhile Soviet Union were perhaps the first to comprehend it.

Excavations made by Soviet archaeologists in Central Asia show that there existed direct links between the southern parts of Central Asia and India as early as the Harappan age and these became particularly deeper in the Kushan period. Central Asian influence took birth in India as the Kushanas and Shakas extended their sway while Buddhism and other aspects of India's religion, culture and philosophy spread to Central Asia in turn.

Judging by the inscriptions found in Central Asia, a large number of monasteries had been built during the Kushan and Gupta periods. The most striking demonstration of this is provided by the Buddhist monasteries at Kara-Tepeb (near Termez, in the first century A.D.) and in Ajina-Tepeh (southern Tajikistan, seventh century A.D.).

In the earlier centuries A.D., trade links between India and China grew apace; these were established by way of the Great Silk Route and also by sea. Indian embassies and Buddhist missions were sent to China. In the third century A.D., Buddhist monasteries appeared in China and translations of Buddhist writings into Chinese were undertaken.

Indian culture exercised a strong influence on literature, architecture and religion of a large number of countries. At a very early stage, Indian began trading with many countries of South-East Asia and later Indian settlements appeared in some of them. The settlers popularised the Sanskrit language in these regions and enriched them with the many achievements of Indian culture.

At the time of the Harappan civilization, trade and cultural ties were established with the submarine. Later, the Indians engaged in overseas trade with Arabia and Africa and consolidated links with countries bordering the Mediterranean, particularly with Egypt.

A new era in relations between India and the west began after the campaign of Alexander the Great, when the Greeks came to acquire first-hand knowledge of India and her culture. During the Kushan period ties between India and Rome grew stronger; Indian embassies bearing rich gifts were sent to Rome and the Romans setup trading centres in Southern India.

The influence of ancient Greece and Rome made itself felt particularly deep when Indo-Greek states were established in North-Western India, and then later in the Kushan period. It was reflected in the art of the period (Gandhara Sculpture), in science and philosophy. Certain Indian astronomical treatises dating from the early centuries A.D. indicate that Indian scholars were acquainted with the work of Alexandrian astronomers and one of the siddhantas (astronomical treatises) actually came to be known as the Romaka-siddhanta (the Roman siddhanta).

It would be relevant to stress that many crucial questions concerning the universe, man and Nature were posed and solved through mutual exchange by Indian and classical thinkers. This interplay points to the underlying pattern of cultural advance shaped the processes of historical development in the ancient period. While maintaining and consolidating trade and cultural links with other lands and people over the centuries, India did not fail to preserve her own essential and distinctive culture, philosophy, traditions and social and political institutions. At the same time, she gave to the world freely and generously. The contribution of ancient India to the common heritage of mankind is truly immense. "A blind reverence for the past is bad so also is a contempt for it, no future can be founded on either of these. The present and the future inevitably grow out of the past and bear its stamp, and to forget this is to build without foundations and to cut off the roots of national growth.

Jawaharlal Nehru

Jawaharlal Nehru underlined this in his book, 'Discovery of India' in the context of role of nationalism. But he also said that "group memory of past achievements, traditions and experiences" is one of the most powerful forces that influence people. Thus when we say that India's relations with socialist countries, particularly the Soviet Union are rooted in history, one obviously recalls memory of past relations to mind. Though one need not go into details here, there is sufficient proof that cultural and economic relation between India and Russian particularly with its Central Asian regions go back to thousands of years. Now let us examine the specific contribution of Indo-Soviet economic cooperation in building the modem Indian nation state. This does not mean that one should ignore the mechanical transplantation of the Soviet model on the Indian economy. But it is not the issue under discussion at the moment nor it is intended to make a critical estimate of internal and external factors, which led to the collapse of the Soviet socialist economic system. We have yet to fully comprehend it. Now China, the biggest socialist country in todays world has evolved its own modi of economic development. Whatever label the theoreticians may give to the 'Chinese Model' the harsh reality is that China is industrialising and modernising its economy on a scale, which has no parallel in the history. Let us leave this at that and critically examine the Indo-Soviet economic cooperation despite its limitations in modernising todays India. It is necessary to recapitulate this point with a view to highlight the state of Indian economy during the British colonial rule.

For our present purpose it is not necessary to describe in detail the chronicle of Britain rule in India for nearly two centuries. We are only concerned at present with India's past in order to bring to light the destructive role of British imperialism in our ancient land, which was once the pride of human civilization. The British rulers destroyed the traditional Indian economy which was based on common ownership of land, on the "blending of agriculture and handicrafts" and thus in all respects was selfsufficient. In the first phase, during the whole of the eighteenth century the "treasures" were transported from India to England and later when the British landed system was introduced into India, heavy duties were imposed on the import of Indian manufacturers, first not England, and later into Europe also. In the nineteenth century, India was turned into an agrarian appendage of British imperialism. We exported the raw material and imported practically everything else. If one recalls even casually what India was in 1946 and what it is today, one cannot but feel proud of one's country and share a sense of fulfillment. In making India what it is today, the Indian people, their patriotism and their hard labour have played a decisive role. And in this process of regeneration it has received abundant, friendly help cooperation from the Soviet Union. To say this does not mean that we should ignore the stupendous task of building the economic and raising the standards of living of the poorest strata of population.

The main problem which Indian faced after she became independent was that in her endeavor to overcome colonial backwardness, she found that there was serious shortage of productive capital, industrial machinery, spare parts, industrial raw material fuel etc. To solve this problem, she needed foreign aid. Thus in the initial period, India mainly depended on the western capitalist countries, particularly on Great Britain and the United States for such aid. It would be a lop-sided assessment to ignore the fact that the foreign private capital did not play an important role in the industrial development of India at that stage. According to a survey of foreign capital in business investment outstanding at the end of March 1974 was Rs. 943 crore. This figure crossed Rs. 2,000 crore in the beginning of the eighties. Foreign capital in companies in India accounted at that stage for about ten per cent of the total industrial investment in the private sector. These facts speak for themselves and highlight how India had to turn to the Soviet Union for capital investments for its industrial development.

The most important characteristic of Soviet economic assistance to India was that whole of it was available in the form of credits at a nominal rate of interest. The majority of the Soviet loans carried 2.50 per cent interest and extended up to 12 years.

The majority of the USA loans carried 4 to 5 per cent interest. Since the Soviet assistance wholly belonged to the state, the question of repatriation of profits every year, and that too in hard currency, did not arise. The repayment of the Soviet credits, as a rule, began after the completion of the deliveries of machinery necessary for the commissioning of a project. This means that in actual practice, the repayment period was spread over 15 to 20 years, including a grace period of 3 to 4 years.

Another salient feature of Indo-Soviet economic cooperation is that the credits were not repayable in hard currency but in Indian rupees. This amount was utilised for the purchase of Indian goods exported to the Soviet Union. This had threefold advantages for our economy. First, the country saved foreign exchange resources including those on some of the commodities, which the country otherwise would have to buy in hard currency, such as crude oil and petroleum products. Secondly, it stimulated Indian export to the Soviet market-a market, which was assured and stabie. Thirdly, it enabled India to industrialise itself and build basic industries.

Another aspect of Indo-Soviet cooperation was that public sector projects built with the Soviet assistance in their production capacities were comparable with those of the developed countries and even today constitutes is strategic component of the economy. It is relevant for instance to mention here that by the beginning of the these projects had produced 48 million tonnes of pig iron, 38.5 million tonnes of steel and more than 30 million tonnes of rolled iron, 70 million tonnes of oil had been drilled, and about 4.30 lakhs of metallurgical and other machinery for heavy industries had been produced. These projects in the early eighties contributed 40 per cent of steel production, 60 per cent of oil production and accounted for 15 per cent of power generation. This is how Indo-Soviet economic cooperation laid the basis for the industrialisation of the country and transformed it from a developing country to a most developing nation. That more than 90 per cent of the Soviet economic assistance went to the share of metallurgy, fuel energies and machine building further reinforces this conclusion. If one takes into account Indo-Soviet cooperation in science and technology, space and nuclear technology in particular, the picture graphically illustrates how this friendly cooperation has made rich contribution in making India self-reliant. It is relevant to mention here that the first Soviet-Indian agreement of February,1955, which gave a credit of Rs. 101.93 crore was directed to build the first phase of the Bhilai Steel Plant. The second Soviet credit worth Rs. 93.71 crore on November 9,1957 was to be utilized for the construction of the Ranchi Heavy Machinery Plant and the Opthalmological Glass Plant in Durgapur, a complex at Korba and the first phase of the Neyveli Thermal power station. The third Soviet credit of Rs. 14.99 crore was given on May 29,1959 for the construction of the pharmaceutical industry-the Antibiotics Plant at Rishikesh, the Synthetic Drugs Plant at Hyderabad and the Surgical Plant in Madras. The Fourth Soviet credit of September 12,1959 was intended for financing the projects of the third five year plan, which included some of the on-going projects in addition to Thermal Power' Stations, construction of the Barauni Oil Refinery, Heavy Electrical equipment plant at Hardwar and prospecting and drilling work for oil and gas. This credit was worth Rs. 281.14 crore, to quote some figures.

On the other hand, India had found a new and stable market in the Soviet Union for its traditional export items such as jute, tea, jute articles, coffee, spices, tobacco, skims and leather goods. With industrialisation manufactured and semi manufactured goods to the Soviet Union, such as pig iron, accumulators and power cables. Another new area of India's exports to the Soviet Union was consumer goods such as hosiery, cotton and woollen fabrics, garments, handcrafts, linen and some of the herbal medicines. And with the industrialisation of the country, the pattern of the Indosoviet trade too had started changing.

By early Eighties the trade turn over between the two countries was Rs. 2,000 crore and the Soviet Union became one of the biggest trade partners of India. It is also relevant to mention that with industrialisation of India and growing demand of consumer goods in Soviet Union, the trade pattern between the two countries also started changing. Till the mid sixties, traditional items of export-tea, coffee, raw wool, leather, spices, jute and jute bags and cotton textiles consistituted 80 per cent of India's export to the Soviet Union but in the early Eighties, their proportion came down to some 50 per cent. This shift should be estimated in the context of expanding trade between the two countries.

This shows that erstwhile Soviet Union became an important light partner of India, primarily because of rupee trade. Trade between the two countries increased from Rs. 1.3 crore in 1956 to Rs. 7,800 crore in 1990-91. India's exports increased from Rs. 1,226 crore in 1980-81 to Rs. 5,255 crore in 1990-91 and her imports increased from Rs. 1,014 crore to Rs. 2,348 crore during the same period. The USSR accounted for 17 per cent of India's exports in 1990-91 while USSR share in India's imports was 5.9 per cent. It is important to mention that the trade denominated in Indian rupees benefited both the countries immensely. India like the Soviet Union, derived greater advantage as its need to source imports without spending foreign exchange was even more than that of the USSR[1].

However, after the disintegration of the Soviet Union this unique model of economic relationship under-went basic changes. A 5-year trade agreement was signed between India and Russia in May 1992 which marked the end of Rupee trade from January 1993 and ushered a new-phase of convertible currency trade. India also extended a line of credit of Rs. 250 crore for the purpose of financing India's exports of tea, coffee and tobacco to Russia. Indian debt to Russia was to be repaid to the extent of Rs. 3,000 crore annually through exports of goods and services. The Indian debt was evaluated at Rs. 31,377 crore, out of this, Rs. 19,044 crore carrying an average rate of interest 2.4 per cent was to be repaid in 12 years. The remaining Rs. 11,733 crore carrying a nil rate of interest was to be repaid in 45 years beginning April 1993.[2] This and other measures laid the basis for restructuring the economic relations between India and Russia in the new conditions.

In August 1998, Russia faced a crisis due to (i) fiscal mismanagement (ii) overdue short-term foreign exchange liabilities. As a result rouble was under pressure. The IMF, provided financial support of $ 22.6 billion to Russian bail it out.

As far as India is concerned rouble devaluation did not have much effect because 80 per cent of its exports is rupee denominated and governed by the Indian export Rs. 3,000 crore worth of goods are explored to Russia every year in discharge of its debt obligation to the former Soviet Union.

Political stability in Russia combined with economic reforms have begun to turn the tide. Russian industries, particularly consumer industries have begun to pick up. Real incomes have begun to rise and rouble in now appreciating.

In 1992-93 India's exports to Russia was 3.3 per cent of its total exports and its imports in the same year was 1.2 per cent of the total imports. In 1998-99 India's exports to Russia was 2.1 per cent of its total exports and its imports in the same year was 1.3 per cent of the total imports.

This shows that after the disintegration of the Soviet Union, Indo-Russian trade has registered no marked change and there are various reasons for this, including tuff competition from western countries and poor image which India has created in the minds of Russian consumers.

No doubt, Russia provides a large market. The market sized is estimated at $ 18 billion. It is growing by 4 to 6 per cent every year especially for foodstuffs, beverages, textiles, leather goods, consumer electronics and cosmetics. The emphasis in the Soviet consumer market is on basic needs. However, it leans distinctly towards all western consumer goods. Russians have learnt to demand the best. Indian exporters can no longer treat the Russian market as a place to dump sub-standard goods. In fact, in many important commodities India has lost market share substantially. Traditionally, Russia has been the largest importer of tea from India together with other products like rice, tobacco, pharmaceuticals, textiles and leather garments. But in tea Sri Lanka is overtaking India.

Similar is the situation with Indian companies operating in Russia. Of the 400 Indian companies that had operations have closed shop and yet more are on borderline. The enthusiasm of a few years back has been eroded by continuing problems and the recession. Cadila, Balmer Lawrie, L&T and Bharat Forge are reported to have lost faith in their Russian operations.[3]

There are ample opportunities to collaborate for Indians to have joint ventures in Russia. The areas include petro-chemicals, telecommunications and development of port facilities in the black sea region. Departmental Stores, fast food chains and hotel industry also offer investment possibilities in Russia. Indian joint ventures in Russia can also help us in penetrating the European market.

There is a good opportunity for a strategic partnership between India and Russia in the field of diamond business. Russia's strong production base and India's processing capabilities 'could be pooled to improve value addition to each other business-resulting from a stable and viable price for Indian processing industry and an assured market for Russia demands. MMTC from the Indian side and Gokhran from the Russian side are expected to identify different types of rough diamonds which could be supplied by Russian to the Indian processing industry at reasonable costs to market it more competition in world markets. Russia would benefit by direct sales which would be more remunerative due to climination of intermediaries.

Many Indian firms have gone to Russia in a big way. Lakme had severed distribution outlets there. Hindustan Lever and Ganpati Exports have increased their exports substantially. Lupin Laboratories and Nirma have their ventures in Russia. Alpha Group, Procter and Gamble and BPL are also setting up their manufacturing units. Similarly Russia could establish joint ventures in India. At the third session of the Indo-Russian Joint Commission, it was agreed that 10 per cent of the rupee debt could be utilise for this purpose. The areas where Russian investment would be welcome are power and oil and gas sectors. Priority would be given to infrastructure project. Russians also appear to be keen to use the large rupee debt because they want to exhaust it as quickly as possible as also to normalise bilateral trade as quickly as possible. So far, Russians have been slow in utilising the rupee finds.

In Russian, there are 74 entities with Indian equity participation mostly in trading. Major direct foreign investment in manufacturing sector in Russia include Engineering pharmaceuticals and food processing. The total Russian investment is estimated at US $ 245 million. Similarly in India there are 23 entities with Russian equity investment, mostly in technical collaboration R & D as also design and drawings. The total investment is put at only US $ 93 million.[4]

Future prospects of Indo-Russian economic cooperation should be examined on the basis of experience of India's economic relations with the

Soviet Union, complementary nature of the economies of the two countries and above all the new economic reforms being introduced in the two countries.

It is relevant to mention here that Russia has made it clear that it will discharge its foreign debt regularly. Russian also declared in 2002 that it intends to join WTO. Significantly Russia's foreign debt has come down to 51 per cent of the GDP and can fall to 45 per cent by the end of 2002. As much as 2.6 billion dollars were accumulated in 2001 as a financial reserve. This money can fully pass into the year of 2003 (the year of the most sizable foreign debt payments Russia must pay about 19 billion dollars). But even in case of a pessimistic variant of a fall of oil prices, for instance, if they drop to 14 dollars per barrel, Russia will not face serious problems with the financing of a deficit free budget, as well as with the fulfilment of the foreign-debts obligations.

This trend should be seen in the context of on going structural reforms which are taking place in Russia at present. Russia has recently inforced laws controlling accumulation of wealth by criminals and mafia gangs. Importantly flight of Russian capital to other countries has dropped from 24.4 to 17 billion dollars.[5]

This analysis shows how Russia is once again emerging as an economic power with its vast natural resources, crud oil, diamonds and its defence manufacturing industries on one hand and expanding internal market on the other. This open new potentialities for Indo-Russian economic cooperation.

Scientific and Technical Cooperation

Let us now turn to some aspect of Indo-Russian cooperation in science and technology.

New avenues and areas of economic scientific and technical cooperation between India and Russia are being explored.

A renewed Integrated Long-Term Programme (ILTP) for Indo-Russian cooperation in science and technology for instance is being actively considered.

The ILTP programme, signed by the President of erstwhile Soviet Union, Mikhail Gorbachev, and the late Prime Minister Rajiv Gandhi in Moscow in 1987, lasted till the year 2000. It has emerged as the world's largest technology. This programme is a reflection of the close cooperation in science and technology that has developed between India and Russia over the last 13 years. The programme had facilitated exchange visits of over 2,500 scientists and generated a close to 300 developments projects in India and Russia.

Moreover, India and Russia have entered into an agreement to expand their cooperation in nuclear physics. A MoU (Memorandum of Understanding) has been signed between the Department of science and technology of the Government of India and Russia's leading nuclear research institute, the Kurchatov Centre. The three year agreement, signed by the officials of India and Russia, will be automatically renewed unless one of the sides decided otherwise.

Nuclear physics has thus become one of the thrust areas of Indo-Russian cooperation under the 13 year ILTP, which would be renewed for another 10 years. The two countries are planning setting up a satellite link between the PARAM 10000 in Moscow and the supercomputer at C-DAC in Pune (Centre Development of Advanced Computing). The C-DAC and the Institute for Computer Aided Design (ICAD) have already prepared a joint work document identifying applications and areas of requirements will be met in Russia and India, besides third world countries.[6]

Multi-faceted scientific cooperation has been thriving between India and Russia, the most significant being cooperation in nuclear realm. As the culmination of this process has come the Indo-Russian agreement on collaboration reactors in India, each of 1000 Mwe generating capacity. The reactor are described as the WER type, incorporating the most advanced reactor technology in Russian and rated among the best in the world. The project is located at Kudankulam in Tamil Nadu.

The Kudankulam project is being implemented under the inter-Government agreement signed between the government of India and the erstwhile USSR in November 1988, which was subsequently amended through a "supplement" in June 1998. In the initial phase, a detailed project report for the project was prepared with the help of Premier Russian design organisation an institutes, a contract for which was signed between NPCIL and the Russian organisation, Atomstroyexport in July 1998.

The project has now entered the second phase of construction-that of civil works-with the ground breaking for the project works carried out on October 7,2001.

The Kudankulam project has several distinguishing features-its design and technology, the impact on Indian atomic reactor design technology, Indo-Russian scientific cooperation terms for implementing the project and not the least, the financial arrangements to cover costs of an atomic project of such a massive size. Notable, too, has been another development related to the project strong pressures form nuclear weapon powers, particularly the United States, on Russia against implementation of the Kudankulam project, invoking terms of the London Club, of which Russia is a member.

To take the financial aspect first, one should note that the soft repayment terms of the Russian loan for the project set new parameters that facilitate implementation of this massive nuclear undertaking without any harsh burden on the Indian economy. The final costing and the financing terms of the project, completed in recent negotiations between the Indian and Russian sides, stipulate that the Russian side will carry out the entire design of the project and supply all the equipment and machinery for the plant. Eighty-five per cent of the cost of the supplies and services from the Russian organisations shall be covered under the State Credit extended by the Russian Government to the Indian Government for the project.

The total amount of credit for the project from the Russian side will work out to about 50 per cent of the total project cost. The credit utilised for the project is to be repaid in 14 equal installments, beginning with the commercial operations of the plant. This will enable loan repayments largely from earnings of power generations.

The scientific and technological aspects of the Russian reactor design have a special bearing for India, for induction of the light water reactor design, based on low enriched uranium as fuel will mean a departure from the existing pattern of aton & power plants in India. These have pressurised heavy water reactors that use natural uraniwn as fuel and heavy water as moderator and coolant.

The view of the scientific establishment is that far form being a technological slow down, induction of the Russian reactor design will mean enrichment of India's nuclear reactor technology. The Kudankulam project will be based on the latest WER, reactor design of pressurised water type (PWR), which is rated as the leading type of nuclear power reactors worldwide.

This perfunctory survey on the course of Indo-Russian cooperation in economy, science and technology clearly reflects that after 10 years. of the disintegration of the Soviet Union, Indo-Russian cooperation has begun to take a new turn.

References

1. Prof. R.L. Varshney Trade Relations between India and Russia Indo - Russian Relations - Prospects Problems and Russia today, pp.93.
2. *lbid*- p.95.
3. *Ibid* p. 97.
4. *Ibid* p. 99-100.
5. National Herald, New Delhi, February 15, 2002.
6. National Herald, New Delhi, November 4, 2002.

15

New Trends in Indo-Russian Relations-A Futuristic Study

G. M. Shah

Introduction

The Indo-Russian relations are based on the strong foundations of good neighbourly ties, liberal political ideology, convergence of national interests, geo-political setting, economic opportunities and international interdependence. The Great Soviet Revolution of October 1917 not only paved the way for the socialistic reconstruction of Soviet Union but it also positively influenced the Indian freedom struggle against the British imperialism to create conditions of- planned economic development in this country. Pandit Jawaharlal Nehru's foreign policy was based on the principle of 'United Asia' and 'one world' of which India and Soviet Union were two important and integral parts. Even after the disintegration of Soviet Union the relations between the Russian Federation and India remained unchanged and there is a great scope for deepening the bi-lateral ties in future as well. The present paper is an attempt to throw some light on the evolution of Indo-Russian relations after the end of the cold war. The study aims at highlighting the shared national security concerns of India and Russia, their defence ties, economic relations and the scope for their united effort in shaping the new world order. The following paragraphs present a systematic analysis of all these areas in a sequential way.

Evolution of Indo-Russian Relations

Immediately after attaining independent statehood, new Russia followed a pronouncedly pro-Western and pro-US policy. Moscow hoped to bring about targeted economic transformation from a centrally controlled command economy to a free market economy integrated with the rest of the world and political transformation from a totalitarian state to a liberal democracy essentially with the help of western political and financial support.

India and other Eastern countries were given a rather low place in the Russian order of priorities at the time. Unlike the former Soviet Union that needed a "special relationship" with India in its politico- strategic rivalry with both the West and. China, Russia did not seem to need India as a strategic ally. It was a period of uncertainty in Indo-Russian relations. In fact, low priority accorded to India in Russian policy was reciprocated by India also. India tried to adjust to the post Soviet world reality. In a reversal of cold war roles, Washington was making up with New Delhi. US arms supply to Pakistan was stopped in 1990 in view of the latter's nuclear programme and ambition on the other hand Moscow appeared to be improving ties with Pakistan. It seemed two different schools of thought existed in Russia at this time regarding the policy towards India. One opinion favoured that the traditional "special" relationship with India should be retained . India should be given priority in the country's policy in South Asia, while at the same time developing good relations with other South Asian countries, including Pakistan. The other School favoured that the epoch of "special" relations with India should be ended.

To the dismay and disappointment of New Delhi, Russia in its early diplomatic moves showed greater readiness than before, to tolerate a Mujahideen government in Kabul and abandon India friendly Najibullah government. It seemed that during this period of uncertainty in Indo-Russian relations, Moscow was seeking some compromise and synthesis between the two divergent schools of through regarding the approach to India mentioned above.

The basic geo-political factors that lay at the root of the decades long uninterrupted Indo-Soviet friendship could not be ignored altogether. On its part, the Russian military industrial complex was very keen to restore defence ties with such a large and lucrative market like India. Defence industry was the only field in which Russia could compete with the West. India was equally keen on the restoration of spare parts and military supplies from Russia as 60 to 70 per cent of defence purchases of India's were from Russia and the former remained as the second largest trading partner of the latter. President Yeltsin's New Delhi visit in January 1993 removed the fog and put Indo-Russian relations on a firm footing. It showed a decision had been finally taken in the Kremlin in favour of according priority to relations with India in the South Asian context. Yeltsin's India visit, in conjunction with his visits to China and South

Korea earlier, was also projected as an attempt to correct the earlier pro-West bias in Russia's foreign policy. It was stressed that Russia was both a European and an Asian power. It had direct geo-political interests in both the regions. Indo- Russian relations were now placed on a sound footing of shard political and economic interests , devoid of rhetoric and platitudes, as was the case earlier.

India and Russian reached a compromise solution on the Cryogenic issue, whereby Russia was to with hold from passing on to India those elements of technology that could be used for dual purposes. But the technology not considered dual purpose was to be transferred. For the balance money Glavkoms was to provide India two additional rocket engines. The government of India decided to go ahead with indigenous development of the requisite technology.

Observers of the Russian scene noted that since the end of 1992 Russian foreign policy was absorbing and reflecting the growing impulses in the country of assertive nationalism disenchantment with the West for trying to browbeat Russia and for inadequacy of aid offered and actually delivered. Claims of Russia's status as an independent great power were repeatedly put forward. Moscow's new assertive mood has been most marked in dealing with other former Soviet republics referred to as the "near abroad" in Russian parlance. It seemed friendship with large Asian countries like India and China fitted well with new policy tack in Moscow. Russia project itself as a truly Eurasian power.

On the nuclear - strategic issue on the NPT and the Comprehensive Test Ban Treaty (CTBT) Moscow stands firmly with the West. In fact on January 14, 1994, president Yeltsin and president Bill Clinton signed a joint statement in Moscow pledging to take energetic means to prevent the proliferation of nuclear weapons. Indo-Russian differences on the nuclear strategic issues, however, were not allowed by the two sides to come in the way of further strengthening of multifarious bilateral tie[3].

There has been again a revival of the talks of Indo-Russian strategic partnership". President Yeltsin and India's (then) Defence Minister Mulayam Singh Yadav during the later's Moscow visit in October 1997 re-affirmed their countries intensions to develop a strategic partnership. Military technical cooperation in the backbone of their bilateral relations. India is the largest buyer of Russian military hardware. It is the only country in the world with which Russia has a long term programme of military technical cooperation, worth more than, $ 10 billion. During the Indian Defence Minister's1997 visit to Moscow, the two sides agreed to prolong such cooperation until the year 2012. A section of the Russion media has commented on the agreement to extend Indo-Russian military technical cooperation until the year 2012 under the heading "Russia will help to Become Great Power".

Strategic ties, a score of agreements, defence deals and common understanding marked Russian -Indian relations during president Putin's India visit in October 2000. The key strategic partnership declaration signed by President Putin and Prime Minister Vajpayee as the delimiting vision of Indo- Russian relations for the next decade emphasizes the continuity of bilateral relations, touching on the earlier 1971 and `1993 treaties of friendship and cooperation that had marked the past era of Indo- Soviet ties and its aftermath. This has opened a new era of strategic relations that can help both countries in the changing international context. The importance of the strategic partnership document lies in the fact that both countries include political, economic, cultural and scientific cooperation simultaneously with defence and geostrategy as part of their understanding of security partnership. This broadens the concept of security itself and balance the earlier relations that privileged defence related security.

The Russian Foreign Ministry spokesman told the *Hindu Staff* Reporter at Moscow on 18th Feb. that during the Indian foreign Minister Mr. Yeshwant Sinha's visit between 19th to 21st February 2003, the Idno-Russian talks would cover Afghanistan, Iraq North Korea and West Asia as well as bilateral relations, terrorism and strategic stability. Mr. Sinha's visit to Moscow is also part of preparation for an annual meeting in April 2003, of the Indo-Russian Inter Governmental Commission for Trade, Economic, Scientific Technical and Cultural Cooperation, which he co-chairs with the Russian Minister for Industry, Science and Technology, llya Klebanov. On 20th February, Indian External Affairs Minister stated in Moscow that defence cooperation between Russia and India will move from buyer-seller relationship to technology sharing and joint research and production. In wake of Mr. Putin's December 2002 visit to India Mr. Vajpayee will be visiting Russia in IInd half of May 2003 to attend tricentennial celebrations of St. Petersburg.

Indo-Russian Relations in South Asian Context

A thorough analysis of the geo-political situation in South Asia shows that certain challenges to Russia's national security stem from that region. They are caused by internal socio-economic and political factors, as well as by the character of relations between the South Asian states in general and India and Pakistan in particular . Some problems arise from general instability in a vast region located close to the boundaries of Russia and several CIS states, from heightened religions and ethnic extremism, separatism, mounting terrorism and crime and expanding drug trafficking . Another hitherto latent danger is uncontrolled migration from the countries of South Asia with their massive poverty and disease, population growth, ecological problems and so on.

Keeping the above mentioned realities of South Asia into consideration there is enough scope for Indo-Russian bi-lateral cooperation to address the national security issues of the two countries . The two countries can take many unilateral, bi-lateral and multi lateral steps to make South Asia, a peaceful zone for human progress and prosperity. The recent statement of Russian Foreign Minister Igor Ivanov after his meeting with Yashwant Sinha at Moscow that India and Russia would continue their support to the Karzai Government in its efforts to stabilise the situation in Afghanistan is an indicator of Indo-Russian resolve to play an effective role the region.

A positive role might be played by Russia by establishment of equal and fair relations between powers outside the region and the South Asian countries, and by the elimination of asymmetry and imbalance in their relations with India and Pakistan. As is known, in South Asia, Russia has traditionally relied on joint action with India. Even after India carried out its nuclear explosions, the implementation of the integrated Long Term Programme of Cooperation in Science and Technology, to the total amount of $ 8 -10 billion is continuing. An understanding has been reached on supplying the Su-30 MK and Su-30 MKI fighters, and an agreement has been signed on the construction of an atomic power station in Kudankurlam in Tamil Nadu with two reactors from Russia. During Prime Minister Primakov's visit to India on 20-22 December 1998 a long term Agreement on Military -Technical cooperation upto 2010 was signed which provides for India to buy high technology weaponry from Russian worth $ 16 billion over the next decade. Primaker told reporters that a lot in the Region depends on the policies pursued by China, Russia and India. If we succeed in establishing a strategic triangle it will be very good". He added that the proposal was made within a framework of partnership between the three countries to bring about greater stability in the world and was not just a formal initiative.

There is a great scope for promoting trade and commercial relations between Russia and India in the changing geo-political situation of South Asia. Indo-Russian Trade had been stagnating at about $ 1.5 billion a year; Russian investment in India in 1991-2001 amounted to a meager $ 129 million, while Indian investment in Russia was altogether negligible at $ 2.3 million. The establishment of Joint Business Council will go a long way in promoting greater awareness about the business opportunities in both countries.

Indo-Russian Relations in the Greater Middle East

Indo-Russian strategic cooperation can pave the way for establishing an Eastern Alliance to check the growing US influence in the 'Greater Middle East." The term ' greater middle east or "new middle east" has been used to signify North Africa, the Levant, the Persian Gulf, Central Asia and South Asia, Adding to the traditional Middle East the eight newly independent states of the Caucasus and Central Asia, India and Pakistan, the 'greater middle East' 'is infact an' enlarged post - cold war Middle East', In other worlds it is ' Washington's 'New Middle East', or a kind of geo-political ideal type construction intended to support US hegemony in the vast region. Judging from the statements and actins of some US officials, the Washington appears to believe that there is now a historic opportunity to reshape the region, owing to the collapse of the Soviet Union, the defeat of Iraq in the second Gulf War, and the acceptance of the Madrid/Oslo peace process by the PLO, the post September 2001 was against terrorism in Afghanistan and move to overthrow Saddam Hussain are partly motivated by the geo strategic interests of US in the greater middle east.

What we term the Greater Middle East and its energy resources may now be the strategic fulcrum and prize in the emerging arena of world politics. Approximately 70 per cent of the world proven oil reserves and over 40 per cent of its natural gas reserves lie within an egg-shaped catchments area from Southern Russian and Kazakhstan to Saudi Arabia and the United Arab Emirates. What is of special relevance are the growing energy needs of Asia including China, India, Pakistan and South East Asia, and the fact that they will all have to compete with Europe and North America for Middle East energy supplies. This will lead to significant changes in the patterns of diplomacy and security relationships ~hat have evolved since the energy crisis of the 1970s and the 1990-91 Gulf war. The Asian countries in general and India and Russia in particular can no longer afford to remain as silent spectators, they have collectively to exert pressure on US to respect the sovereignty and territorial integrity of Independent nations.

Conclution

To sum up it can be concluded that there is a great scope for deepening the Indo- Russian relations not only to create conditions for improving the socio-economic conditions of their people but also to play an important role in shaping the future world order. The unipolar world order which came into existence after the collapse of the Soviet Union can be replaced by the multipolar world order if the Asian Powers in general and India, Russia and China in particular come closer to each other to form on Eastern Alliance against the growing influence of one single super power. The European Union in general and Old Europe (including the countries of France, Span and Germany) in particular can also emerge as a powerful grouping to counter the Anglo American hegemony in shaping the future world order. The Huntington's clash of civilisations needs to be replaced by the dialogue among power blocs for sharing the global resources in an equitable and sustainable manner. It is in this context, the Indo-Russian strategic partnership needs to contribute to play the role in shaping the 21st century world order.

16

India -Russian-China-Prospects for Trilateral Cooperation

Nirmala Joshi

During Russian Prime Minister Yevgeny Primakov's visit to India in December 1998 he proposed at an informal level that India-Russia and China should come together and form a strategic triangle in the interest ofpeace and stability in the region. The initial response of India was one of caution which could be explained by the fact that strategic triangle implied common perceptions and convergence of interests vis-h-vis a common threat. Similarly China expressed no opinion on this idea. China too must have had reservations about this idea given its own state of uneasy relations with India. Hence, at that juncture it was difficult and even now to perceive of a convergence of strategic interests between India, Russia and China. This does not, however, mean that the idea of cooperation among the three major countries of Asia is impossible. India, Russia and China occupy a huge landmass of Asia, a look at the map will convince any reader. They are contiguous to each other, except that Pakistan and Central Asia separate India and Russia. While the idea of a strategic triangle appears distant, in the immediate future what is worth pursuing is the objective of promoting trilateral cooperation between India, Russia and China.

In the post Cold War era the world order is no longer dominated by an ideological divide. The bipolar world order has given way to a trend that can be characteried as cooperation among nations. It is a change from the earlier Cold War mindset of a zero sum game to cooperation for the ensurance of ones' own national interests. In terms of security it means that it is comprehensive and global. Security today is not merely territorial integrity and sovereignty but the protection of areas such as economic security including energy, social and political stability, smuggling of weapons, drug trafficking, flow of refugees etc. The meaning of security has widened considerably. Today nations opt for cooperation mainly because the issues confronting mankind are global in nature and such issues have to be confronted in a collective manner. The issues are of common concerns such as environment, ecology, economic issues and the recent addition of campaign against terrorism. The trend towards greater cooperation does not, however, mean that competition, rivalries etc. are over. Differences among nations do exist. In fact the present day world order is marked by cooperation and competition.

Given the dominant trend of cooperation among nations it is not difficult to envisage cooperation between India, Russia and China. As mentioned the three countries are major Asian nations, contiguous to each other and importantly occupying a huge landmass of Asia. Straddling across Europe and Asia the Russian Federation has enormous natural resources including vast amount of energy sources. Its Siberian and the Far East regions are richly endowed with natural resources. Russia has a highly skilled and technical manpower; its contribution to further development in India and China could be beneficial. India and China are the two most populous nations in the world which means that they are a large market for each other's products.

Meanwhile as the Twenty-first century progresses, Asia is likely to occupy a center stage in international system. While on the one hand Asia has seen economic prosperity it also has sources of dangers, which, if not, checked could also have a disastrous impact on Asia. The arch of instability stretches from the Persian Gulf to the Philippines contains sources of tensions such as global terrorism. Countries who have a poor track record for governance and human rights provide fertile ground for other negative tendencies to grow. In American perception the "Axis of Evil" that is, Iraq, Iran and North Korea are located in Asia. In this context the U.S. and Russia would lime to push non-proliferation especially preventing terrorists from acquiring nuclear weapons to be given the top most priority. President Vladimir Putin has proposed that the arch of instability be converted into an arch of stability. hi this objective India, Russia and China could play a vital role.

From this perspective the Central Asian region assumes significance. For geopolitical reasons all the three countries are interested in peace and stability in Central Asia. India, Russia and China face the biggest challenge to their integrity from forces of religious extremism, separatism and terrorism. All the three countries have a common perception that

Afghanistan has emerged as the epi center of such negative activities, especially after the Taliban came tom power in 1996. For over a decade India has been the challenge of militancy in its state of Jammu and Kashmir. Cross-border terrorism and the support of various militant groups fighting against the Indian Union from across the border in Kashmir has posed a serious threat to the integrity of the Indian Union. The talk of Jihad against India declared by the militant groups enjoying sanctuary and support from Pakistan and Afghanistan has made the situation in Kashmir extremely difficult. Similarly the Chechen separatist rebels have received support from Afghanistan. In fact the Taliban regime had recognised the independence of Chechnya - the only country to do so. Forces of religious extremism are slowly gaining momentum m. China's Xinvang province. After the break-up of the Soviet Union in 1991, Uighur nationalist sentiment increased. The establishment of Turkic countries in Central Asia had an appeal to the Uighurs. Here Uighurs an ethnic group that is also spread into Kazakhstan, Kyrgyzstan and to some extent in Uzbekistan, have political demands. The Uighurs in China are a small group and the group is slowly acquiring religious overtones. China is aware of the fact that rebel Uighurs were being trained in Afghanistan and through the narrow border entered Xinjiang. In short the perception of Afghanistan under the Taliban was similar. India and Russia also accepted that Pakistan was the supporter of the Taliban. Perhaps Pakistani calculation was to have a friendly government in Afghanistan unlike the earlier years when the governments were unfriendly and pro-India. In Indian and Russian perception Pakistan was as much at fault as Afghanistan. While China was aware that Uighur separatist received training and sanctuary in Afghanistan, it is not clear whether it accepted Pakistan to be the Afghan-Taliban supporter.

However, Indian, Russian and Chinese were interested in peace and stability in Central Asia. Any destabilization of the secular regimes of Central Asia would pose a bigger challenge to the three countries. It is in the interest of all the three countries to see that the secular regimes presently in power in Central Asia are not dislodged by forces of Islamic extremism. In the Fergana valley of Uzbekistan radical Islam has already gained a small foothold. In the eventuality of Central Asia being swept by forces of religious extremism, then a vast integrated region dominated by religion would come into existence. It would provide a strategic depth to Pakistan. Peace and stability in Central Asia is linked to peace in Afghanistan. From the long-term perspective durable peace can be ensured with accelerated development and open political system with good governance. India, Russia and China can easily work towards this objective.

In order to ensure the security of Central Asia the Collective Peace Keeping Force of the Commonwealth of Independent States (CIS) guarded the Tajik-Afghan border. The hordes of extremists were prevented from destabilizing Central Asia. But as the intensity of the danger increased the Shanghai Five, comprising of Russia, China, Kazakhstan, Kyrgyzstan, Tajikidstan joined by Uzbekistan evolved into the Shanghai Cooperation Organisation (SCO). The SCO expanded its agenda to include the fight against Islamic fundamentalism and terrorism. The SCO has initiated certain measures like the formation of the anti-terrorist center at Bishkek. The Rapid Deployment Force was created, agreement to coordinate their policies, exchange of information etc. were other aspects of cooperation among SCO. In. June 2002 at the St. Petersburg Summit meeting of SCO countries the organisation was institutionalized by adopting a charter. Russia wants the SCO to emerge as a regional organisation and open to other members. During the recent visit to India in December 2002 President Putin accorded high priority to trilateral cooperation and has expressed his desire to include India in the SCO. On its part India would be willing to joint it, but Chinese response to India's candidature has been elusive so far. Nevertheless China evaluates the SCO in a very positive manner. In the words of Sa Benwang, Vice-Chairman of the China National Committee of the Council for Security Cooperation in Asia and the Pacific "the Shanghai Cooperation Organisation that China has actively initiated and participated in has become a successful mode of new-type international relations and new type regional cooperation and the Shanghai spirit with mutual trust mutual benefit, equality consensus through consultation, respect for multiple civilizations and seeking common development at the core has played an exemplary role in promoting the establishment of a new security concept."[1] After 9/11 the fight against terrorism assumed global dimensions. The horrifying acts by terrorists committed in New York and Washington were condemned by all the three countries. India and China strongly condemned the outrageous act of 9/11. While President Putin aptly summed up the world horror by describing it as "a plague of the Twenty-first century." India, Russia and China have supported the global campaign against terrorism. The three countries also supported the United Nations a" Security Council resolution sanctioning campaign against Afghanistan. While supporting the U.S. led international coalition of forces and the military presence in Central Asia, there is an underlying concern, though not similar and not to the same extent, as to the length of stay of these forces. There is no doubt that India, Russia and China have complementarity of interests vis-A-vis the US. In the couple of years India has been able to bad up a close and friendly relationship with the US.

There is now greater convergence of views on issues like South Asian security. Indian decision makers feel that the US alone could restrain Pakistan and stop it from supporting cross border terrorism. Recent statements of Indian leaders suggest that the ability of the U.S. to restrain Pakistan is limited. India would have to tackle the problem on its own strength. The economic interaction has intensified. For Russia the campaign against international terrorism opened a window of opportunity to come to better understanding with the West especially the USA- Russia needs credits and trade with the West. The US-Russia summit of May 2002 saw some very significant agreement, the Energy Dialogue is indeed a breakthrough one. Russian foreign policy focused on the West, until the stand on the Iraqi crisis which highlighted Russian assertiveness vis-a-vis the US. China poised to emerge as the future power is also in need of American investments in order to maintain its economic growth. Hence neither India, nor Russia or China would like to be perceived as forming a grouping against the US. For all the three countries relations with the US are crucial. Nevertheless, the physical presence of the West could also add to heightened tensions and concerns. At this juncture it is difficult to say when the campaign against terrorism would end. It appears that this fight is going to be a protracted one. In that eventuality there is a possibility that the Western presence could arouse antagonistic sentiments. There are reports that the Al Qaeda and Talibans are regrouping themselves. Besides the focus of American policy has now shifted to Iraq. The campaign against terrorism and Afghanistan will not receive the kind of attention the situation warrants.

It is more than over a year since the American led international coalition forces are stationed in Afghanistan and Central Asia. The coalition forces are in Central Asia with the approval of Russia. Despite uneasiness in certain quarters about the stationing of Western forces in an area that holds significance for Russia, the Russian leadership permitted their presence for the purpose of combating terrorism. Even now voices of disagreement on this issue can be heard. For instance in an interview Russian General Lenoid Ivashov now Vice-President of the Academy of Geo-Political Problems felt that Russia faced a political paradox at the turn of the century. By supporting US led struggle against international terrorism, Russia has also complicated its positions in the CIS countries. In his view the Central Asian leaders have made a mistake by inviting the US led coalition forces. [2] For China the presence is also worrisome. Stationing of American troops in Manas in Kyrgyzstan makes the Chinese Western region vulnerable. Manas air base is just 200 km from the Chinese border.

Many analysts and observers of Central Asia feel that the Western presence in the region has a hidden agenda. The agenda to control the vast energy sources and to influence the states of Central Asia. It is estimated that Central Asia is the third largest reserve of energy sources - oil, gas and hydrocarbons after Persian Gulf and Iraq. India and China's needs for energy are likely to go up in the years to come. India has been trying to ensure its energy security by diversifying its sources of energy. Most of India's requirements are met from the Persian Gulf. But given the uncertainty in the region, it would be tacitly wise to seek new sources. Central Asia offers one such area. But its land locked status is a big obstacle. Efforts to procure Central Asian energy are being made via Iran. Recently President Syed Khatami of Iran was in India and the question of transporting oil from Central Asia was discussed. Similarly China is also seeking to obtain energy from Central Asia. An American company Chevron is exporting Tengiz crude oil to the refinery at Urumqui in China's Xinjiang region by rail. Given Kazakhstan potential resources and China's needs in future, the latter has invested in oil field in Western Kazakhstan. The Chinese National Oil and Gas Cooperation (CNOGC) has invested in Kazakhstan. [3] In view of the growing concern for energy security, India, Russia and China could cooperate for mutual benefit.

At the broader level India, Russia and China agree that the world should be a multi polar one. A multi polar world order would be one that is fair, just and democratic in which all nations are equal and enjoy equal security. Russia has been vigorously championing the idea of multi polar world as against the tendency of unitlateralism. Unilateral approach to international relations would lead to the unchallenged supremacy of the USA. Such a tendency of unilateralism would lead to bypassing the UN. Russia and China signed an agreement favouring a multipolar world in 1996. On its part India has upheld that the world order is not an unipolar one as new centers of power and influence are emerging. While acknowledging the need for a multipolar world Indian approach is not in terms of blocs but the need to maintain a balanced and a stable world order. An unipolar world could lead to instabilities and the utmost need was to have a balancing force. Similarly, China also attaches importance to the centrality of the UN in a multipolar world.

One of the impact of the events of 9111 has been that China has developed a positive attitude towards the idea of trilateral cooperation. Possibly the renewal of Pakistani American cooperation could have had an impact on Chinese strategic thinking. Besides with American presence in the center of Eurasia, the need for normal relations with India could have been a contributory factor as well. During the session of the U.N. in September 2002 the Foreign Ministers of India, Russia and China conferred with each other on the resolution on Iraq. Since the position of India, Russia and China on the crisis in Iraq is similar the possibility of coordination in future is also bright. Noting the growing responsibility of the three nations in establishing a system of security and stability in Asia, Russian Foreign Minister hoped that there would be coordinated effort to promote the interests of the three nations. [4] It perhaps with the idea of furthering the cause of trilateral cooperation that President Putin embarked on his Asian tour by visiting China and later India in December 2002. In a T.V. interview, former Russian Prime Minister Primakov said "It is the shared interest in maintaining security and stability in Central Asia and Afghanistan that may give flesh and blood to the idea of the Moscow Beijing-Delhi triangle. [5] However, no concrete steps to further the trilateral cooperation have been taken was stated by Prime Minister Atal Bihari Vajpayee in the Rajya Sabha .[6]

At the economic level there is potential for India, Russia and China to cooperate with each other in areas such as high technology, machinery, energy, pharmaceuticals, telecommunications, chemicals etc. Joint ventures could be set up in any of the abovementioned areas. At this exploratory stage of trilateral cooperative endeavour it would be worthwhile to identify areas of common interests. These could be participating jointly in constructing transport corridors (one envisaged rail connection from Bangladesh to Kazakhstan) or building of oil pipelines, improving banking facilities etc. Besides cooperation at various multilateral fora could strengthen their bargaining positions. By coordinating their policies on global economic issues India, Russia and China could drive benefit in the long run. Other issues of common concern are combating organised crime, drug trafficking and smuggling of small weapons. These are some of the problems that have affected India,'Russia and China at some time or the other. Exchange of views and experiences on these matters would strengthen trilateral cooperation.

In the past a lot of energy was expanded in maintaining adversial. relations - SinoSoviet and Sino-Indian. Given the changed paradigm of international relations where the dominant tendency is cooperation, it is possible for India, Russia and China to initiate such trilateral cooperation in areas of common interest and concern. Such exploratory initiatives have been launched by the academic community of the three countries, the dialogue should move now to a higher plane. There are undoubtedly constraints in the way of such cooperation. Much will, however, depend on the state of bilateral relations among countries.

Indo-Russian relations are warm and friendly. After the break-up of the Soviet Union in 1991 Indo-Russian relations were in a state of neglect This was a very short phase. President Boris Yeltsin's visit to India paved the way for a meaningful and productive relationship. The Treaty of Friendship and Cooperation of 1993, the Moscow Declaration on the Protection of Pluralist Societies laid the foundation of strong and friendly relations. The crux of this relationship lies in shared geopolitical and security interests at the regional level. Common perception of threats and interests brought India and Russia closer to each other. Over a decade of Indo-Russian ties have evolved towards a Strategic Partnership, signifying a high qualitative relationship. In Russian thinking partnership idea can be promoted with those countries whose policies Russia views as not being detrimental to its national interests and security, and which do not run counter to the UN Charter. Russia understands partnership as the combination of equality, mutually advantageous cooperation and good neighbourliness. Mutual trust is at the core of such a relationship. In the process India and Russia have supported each other on issues of crucial significance to each other. A new chapter to the Strategic Partnership was added during Prime Minister Atal Behari Vajpayee's visit to Moscow in November 2001 and during the visit of President Putin to India new initiatives would further strengthen the Indo-Russian Strategic Partnership.

Similarly Russo-Chinese relations in the course of over a decade have overcome the acrimony of the past and have moved to the level of strategic partnership. The two countries have not only solved the contentious boundary issue but have also initiated dynamic interaction in defence, economic, political and strategic fields. Their views and interests on regional and global issues coincide a great deal. The two countries have also launched measures to institutionalize their growing friendship. The Shanghai Cooperation Organisation reflects their common concern at the regional level. The Sino Russian Treaty of 2001 is an important landmark in the relations. In short Russian Chinese relations are friendly and marked by a high degree of understanding. This is not to suggest that there are no diffierences in Russian-Chinese relations. The issue of illegal Chinese migrants into the sparsely populated Siberian and Far Eastern region could assume threatening proportions.

On the other hand Sino-Indian relations are still inching towards normalization. There are serious obstacles to a radical improvement in Sino-Indian relations. The vexed boundary question, Pakistani factor in China's South Asia policy are issues which have hampered any improvement. Nevertheless these issues are so deep and wide that there are no easy solutions. Indian policy, however, has been to constructively engage China. Some observers feel that there has been a notable shift in Chinese policy, is its rapprochement with India. Chinese Prime Minister Zhu Rongji made the first visit by a Chinese Prime Minister to India in over a decade in mid-January 2002, as Indian troops were on a war footing with China's long-term ally Pakistan .[7] High-level diplomatic exchanges between India and China are a regular feature and economic interaction is gathering new and slow momentum.

Conclusion

On its part India should pursue the idea of trilateral vigour for three reasons. One such cooperation would provide India space for maneuverability in its negotiations with the West. It would also bring about greater balance in its policy. Secondly, from the perspective of its deep geopolitical and security interests in the region (Central Asia), trilateral cooperation holds enhanced significance. The level of activity in the Central Asian region has intensified. On the one hand is the military presence of the West and on the other hand Russia is making serious attempts to build new security structures in the region. The Shanghai Cooperation Organisation has been institutionalized and President Putin hopes to create a Collective Security Treaty Organisation. How these two organisations will shape up and how effective an instrument they will emerge is difficult to say at this juncture, but India could be left out from an area that is of vital importance to it. Thirdly, the role of Asia is growing in international politics and as one of the major Asian countries India could drive benefits by cooperating with other major Asian countries. From this perspective India should make serious effort to see that trilateral cooperation moves forward.

References

1. Sa Benwang, "Preliminary Analysis of Main Features of China's New Security Concept", Foreign Affairs Journal (Beijing), No. 665, September 2002, p. 35.
2. Leonid Ivashov, "Russian General Comments on Topical Geo-Political Issues", Nezavisimaya, No. 7, Daily Review Moscow), January 2002,
3. R.G. Gidadhubli, "OR Politics in Central Asia", Economic and Political

Weekly (Mumbai), January 30, 1999, p. 262.

4. The Hindu (Chennai), 7 November, 2001.
5. *Ibid.*, 9 December, 2002.
6. *Ibid.*, 12 December, 2002.
7. Robert 0. Keohane, "The Public Delegitimation of Terrorism and Coalition Politics", in Ken Booth and Tim Dunne, eds., Worlds in Collision Terror and the Future (London, 2002), p. 145.

17

A Balance of Coalition Needed Among India, Russia and China

Chandra B. Khanduri

In September, last year the Foreign Ministers of India, Russia and China - Yashwant Singh, Igor Ivanov and Tan Jlaxuan met during the UN General Assembly nod held an informal tri-lateral talk. Over a lunch hosted by Mr. Ivannov, the three ministers not only widely disparate in their names, but she attitudes, seemed to drive at a consensus on three current problems which all three countries were facing the need for a world order that was based on the accepted charter and covenants of the UNO, Combating terrorism as a collective threat; and jointly, without looking Confrontationist to the US policy of a regime change in Iraq, how to press forward the Idea of a non-military intervention. In the latter case not only Russia, but Indis and China have had large stakes in all.

There was also, an expressed desire to solve the problem that proverbially 'dog' the three countries. The Russians on the other band, ardent advocates of cooperation as in the past, have been propagating the need for a trilateral consensus, if not agreements owns all issues of common and International concerns. But gradually and slowly, there seems to be a tri-lateral consensus, at least on Iraq. As a result, despite US-enforced UN Resolution on Iraq November Ist and for Iraq to My declare all its so-called weapons of mass destruction, (W.M.D.) by December 23rd it is trading for time for Suddam Hussein, without any guarantee of the US not attacking Iraq, some breathing space had nonetheless been achieved. Fortutously, the declaration by North Korea of its resumption of nuclear test, dumping of the NPT, from November 28, 2002, added to the complexity of the situation. Although, despite UN Inspectors' clear certification of nos possession of W.M.D., has mobilised a large assaulting force, against Iraq, there are, hopes, against hops that this is only a muscle-flexing and would be regarded as a "manoeuvre of advantage

Out of this predicament, and earlier US overtures, it is the uneasy feelings of the rest of the world against the UNILATERALISM of the sob Suprepower that has given an, eerie reeling to all. To many it looks to be re-emergence of a US as a 21st Century 'colonial power' with great imperial aspirations. The hesitant tri-lateral meeting of the three big of Asia therefore, seem to have boom the direct outcome of this now kind of threat which the world seems to perceive from the world richest and mightiest power.

Every threat, whether real or embroidered is like a Newtonian Law of action, reaction. The threat the American action seem to generate appears to result in a struggle for security in its larger shapes and ramifications. The International agreements the US, for example might once have supported, to paraphrase the Bulletin of Automatic Scientists (July-August, 2002) have 'fallen like leaves in the breeze'. Rejected, shelved or modified for one reason or the other, the US has evaded the issue of ratification of the 'comprehensive Test Ban Treaty' (CTBT); it has refused to sign the 'Mini Ban Treaty', the Chemical Weapons Convention, the Bioweapons Protocol, the Child Soldier's Protocol the Small Arm Action. It has refined the trial of its servicemen by the International Criminal Court, whereas Milosevic faces trial by the saw court. These are small as compared to the 'dustbinning' of the Anti-Ballistic Missile Treaty, which the US regards as being in conflict with Its NMD. Still worse is its damping of the NPT, besides calling the Kyoto. Protocol as flawed Treaty because of its being Unscientific' and[6] unsupportive to the developing nations'. This 'going alone' by the US, with its economic ad military strengths, Global sweep, its post September 2001 Operation Enduring Freedom postures all ever the world but specifically in Central and South East Asia, its relentless pressures for exploitation of its own priorities for energy and other concerns, besides turning a blind eye to happenings in Pakistan, East Turkestan, Checnya and Kashmir, have apparently made Russia, China and India sit up Virtually.

Russia is deeply concerned, if not openly resentful of the American presence in Central Asia. What was once solely a region of Russian area of interest and influence from the days of Catherine the Great (1762-96) has been penetrated by the Americans. (It is like the Chinese entry into Tibet in 1950 and its dragonisation and the loss of a buffer state to India against China and its repercurssions reporcursdan that continue to re-echo to the Himalayas.)

With the growing influence of the US in Uzbekistan, Tajikistan (where US bases are established). Turkmenistan (which abounds in oil and gas),

Kazakhstan and hyzstan there is a scramble for what the US Government calls a *Eurasion Energy Corridor*, that is to link *Baku* with *Ceyhan*.

Energy Alliances

Terrorism apart, the tapping of the energy sources of this region has inevitably led to the Chinese extending their oil pipe line from Kazhakstan-Turkmenistan. Under the circumstance Russian importance re-emerges. "Russia's complex" said Vladimir Lukin, the Deputy Chairman of the State Duma," may become a basic element of global security especially against the background of increasing challenges in the world energy complex". He was speaking at the opening ceremony of the All-Russian oil and Gas Week in Moscow on October 14th, last. It was to highlight the importance of the Russian oil and gas as an alternative and stable sources vis-a-vis the more abundant yet unstable Middle East oil and sources. "Russia is a longterm option for the world", says President George W. Bush. Everyone is looking at it optimistically. Obviously with 66 billion barrels of oil and 47.6 trillion cubic meters (1680, trillion cubic feet) of gas, no one can ignore Russia. And if Putin continues to manage his strategic priorities well-as he is doing-Russian emergence as a great power is a decade off.

In a fast moving world, one of the lessons of current history that the rich nations have learnt is to diversify energy and other sources. This one was the major lesson of the Arab-Israeli wars of 1973 when the Arabs reduced the supply and hiked the prices some ton-fold. So is the state of political situation in the Middle East again In 2002-2003. While of world's known oil resources, two thirds are, Indeed, in the Middle East, the Eastern Europe and former USSR, have about one fifth of it. This, therefore, assumes a very large importance in the energy market.

The Emerging Alliances

Besides the CIS, the Russians have formed what has come to be knowns as the *Caucasus Four* comprising Georgia, Armenia, Azerbaijan, besides Russia. The Chinese too have promoted the six membered Shanghai Cooperation Organisation (SCO) comprising China, Russia, Kazakhstan,Tajikistan and Uzbekistan. This, thus, is a fall out of the Afghanistan situation, leading obviously to the US presence in Central Asias, besides the looming threats of 'three evil forces', namely, terrorism, separatism and extromism.

Regional forums and alliances are thus already developing to the region with Russia and China in the lead, with profound potential for future developments. These undoubtedly, will grow further as NATO expands, into the Baltic region the energy supply assumes more reliability vis-a-vis the volatile unstable Middle East, and God forbid, the fundamentalists once again destabilise a fragile democracy in Afghanisatn and neighbouring Pakistan which, in fact, has become the mother of all terrorism in South Asia.

Without elaborating further, the Chinese are really rattled about the East Turkestan terrorist forces, led by the East Turkestan Islamic Movements demanding an 'East Turkestan Islamic State'. Like Al Qaida, an host of separatists in Kashmir, Indonesia, the Philippines, Nepal, Chechnya, the ETIM are regarded as international terrorists.

Commonality of Perspectives Get Highlighted

If Kashmir has turned into a fistula in the side of India, Chechnya an 'Achilles Heel' for Russia, then Xinjiang is a festering wound for China. All three are the angst of three bigs of Asia, and admittedly, require a concerted effort, if possible a collective endeavour to the 'Islamic jihad' inspire supported by Muslim fundamentalists all over the world, these nuclei of fundamentalism have every potential to proliferate especially in India. They have to be liquidated.

Secondly, while Russia and China, Russia and India have a strategic partnership, the same need to be developed between India and China for a lucrative and meaningful mutual benefits. China, it must be said, has been clearly reticent about it; so perhaps India has been cautious to begin an initiative afresh.

This initiative that, in fact, had begun in a euphemistic bang in 1954 with *Panchsheel* and *Hindi Chini Bhai - Bhai*, ended in a literal whimper by 1962. The Chinese invasion of India's northern borders and continued Chinese belligerence, without doubt, remain wholly responsible for it.

Whatthen are the Differential Calculus Between Idnia and China

The Border Disputes since 1954-62 Demand New Solutions

China should compensate India be leasing, say for 100 years or more an equal part of the Tibetan territory, in for instance in the Chumbi Valley; or readjust positions in Western Tibet in the region of Mansarovar.

Do not consider India as an adversary as was done during Mao Zedong's time.

Open all border passes to allow unhindered movement of trade and commerce as was envisaged in the 1954 "Treaty and Intercourse". Admit entry of the Dalai Lama into Tibet and accept Tibetan autonomy.

China and Russia

China and Russia have also border dispute, mainly in the Usuri Tract, which remains unroselved. Clubbing those border disputes as the major cause of distrust and as serious stumbling blocks (especially between India and China), China should consider the 'ball in Us court'. It must take adequate and prompt initiative to rebuild confidence of India and show her residence with Russia.

Balancing Coalition and Alliances-A Necessity

There is no doubt, a need for the 'three bigs' of Asia to unite in their eadeavour to create and activate a mechanism not only against terorism (which is an elusive threat and should be ealt with as a contingency), but against the growing unilateralism - even a new kind of American colonialism. Russia, no doubt plays a key role, China of late has emerged as a great power of the future to reckon with. But to be a truly enduring structure, China should find solution to the 40,009 sq km of Indian territory it has occupied since 1962. This will ensure regional and global stability. It is hoped It will. For, China's future has large implications for both regional and global stability.

It is not only the bastion of Communism - the ideological balance to Western capitalism and ideology - but at stakes are the lives and welfare of 1.2 billion people and their 14 neighbours - next only to Russia's 15. Although its Gross National Product is just a quarter of Japan's $ 4.4 trillion, it is outpacing this world's second largest economy with its steady 7 to 8 percent annual growth. It is expected to outreach it in next two decades or so. As it is, China's, Central Bank has the second largest foreign currency reserves in the world. Confident of its Military prowess, including nuclear, China has begun to look up at its space programmes too. This is being accelerated on account of decision of the USA, to adopt its NMD and unilaterally abrogating the ADM Treaty to an euphemistic 'dust-bin' of history.

India on its part, despite the problems of population, poverty, Internal dissonance, and corruption is striving hard to move ahead with economic developmats. Militarily it is strong and Is capable of handling the apparent threats that might post in future. Overall, a nuclear power, India is respected in the comity of nations and has a large potential to emerge as a regional power In South Ask. And although India and the US are cooperating In several reglem Including military, it cannot be said India is at case with the unilateral policies of the US. And while like China and Russia, India should 'go along' rather than confront USA, it would serve the came of global strategic balance and development, if the 'big threes' of Asia develop in strategic thoughts and plans.

There is therefore, so better way to strengthen friendship and tri-lateral equation and rapprroahement other than by whole heartedly supporting India's case for admittance as a permanent member of the Security Council. Of the two, Russia and China, the latter could reciprocate India's magnanimity by persistently sponsoring and promoting this nove, since it was India, who, against the stiffest resistance of the American led Western world, saw the Communist China's entry into the UN.

Summation

The concept of a strategic balance of coalition among India China and-Russia, that is being advocated, is being advocated, is *unlikely* to find full favour even among the most knowledgeable and professional *elites* in all the three countries. Some will be clearly skeptical others pessimist. There is, nonetheless, a need to generate optimism on this account.

Skepticism and pessimism, survive only if they are supported by reflections and truth. Perhaps it is true that China's reticence may abort the concept, at present temporarily. But the long-term based strategic needs of the three countries that form Almost one-third of the world's population, all three of whom are determined to maintain peace and stability in the Asia-Pacific region, demand coalition and formation of alliance. And although, Asia as a whole, has hardly had a common Civilization, but it houses Asia's three major civilizations, all the major religions of the world and nine-tenth of energy resources, to name only a few. A pioneering spirit, therefore, is called for achieving this coalition of the future, if Asia is to achieve its rightful place, like Europe, or the two Americas.

They may make uncertain allies, but allies they can be. Our politicians and pundits, it is hoped, will play their role in facing and sustaining this alliance - the politicians will have to cater for the preseut and the pundits, articulate a bright horoscope, for the future.

Note - During the state visit to India of Vladimir Putin, he is purporated to discussed the feasibility of a coalition. The Indian and the Chinese Governments (where Putin Pre-staged his Indian visit) are said to be agreed upon the basic concept. Future developments will show how this could be shaped.

18

Commonalities of Indian and Russian Interests in Central Asia

Meena Singh Roy

The subject matter of Convergence of Indian and Russian Interests in Central Asia can be seen in the changing geo-political environment of this region. Both India and Russia have some common interests in Central Asia, which can be explored and given a more concrete shape. After the disintegration of the Soviet Union, the emergence of Central Asian states in the international political firmament has brought Russia (in its near-abroad foreign policy) and India closer in looking for some broader areas of cooperation. No doubt, this has gone through ups and downs at some point yet future relation between the two would be sustained by commonality of interests. In the post Cold War scenario the soundness and strength of the Indo- Russian relations should not be underestimated. The present paper attempts to analyse Indo- Russian cooperation in the backdrop of their converging interests in Central Asia.

Indo-Russian Relations should be viewed in the context of new global realities. In the post Cold War scenario United States has emerged as a sole super power, working towards establishing the new world order. Russia has been reduced to the middle level power struggling to improve its economy. If one looks at the foreign policy priorities of Russian Federation, one notices a gradual shift in Russian policies. Its priority remains the economic recovery. In the current Russian foreign policy goals one finds that the role of economic diplomacy is continuously increasing and is being reflected in its foreign policy both at global and regional levels. While explaining the Russia's foreign policy goals Mr. Igor S. Ivanov has stated that "The Central goal of Russian foreign policy was and remains creating the optimal external conditions for continued domestic transformation that strengthens the government, improves the economy, and increases the well being of Russian citizens"[1].

Therefore, for economic reasons Russia needs Europe and US. This in turn puts west at the top priority of Russian foreign policy. After 9/11 there has been greater cooperation between Russia and US they have functioned as partner in fighting the menace of terrorism. There has also been greater cooperation in the international energy market.

Russia's relations with NATO, strained over the alliance's expansion into Eastern Europe have improved rapidly after 9/11. Russia and NATO have also agreed to build a missile defence shield for Europe. A Russia NATO council has approved the first phase of cooperation programme to deploy a non-strategic anti- missile defence in Europe.[2] Russia-Pakistan relations have also entered a new phase. These factors need to be taken into consideration while analysing current and future Indo-Russian relations.

Indo-Russian Convergence of Interests in Central Asia

India and Russia, two great powers located in close proximity to each other, have had common approaches to various important international problems. During the last fifty years they have worked in close cooperation towards establishing greater peace and stability in Asia. After the disintegration of the USSR and emergence of Central Asian States India and Russia have been cooperating on various issues pertaining to the security and stability in Central Asia and Afghanistan. The commonalities Indo- Russian interests in Central Asia can be explained under following subject headings.

Geo-Strategic Significance of CARs

India as well as Russia considers Central Asia to be an important region with vital geo-strategic and economic interests.[3] The geo-strategic importance of Central Asia draws India and Russia together in this region. Both are keen on maintaining peace and Stability in this region. After the end of Taliban rule in Kabul and establishment of friendly regime in Afghanistan India wants to consolidate its political and economic position in CARs. India also looks at Central Asian energy resources as alternate source. India is making every possible effort in cementing its existing ties with these republics with an aim of establishing a peaceful and cooperative framework in the region. These efforts were strengthen by the visit of Indian Prime Minister in June 2002 to attend the 16-nation summit of Conference on Interaction and Confidence-Building Measures in Asia (CICA) in Almaty. There after also there has been several visits at ministerial level to strengthen these ties. Central Asia has been of great significance to India in past as well as today. India's objectives in this region have been very clearly spelled in various speeches made by our ministers and by several government statements. These could be summarized under following headings

- Establishing stability and peace in this region
- Working against the spread of terrorist network
- Ensuring its energy security
- Wanting central Asia to be part of an expanded trade network
- Increasing trade and economic relations with this region
- Working for the greater regional cooperation
- Controlling drug trafficking in the region

India's attempt has always been to increase its political, cultural and economic ties with these republics, and not to expand its military influence in this region. Nevertheless, post 9/11 it has started building its military technical cooperation with this region. Intelligence sharing, joint military exercise, providing training and assistance to Central Asian forces, joint manufacturing of transport aircraft (with Uzbekistan) and possibly upgrading military hardware are some of the features of this military cooperation. In this context the external affairs minister, Yashwant Sinha during his recent visit to Tajikistan, Kyrgyzstan and Kazakhstan stated that in reaching out to Central Asia, India is not competing with any of the internationai players that are engaging the strategically important region. He said, "We are not in central Asia to replace anyone. We see Central Asia as part of India's extended neighbourhood and our presence there is to promote a mutually inclusive relationship."[4] India sees CARs as a potential partner in fighting the menace of religious extremism, ensuring its energy security and expanding its trade network. Central Asia is Russia's soft underbelly and vital to its interests. But preoccupation with its own political and economic turmoil did not permit Russia to pay much attention to these newly independent former Soviet Republics after their independence in 1991. Despite its past linkages and geographical proximity Russia's central Asia policy was kept at the back burner. For some time, Moscow had no coherent policy towards the CARs. Central Asia remained on the periphery of Moscow's attention and the CARs were not regarded as "important objects of Russian foreign policy activities.[5] But later, the

CARs came to be recognized as an integral part of the zone of Russia's special interests."[6] Since 1992 necessity of active development of relations between Russia and Central Asian states have been stressed. Russia has been working towards greater economic integration and Politico-Military cooperation in this region. Recent developments in the region have offered a new opportunity to Russia to bolster its position in Central Asian region.At strategic level new regional alliance Collective Security Treaty Organisation (CSTO) has come into existence. This regional alliance comprises of Russia,Kazakhstan, Kyrgzstan, Tajikistan, Belarus and Armenia.Through Eurasian Economic Community (EEC) Russia is trying to promote economic cooperation in the region.[7] Russia has also established airbase in Kant, 20 Ian from the Kyrgyz Capital.[8] In post 9/11 and Iraq war Russia has been very successfully reasserting its authority in Central Asian region which is considered to be the Southern Security belt of Russia.

The Central Asian population is not radicalized, but their prospects for economic prosperity are quite elusive. The region is also rife with traditional rivalries, fueled by a growing competition for land and water. Russia alone does not have the resources to support Central Asia economically, to be source of credits and loans. But Russia remains economically important in Central Asia. It provides the region with important hidden subsidies by supplying it with goods and fuel at belowmarket prices. Landlocked Central Asia carries out the lion's share of its trade with the West through Russian transport links and at favorable tariffs. In the given political situation it is more advantageous for Russia to coexist in Central Asia with the United States than with China. Though Central Asia is interested in US patronage. Kazakhstan, Kyrgyzstan and Tajikistan retain special ties with Russia. General Bolot Januzakov, the public relations advisor to President Akaev and the former chief of the national security service is of the view that "The simultaneous presence of all three (Russia, China and US) in Beshkek is in our national interest." According to him the Kyrgz state budget receives considerable funds from the US-led coalition, and that the revival of local defence factories[9] with Russia's assistance will provide regular employment for hundreds of people. Kyrgyz military factories are already receiving orders from or through Russia. Kyrgyzstan is not able to reach the world market itself therefore, by reviving its ties with Russia to restart the closed defence industries will be profitable for Kyrgyzstan. It appears that CARs would be more comfortable accepting US presence in the region while maintaining ties with Moscow if US-Russian partnership in this part of Eurasia were to become a reality. When we look at overall geo political situation we find that Central Asia is classic case of big power small power syndrome where CARs are between two big powers, China and Russia. Here U.S., the sole super power, is trying to acquire influence and foothold in this region[10] to achieve its short-term and long-term goals. The US is challenging Russia's historical influence in the region by also nurturing close military partnership with the Central Asian States. Uzbekistan and Kyrgyzstan are providing military bases for use by US troops supporting operations in Afghanistan, while Kazakhstan and Tajikistan have opened their airspace. In such a scenario balancing act is being attempted by Central Asian States. Russia while supporting the U.S. campaign against terrorism does not want to lose Central Asia to the U.S. It wants to retain its hold over the region, which is strategically as well as economically significant for Russia. China as an emerging power with its vested interests in this region is trying to counter balance the American influence through its efforts in Shanghai Cooperation Organisation (SCO) along with Russia and CARs. Geopolitical developments in West Asia and Central Asia are encouraging China and Iran to develop stronger political and economic ties. The major factor in the expansion of Chinese and Iranian relations is a shared concern about US "unilateralism." Both Chinese and Iranian officials have expressed concern about possible" encirclement" by US forces, which are now based in Iraq, Afghanistan, Kyrgyzstan and Uzbekistan. India as an extended neighbour is trying to forge its ties at bilateral with CARs, Russia, Iran and US and at multilateral level as a part of antiterrorist coalition.

Terrorism/ Religious Extremism

India, Russia and CARs share a common interest in blocking the dissemination of radical Islam in this region. Given the global nature of terrorism collective efforts by like minded nations is required. In this respect India along with Russia and Central Asian Republics has taken major initiative to counter this menace of terrorism. India and Russia have much to gain in continuing the level of intense cooperation as their relations are based on pragmatic considerations. Russia highly values its good partnership relations with India and India views Russia as real and reliable strategic partner. Both the countries are committed to cooperate bilaterally and at the multilateral level on strategic issues for development of a multi-polar world based on a new cooperative security order[11].

Both are facing challenge from religious extremism and terrorism emanating from Afghanistan and Pakistan. India understands Russia's problems in Chechnya and Russia has shown complete understanding of India's stand on Jammu and Kashmir. After recent visit of Mr.Yashwant Sinha to Moscow in May 2003 once again the Russian Foreign Ministry made its position very clear by stating that "the full implementation of obligations assumed by Islamabad to stop infiltration of terrorists across the Line of Control into Jammu and Kashmir and destroy all terrorist infrastructure on Pakistancontrolled territory would foster the sprit of cooperation in South Asia"[12] It has always stood by India in its critical situation in international organizations. Pakistan, which recently took over as president of the UNSC, proposed to raise the Kashmir issue but Russia opposed Pakistan's move to take up the Kashmir issue in the U.N. Security Council by stating "This issue is not on the agenda of the World body"' [13]

Despite US military achievements in Afghanistan, vulnerability of the region (because of inherent internal problem) falling back in the hands of extremist forces remains. India and Russia both affirm that fight against terrorism has better chances of succeeding in face of coordinated efforts. In this respect, steps have already been taken by respective governments in the form of joint working groups on combating terrorism. The institutional linkages between National Security Council of Russia and National Security Council of India can be seen as a right step in this direction. Indo-Russian cooperation has been further consolidated by Prime Minister's visit to Moscow in November 2001A major outcome of this visit was the Moscow Declaration on International Terrorism. The signing of agreement on international terrorism reflects the close corresponding views of both the countries on this issue. Under this declaration both agreed for "the adoption on the basis of international law of decisive measures against all States, individuals, and entities which render support, harbour, finance, instigate or train terrorists or promote terrorism. It is essential that all States, without exception, should pay particular attention to the prevention of access of terrorists and extremist organisations and groups to financial resources on the basis of international law."[14]

The declaration reaffirmed the central role of the United Nations in the struggle against terrorism. In this connection they called for early completion of negotiations under U.N. Comprehensive Convention on International Terrorism and the Convention for the suppression of acts of Nuclear Terrorism, which would enable nations combating the global menace of terrorism more effectively. It was also agreed that international terrorism could not be fought by double standards. Both the countries have welcomed Security Council Resolution 1373 of September 28,2001 and the establishment of a Counter Terrorism Committee focused on monitoring of implementation by states of their international obligations in the struggle against terrorism-primarily with the view to reliably curtailing any type of support-moral, material, arms supplies, through propaganda, shelter, etc.[15]

With such a relationship between India and Russia there is all the possibility of multilateral cooperation among CARs, India and Russia in fighting the menace of Islamic extremism. The Russia and U.S. have also emphasized the critical importance of durable peace, stability and prosperity for the countries of central Asia, and the need for a regional approach to the task of restoring Afghanistan. Both the countries have agreed to support expanding anti-terrorist cooperation within the framework of United Nations, the Organisation for Security and Cooperation in Europe, NATO and other international structures, as well as on a bilateral basis. The U.S, and CARs are already coordinating their efforts in this respect At a regional level Russia, China and CARs are pooling their resources through SCO to fight terrorism. India is working jointly with CARs and Russia to fight this menace.

Imperatives for the Regional Cooperation

Building a viable security order and stability in central Asia and Afghanistan continues to be the prime concern of the international community. For regional stability it is important to ensure that Central Asia does not become the next Afghanistan and Afghanistan

doesn't fall back in the hands of radical form once again.[16] While domestic measures are essential, the collective mechanism is required in tackling the problem of terrorism. Looking at the cooperative mechanism at the regional level in Central Asia one finds that issue of terrorism is being addressed at various level in forums like Shanghai Cooperation Organisation (SCO), CIS and conference on Interaction and confidence Building in Central Asia (CICA). The Organisation for Security and Cooperation in Europe (OSCE) and United Nations Office for Drug Control and Crime Prevention (UNODCCP) alongwith Central Asian states are also working at multilateral level to fight this menace. On December 2002, Afghanistan signed a non-aggression pact[17] (Kabul Declaration) with all six of its neighbours, a collective attempt towards establishing peace in the region. Under Collective Security Treaty Organisation Russia and three other former Soviet republics have also created joint rapid reaction force to fight the growing threat of Islamic militancy. In addition, Kyrgyzstan and Tajikistan are also working on two military cooperation agreement. These include an agreement on confidence-building measure within the border area and a defence cooperation treaty. Kyrgyzstan has signed similar treaties with Russia, Kazakhstan and Armenia.[18]

This problem is also being addressed at bilateral level not only among Central Asian States but also with other countries. India is cooperating with CARs at bilateral level and has signed memorandum of understanding (MOUs) with these Republics. It has joint working group with Russia, Afghanistan and CARs. India also supports the measures taken by CICA in its recently held meeting at Almaty. At bilateral level India and Russia are committed to cooperate bilaterally and at the multilateral level on strategic issues for development of a multi-polar world based on a new cooperative security order.[19] "-India and Russia have formed the joint worldng group on combating terrorism. The institutional links between Russian Security Council and National Security Council of India can be seen as a right step towards achieving this goal. Indo-Russian cooperation was further consolidated by Prime Minister's visit to Moscow in November 2001.A major outcome of this visit was the Moscow Declaration on International Terrorism. The signing of agreement on international terrorism reflects the close corresponding views of both the countries on this issue.

Both the countries have also welcomed Security Council Resolution 1373 of September 28,2001 and the establishment of a Counter Terrorism Committee focused on monitoring of implementation by states of their international obligations in the struggle against terrorism-primarily with the view to reliably curtailing any type of support-moral, material, arms supplies, through propaganda, shelter, etc.[20] Further, in a personal message on April 4,2002 from the Russian President, Vladimir Putin, to the Prime Minister, Atal Behari Vajpayee, the two sides discussed the participation of Central Asian States in antiterrorist activities.[21]

With such a relationship between India and Russia there is all the possibility of multilateral cooperation among CARs, India and Russia in fighting the menace of Islamic extremism. The Russia and U.S. have also emphasized the critical importance of durable peace, stability and prosperity for the countries of Central Asia, and the need for a regional approach to the task of restoring Afghanistan. Both the countries have agreed to support expanding anti-terrorist cooperation within the framework of United Nations, the OSCE, NATO and other international structures, as well as on a bilateral basis.

The importance of developing comprehensive efforts to combat and prevent terrorism has been the focus of OSCE and ODCCP in various conferences organized in different capitals of CARs and other cities of world. These organisations have been working towards creating right kind of atmosphere among nations to cooperate and fight the problem of terrorism They have also been urging countries to encourage sustainable economic development and to consider providing financial and technical assistance to the Central Asian States. India has been participating in every effort, which OSCE has been taking to combat the problem of terrorism.

Central Asian Republics have also been raising their voices for greater participation of India in Central Asia. The Kazakh and Kyrgyz president have proposed India's membership to the key Central Asian grouping, the Shanghai Cooperation Organisation (SCO). India has never lobbied for its membership in SCO nor has formally applied for membership as reported in some of the recent writings, but India has displayed interest in SCO. In fact India tends to lose rather than gain by joining this organisation until SCO membership rules are finalized. Moreover, China is trying to reorganize SCO as a bloc to counterbalance increasing US influence in the region.

While assessing the effectiveness of regional organisations it can be said that SCO especially after the US led war against terrorism is likely to function as week organization in search of a unifying operational framework.[22] The CICA a Kazakh initiative, which focuses on collective security against global terrorism, has been comparatively slow in its working. Despite its various strengths CICA still is at a preliminary stage and has to go long way. So far it does not have structured mechanisms for practical cooperation between its members, including in the military sphere. At present it intends to function primarily as a forum for dialogue. Therefore, its role as an effective organization fighting terrorism in this region has yet to be seen. Russian is trying to reassert its influence in the region through its efforts under CSTO. At there recent meeting in Bishkek, security councils' secretaries comprising the CIS, CSTO, as well as observers from Azerbaijan, Georgia, Maldova, and Ukaraine, discussed measures to establish a security belt along the southern borders of the CIS.[23] In future, Russia is likely to play a significant role. Influence of Russia in CARs is likely to increase due to US occupation in Iraq. The US involvement in rebuilding Iraq will shift its priority to west Asia rather than Central Asia. Although this does not mean that US will have any less important role to play, possibility of its resources being diverted towards west Asia is more likely. In the present world order US seem to be the sole power shaping up the future events not only in West Asia but also in Central Asia. India with its increasing ties both with US and Russia is likely to work towards greater cooperation with these countries in fight against terrorism and establishing peace in the region

Cooperation in Energy Sector

The most important area where India and Russia can work together is energy sector. Russia is a major energy power with rich experience in energy diplomacy. Its reemergence as an energy power is an important change in international energy security structure. In November 2002, the Government of Russian federation officially approved the outline of Russian Energy Strategy towards 2020, stressing that Russia should promote its economic recovery and maintain its geographical interests by means of developing energy diplomacy. On May 24 2002 President George W. Bush and President Vladimir Putin issued a joint statement announcing a new energy dialogue whose purpose was to "strengthen their overall relationship and enhance global energy security and international strategic stability."[24] In the post 9/11 -scenario Russia and US are cooperating with each other rather than conftonting each other in Caspian region. India is already cooperating with Russia and Central Asian States in this sector. Some headway was made in this direction during Prime Minister Atal Behari Vajpayee's visit to Kazakhstan. India has already invested in Sakhalin oil field of Russia. India is expected to get about five million tones annually of oil and eight million cubic meters of gas per day from 2005 from this offshore project near Alaska. India is likely to acquire a stake with Russia as partner in the proven Kazakh oil field of Kurmangazy. On November 12, Russia's Gazaprom announced its plan to construct an undersea gas pipeline between Iran and India for exporting Iranian natural gas to India via Pakistan. According to the announcement, the Russian Company has reached an agreement in principle with Iran for the project. In this respect Pakistani consent has also been received. The US3.2 billion-pipeline project will be a major political and economic achievement for Iran, Russia and India if it becomes a reality in near future.[25]

Stand on Afghanistan

The position of New Delhi and Moscow on the Afghan crisis, on its regional impact on worldwide efforts to eliminate terrorism is absolutely identical. Any negative development in Afghanistan would have serious security implications not only for India and Russia but also for CARs. India has always been concerned about security in its northern and northwestern border areas. India has more than 15 million Muslim population. Taliban brand of highly radicalized Islam would inflame delicate communal tensions at home. Russia has an ethnic problem in Chechnya and also a sizable Muslim population (15 percent). Under Taliban rule Chechen rebels were getting full support to carry out their terrorist activities in Russia. In case of CARs Afghanistan remains crucial factor in the overall security situation. Taliban ruled Afghanistan was a source of instability in Central Asia for long. Therefore, a stable and friendly government in Afghanistan is what India, Russia and CARs favour. They want the situation to evolve in such a way that Afghanistan no longer remains the hub of religious extremism and terrorism. Therefore stable Afghanistan is in the interest of CARs, India and Russia. This also opens up new opportunity for cooperation among these states. In the reconstruction of Afghanistan these countries have a major role to play. They have common interest in creating peace and stability in this region.

Drug Trafficking

Related to the problem of religious extremism, and one that confronts India, Russia and CARs is that of drug trafficking. Drug trafficking still remains a major challenge and threat to the stability in the region. There has been very little change in this respect even in the post Taliban Afghanistan. In this context Tajik Foreign Minister Salohiddin Nasriddinov has stated that "the amount of narcotics being transported from Afghanistan through the neighbouring countries and on to Europe.... Is growing. This is because over the years the international community has been fighting terrorism" and forgotten that drug business has been the main occupation of the people of Afghanistan.[26] Whereas the Taliban destroyed many of the poppy fields in the areas of Afghanistan that were under their control, the territory held by Northen Alliance -which bordered Tajikistan-continued to produce large quantities of the crop[27] such that Tajikistan became a major route for the smuggling of drugs to western Europe. With the end of Taliban rule in Afghanistan concerns have grown that the amount of drug trafficking through Tajikistan would increase, given the lack of economic incentive that Afghan farmers have to produce other crops. The Karzai government has limited resources to support farmers in crop-substitution programmes. In the early January it was acknowledged by the Tajik border guards that only 10 percent of the drugs smuggled [28] across the Tajik-Afghan border are intercepted.[28] In an April 26 speechPresident Imomali Rahmonov said Tajikistan ranked fourth in the world in drug seizures, intercepting roughly three tons of narcotics with an estimated street value of $ 1.4 billion since the start of 2003.[29] Russian border guards have seized about 800kg of drugs, including about 550kg of heroin, in various sections of the Tajik-Afghan border in April 2003.[30]

The United Nations Office on Drugs and Crime (UNODC) reports clearly show that Afghanistan would be returning to its position as world's foremost opium producer. In an annual survey released in late October, the estimates mark a dramatic rebound from last year's (2001) low of 185 tonnes to 3,276 (2002). The UNODCs 2002 estimates point out 3 that 2003 poppy crops could move to 4,581 tonnes. [31] The increase in production has been accompanied by a similar increase in the number of heroin refineries across the country.[32] A range of leading military commanders and provincial officers are deeply involved in opium and heroin production and trafficking, which has increasingly turned from conduits through Pakistan and Iran to the northern route to Europe via Central Asia and Russia[33] .

The problem is quite serious in Russia and CARs. Drugs are penetrating into Russia along two main channels. First from the "golden triangle" of Southeast Asia via the Far East; the second from Southwest Asia-mainly Afghanistan and Pakistan-via Central Asia and the South Caucasus. Lieutenant General Alexander Sergeyev, head of the department for combating illegal circulation of drugs in Russia said at a press conference in Domodedovo in June 2000, that Russia needs "a second safety belt to block the drug channels from Afghanistan, primarily the ones that are used for transporting drug to Europe". He noted that, "in spite of the first safety belt around Afghanistan, drugs get from this country to Europe through Turkey and the Balkans. Now, drug traffickers' routes have moved to the north drugs are now transported to Western Europe through Tajikistan and Russia.[34] Bruno Dato, the head of the Moscow regional bureau of the U.N. department for drug control and crime prevention said "over 20 million people on the planet (about 4 per cent of the worlds population) are drug-abusers. The annual revenue from this illegal drug turnover comes to approximately $50 billion. It is the total gross income of two thirds of the U.N. member countries. According to Dato's estimate Russia will have about 3 million drug-takers by 2010. He also stated that a majority of heroin; marijuana, opium and cocaine comes to Western Europe and the USA from Central Asia, in particular, from Afghanistan and Pakistan. [35] The problem of drug trafficking has a serious implication for India's security as well. The extremist groups operating in Jammu and Kashmir are using the income generated by drug trafficking. Therefore, India, Russia and CARs have common interest to pool their efforts to address this problem of drug trafficking. During recent visit of Mr. Sinha to Russia both the sides paid special attention to strengthen bilateral and multilateral interaction in confronting new threats and challenges of terrorism and narcotics.[36]

"North-South" Transport Corridor

Both India and Russia want central Asia to be part of an extended trade network through north-south corridor. This inter-governmental agreement between India, Iran and Russia was signed in St.Petersburg on

12 September 2002. This agreement has been ratified by all the three signatory states and came into force on 16 May 2002, This corridor will facilitate easier movement of goods along the corridor connecting India through the sea route to Iran and then via the Caspian Sea to the Russian Federation and to Europe. This route will not only open the corridor for trade between Russia and India but also to CARs. India has also agreed to construct a 200-kilometer stretch of road in Afghanistan to facilitate transport of goods from the Iranian port of Chabahar to Afghanistan.[37] India, Iran and Afghanistan signed a memorandum of understanding on trade and transit issues in Tehran on 6 January 2003. The memorandum provides for the building facilities on roads and at ports via Chabahar-Zabol-Zaranj-Delaram route.[38] This route would increase the connectivity not only with Afghanistan but in future through Tajikistan with Central Asian states as well.

Science and Technology

This is another important area where Indian and Russian can work together in CARs. Both the countries can develop the human resourse potential in this region. India and Russia has the best scientific manpower but the need is to pool this manpower. In this context, example of Tajikistan can be given. There is dire need of electricity in Tajikistan whereas Russia has surplus electricity. Therefore Indian manpower can work with Russia (which has the technology) and the whole of Tajikistan could be lighted with this collective effort.

Export of Indian software and hardware to this region could be another important area of cooperation. India has already shown its desire to build a major software development center in Central Asia. Potential in the auto manufacturing, mainly the light motor vehicles (LMVs) also exist.

Defence Cooperation

In defence sector the commonality that exist between India and Central Asian States is that both use Russian equipment. After the disintegration of Soviet Union most of the industries in these republics were closed. Now it needs to be seen if these industries could be restarted with the help of Russian R&D, Central Asian infrastructure and Indian investment. Would this be a profitable business for all? Would such cooperation be possible? Remains to be seen. India has been increasing its military ties with CARs after 9/11 as has been mentioned earlier. In future more possibility of mutual cooperation in the defence sector could be expected between CARs, India and Russia. For India Russia still remains the major supplier of Arms and ammunitions.

President Putin's Visit and Indo -Russian Cooperation

Russian President Vladimir Putin's visit to India in December 2002 undoubtedly opens up a new era of friendship and cooperation between India and Russia. This visit can be evaluated at two levels. At bilateral level this could be seen as step towards reinforcing the overall India-Russia relations, providing it more substance and long-term sustainability to the existing strategic partnership between the two nations. And at multilateral level this could be seen as an achievement in addressing the problem of terrorism and evolving the mechanism in combating it, and also cooperating in energy sector, not only in Russia but in Caspian region as well. Issues of Terrorism, cooperation in defence sector, atomic energy and space technology, cooperation in energy sector, commitment for strengthening non-proliferation and disarmament goals, strengthening of U.N.'s central role in promoting international security in a multi-polar world, issue of Iraq and situation in Afghanistan and Central Asia were the major highlights of the meeting between the two heads of states. During this meeting both agreed to intensify and widen their cooperation in multilateral foras. President Putin and Prime Minister Vajpayee signed The Delhi Declaration on Further consolidation of Strategic Partnership between India and the Russian Federation[39] and seven other agreements on economic, technical, and scientific cooperation. Delhi Declaration aims at elevating the strategic partnership to an even higher and qualitative new level in both bilateral and multilateral relations. The declaration clearly states "Bilateral cooperation as well as cooperation with other countries would be further enhanced to meet the various challenges of globalisation, in particular the mitigation of its negative manifestations. Globalisation and national identity represent complementary components of world order. Recognition of and respect for diversity is a necessary precondition for human progress, and essential component of the Dialogue between Civilization"[40]

Both the countries reiterated their commitment towards strengthening non-proliferation and disarmament goals. In this respect Delhi Declaration very clearly pointed out that "India and Russia are convinced that the promotion of the disarmament process, including reduction and eventual elimination of nuclear weapons, is one of the most important components of security both in Asia and in the world at large. We call for early start of multilateral talks aimed at a comprehensive arrangement on non-deployment of weapons in outer space, non-use or threat of use of force in respect of space based objects and preserving the use of space for full range of cooperative, peaceful and developmental activities."[41]

Situation in Afghanistan and Central Asia was noted to be of vital security interest to both the countries. It was mentioned, "there is a need to continuously assess the evolving Afghan situation and intend to continue and expand the close cooperation on Afghanistan." In this context both sides emphasized that coordinated effort in the reconstruction of Afghanistan should be driven by Afghan priorities. Further, the need for the UN and the international community to remain engaged for ensuring the revival of Afghanistan as a sovereign and independent state, free from terrorism, drugs and external interference was stressed by both the countries. Both sides considered security and stability in Central Asia to be of vital significance to them and supported further consolidation of secular and democratic order in the Central Asian region. India and Russia both firmly condemned all types of terrorism, based on any ground, political, religious or ideological. It was emphasized that the countermeasures should be directed also against those states, entities and individuals who support, fund or abet terrorists or provide them shelter or asylum to engage in cross-border terrorism. There should be no double standards in the fight against terrorism. Both the sides reaffirmed the relevance of the Moscow declaration on International Terrorism of 6 November 2001. Both countries agreed to enhance bilateral cooperation in order to combat terrorism, including in the context of the cooperation under the aegis of joint Working Group on Afghanistan and Group on terrorism set up by the national security council of India and the Security Council of the Russian Federation. The cooperation in this sphere was further strengthened by a *Memorandum of Understanding (MOU) on Cooperation in Combating Terrorism by* which both the sides agreed to set up an Indo-Russian Joint working Group on Counter-terrorism. This would be an inter-agency group on both sides and would be coordinated by their respective Foreign offices. While referring to cooperation in nuclear field in a brief press conference, President Putin said that Russia was willing to enhance its cooperation with India to increase the capacity in nuclear power generation beyond the Koodankulam project within the framework of international rules and obligations. He stated, "We are ready, we are prepared, and want to develop our relations with India including in nuclear field.'[42] But at the same time he emphasized the need to tighten international restrictions against states possessing nuclear weapons and alarmed about the possibility of failing in the hands of terrorists. While sharing India's concerns on Pakistan -sponsored cross-border terrorism in Jammu and Kashmir President Putin said "that everything should be done in order to settle all the disputes including the dispute between India and Pakistan by peaceful means." In a joint statement, " Both sides stressed the importance of Islamabad implementing in full its obligations and promises to prevent the infiltration of terrorists across the Line of Control into the State of Jammu and Kashmir and at other points across the border, as well as to eliminate the terrorist infrastructure in Pakistan and Pakistan-controlled territory as a prerequisite for the renewal of peaceful dialogue between the two contries to resolve all outstanding issues in a bilateral framework as envisaged in Shimla Agreement of 1972 and the Lahore Declaration of 1998"[43].

Both sides noted that expanded cooperation in the field of military technical cooperation, especially joint research, development and training, as well as inter-services contacts, were consistent with the national security interests of both countries and for the cause of peace and stability in Asia and beyond.[44] In this context President Vajpayee said that India-Russia Defence Cooperation has transcended a buyer-seller relationship and now encompasses joint research, design, development and co-production.

On economic and trade relations, both countries signed *Joint Declaration on Strengthening and Enhancing Economic, Scientific and Technological Cooperation between the Republic of India and Federation of Russia.* This agreement is aimed to change the rules of engagement on economic relations between the two countries from a buyer-seller one to a diversified one where both countries can undertake joint projects in third countries. In this context Mr. Vajpayee said, "We are trying to bring the economic and trade relation up to the level of our political relations."[45] Mr. Putin called for improving the "infrastructure of business" especially in sectors like communications, transport, finance and high technology. Russian President also suggested the conversion of a part of India's debt into setting up of Indo-Russian joint ventures to enhance the bilateral and trade relations between the two countries. He also said that one of the strategic task is development of transport infrastructure. For executing that "We have created a Coordination Council of the International Transport Corridor North South and two special working groups. Such project would help in reviving economic integration on Eurasian Continent"[46]

A Protocol between India and Russia on the Protection and Use of Intellectual Property Right to an existing Scientific and Technological Cooperation agreement, an MOU in the field of communications, an agreement between Karnataka and Samara region of Russia on trade, economic and cultural cooperation and two agreements between Canara bank and a Russian bank were also signed. Canara Bank has agreed to extend a $10 million credit line to address issues relating to acquisition, distribution, protection, sharing and transferring of IPRs, created in the process of joint activity within the framework of the existing 1994 agreement on scientific and technological cooperation.[47] An MOUon cooperation in thefield of *Telecommunications between the Ministry of Communications and Information Technology of India and Ministry of Communications and Information of Russia was also signed.* Under this MOU, the Ministries of Communications of the two countries will exchange information on telecom sector, develop and apply advanced technologies in the field of telecom, and exchange experts and sharing training facilities in this sector.

Conclusion

Despite ups and downs, India's relations with Russia have developed in a unique and specific way and future relations would be sustained by commonality of interests. Without any doubt it can be said that the current Indo- Russian relations are based on the new global reality. In this context President Putin's visit in December 2002 could be seen as reflection of long- standing partnership and continued warm ties between Moscow and New Delhi. However, in the post-Cold War environment both India and Russia have much to accomplish together. It would be more practical to seek a joint venture with Russia, an Indo-Russian consortium for socio-economic development of Central Asia. The region needs to be strengthened as a bulwark against the spread of religious extremism and terrorism. Post 9/11 US has also been playing a key role in this region in close cooperation with Central Asian states and Russia in combating terrorism and fighting al-Qaida forces in Afghanistan. In future one would see US working in partnership with Russia in Central Asian region, while Russia would try to reestablish its hold over this region, US would continue its long term engagement in this region and in many ways would be instrumental in formulating the future course of political and security developments in the region. Long term US military presence in Central Asia is likely to push this region into rivalry among the great powers for gaining influence in this region.

While Pakistan and China are not particularly eager to see India in the Central Asian Region, Russia, Iran and Afghanistan remain an accommodating friends therefore India should try to increase its connectivity to central Asia through these countries as all the three have land borders with CARs. Attempts in this direction have already been initiated. In the new unfolding situation India should try to counterbalance Pakistan in the region while cooperating with the US and Russia. It is already in a process of forging its ties both at bilateral and multilateral level with CARs, Russia, Iran, Afghanistan and US. These powers have a shared interest in security and stability in Central Asia and Afghanistan. Asia is possibly the only continent still beset with perennial conflicts.

Perhaps a regional grouping of India, Russia, Iran, CARs, Afghanistan can constructively address the existing problems in the region and work towards the strengthening of strategic stability in Asia.

References

1. Igor S. I vanov, *The New Russian Diplomacy*, The Nixon Center and Brookings Institution Press, Washington D.C., 2002. p. 141.

2. Vladimir Radyuhin, "Russia-NATO defence pact for Europe", *Hindu*, 14 May 2003.

3. For details see Meena Singh Roy, "India's Interest in Central Asia" *Strategic Analyses* Vol (2) Jan March 2001 pp. and "Russia and Central Asia Problems and Prospects" *Strategic Analyses*, Vol. 25 (3) June 2001.

4. Atul Aneja"Central Asia is our extended neighbourhood. says Sinha", Hindu (Delhi), February 2, 2003.

5. Uwe Halback and Heinrich Tiller," Russia and its Southern Flanck", Aussenpolitik English ed,) Vol. 45, no. 2, 1994, p. 56-157,162; and Boris Z. Rumor, "The Gathering Storm in Central Asia", Orbis, Vol. 3 (1), Winter 1993, p. 90.

6. Irina Zviagelskaia, "The Russian policy Debate on Central Asia", former Soviet Project, The Royal Institute of International Affairs London, 1995, p. I

7. Radio Free Europe/Radio Liberty Central Asia Report vol. 3, no. 16, May 2003.

8. ITAR-TASS news agency Moscow, As reported in BBC Global Momtoring-Central Asia (Henccforth BBC-GM-CA), 30 April 03.)

9. Beshkek government sources claim there are plans to revive several Russian-build military installations along the shore of the Issk-Kul Lake. Before the collapse of the Soviet Union, Krygyz-made underwater military equipment was tested here. Several Kyrgyz defence factories, idle since the collapse of the Soviet Union, are back in operation and working on Russian military hardware. Sultan Jumagulov, "Kyrgyzstan plays" dangerous" game," IWPR'S Reporting Central Asia, no. 150, 1 October 2002.

10. The United States has established a major operations base at Khanabad airbase outside Tashkent in Uzbekisuin, from where it ran the air war in northern afghanistan and coordinated Special Forces operations throughout Mghanistan Eleven coalition countries have set up a

1500-man base at Manas airport in Bishkek, Kyrgyzstan, which now serves as the main transportation hub for supplies to allied forces inside Afghanistan- US officials have surveyed the airbase in Chunkent, in southern Kazakhstan. And in southern Tajikistan, French aircraft are using the Kuliab airbase.

11. Joint Statement of India and the Russian Federation on Strategic Issues, November 6,2001, <www.meadev.nic.in/jt.stmt.moscow>

12. Valadimir Radyuhin,, "Pak Must destroy terror reservoirs, says Sinha" Hindu (New Delhi) 18 May 2003.

13. "Russia Opposes Pak.move to raise Kashmir Issue at U.N.", *Hindu*, 7 May 2003.

14. Moscow Declaration between India and the Russian Federation on International Terrorism, November, 2001 "www.meadev. nic.in/ ds.pm.nov.htm.

15. India and Russian Federation Joint Statement, February3, 2002, New.

16. "Securing Central Asia", *The Times of Central Asia (Bishkek)*, Vol.4 (8) (155), February 21, 2002, p. 4.

17. "Central Asian Officials sign Regional Security Pact in Kabul" The Times of Central Asia, Vol.4 (52) (199) December 26, 2002.

18. "KyrgyzstanTaJikistan Drawing up Military Cooperation Accord",

<http //www.cacianalyst.org/view article.php?articleid=713>

19. Joint Statement of India and the Russian Federation on Strategic Issues, November 6,2001, www.meadev.nic.in/jt.stmt.moscow .

20. India and Russian Federation Joint Statement February3, 2002, New Delhi.

21. Sandeep Dikshit "Russia, India to Strengthen Nuclear Cooperation

Hindu (Delhi) April 5, 2002.

22. For greater details see Sergei Blagov "SCO Continues to search for Operational Framework. "<http//www.eurasianet org/departments-linsig+/articlcs/eav06llO2a. shtml>

23. Albert Bagdanov, op. cit.

24. Feng Yujun, Ding Xiaoxing and Li Dong, "Russia's new Energy Diplomacy and Its Impact" Contemporary International Relations,voll2(10) October 2002. p. 2-3.

25. Hoomen peimanni " An Economic and Political pipeline" A httv// www.atimcs.com/atimes/Central-Asia/DK2OAgo2.html.

26. Bruce Pannier, "Central Asia Russia Urges Cooperation in Fight Asainst Drug Trafficking"<*http.//www.eurasianet.org/departments/insight/arficles/pp111602.shtml*>

27. United Front -Controled Badakkhshan has now emerged as the third most important opium-producing province.Poppy cultivation in this province rose from an estimated 2,485ha in 2000 to around 6,3000 in 2001.

28 Tajikistan, EIU Country Report, May 2002, p. 38.

29. "Drug Trafficking emerging as top National Security Threat to Tajikistan", httv//www.eurasiane.org/departments/insight/articles/eav050803.shtml

30. ITAR-TASS newsagency, Moscow, BBC-GM-CA, 30April 03.

31. Anthony Davis and Pieffe-Arnaud Chouvy "Afghanistan's Opium Production Rise Post-Taliban", *Janes Intelligence Review*, Vol. 14(12) 2002, p. 38.

32. More than 50 refineries have begun operation in north in the year 2002.

33. Anthony Davis, no. 25.

34. " Russia Suggests Creating Second Safety Belt" *The Times of Central Asia* (Bishkek), Vol. 2, No. 26 (69), June 29, 2000.

35. " Russia Suggests Creating Second Safety Belt" *The Times of Central Asia* (Bishkek), Vol. 2, No. 26 (69), June 29, 2000.

36. Vladimir Radyuhin, "Palc Must destroy terror reservoirs, says Sinha", Hindu (New Delhi) May 18, 2003.

37. Amit Baruah, "India to build key road in Afghanistan", Hindu, 21 November 2002.

38. *Voice of the Islamic Republic of Iran*, Mashhad, BBC- GM-CA, 6 January 2003.

39. Delhi Declaration on Further Consolidation of Strategic Partnership between the Republic of India and the Russian Federation, December 4 2002. *http//Meadev.nic.in/speeches/4 decdelhi- decorationrussia.htm.*

40. *Ibid.*

41. *Ibid*

42. Joint Press Interaction of H.E. Shri Atal Bihari Vajpayee, Prime Minister of India and H.E. Mr. Vladimir Putin, President of the Russian Federation held at Hyderabad House. December 3 2002. *httpl1meadev.nic.in/news/jointmedia-putin-pm.htm*

43. India Russia Joint Statement, December 4 2002. *http//meadev.nic.in/speeches/ 4decdelhi-jointstmt.htm*

44. India Russia Joint Statement, December 4 2002 *.http.- //meadev.nic.in/speeches/4decdelhi- jointstmt.htm*

45. Joint Declaration on Strengthening and Enhancing Scientific and Technological Cooperation between the Republic of India and the Russian Federation, December 4 2002. *http//meadev.nic.in.speechs/4decdelhi-jointdec.htm* Indrani Bagchi, "Dismantle terror infrastructurePutin p to Pak," *The Economic Times* (New Delhi) December 5, 2002.

46. "Putin for Converting Indian debt into JVs," *The Economic Times*, December 5 2002. Also Joint Declaration on Strengthening and Enhancing, Scientific and Technological Cooperation between the Republic of India and the Russian Federation, December 4 2002.

47. Documents Signed on 4 December 2002 During the visit of the President of the Russian Federation to India from 3-5 December 2002 *http//meadev.nic.in/speeche/4decdelhi-docsingd.htm*

19

Trade Relations between India and Russia

R.L. Varshney

The former USSR was an important trade partner of India. By developing the rupee trade, they kept foreign currencies out of all their trade transactions. As a result, trade between the two increased from Rs.1.3 crore in 1956 to Rs.71800 crores in 1990-91. India's exports increased from Rs.1, 226 crores in 1980-81 to Rs. 5, 255 crores in 1990-91 and her imports increased from Rs.1, 014 croress to Rs. 2, 548 crores during the same period. The USSR accounted for 17 per cent of India's exports in 1990-91 while USSR share in India's imports was 5.9 per cent.

Trade denominated in Indian rupees benefited both the countries. India like the Soviet Union, derived greater advantage as its need to source imports without spending foreign exchange was even more than that of the USSR. India obtained substantial quantities of crude oil and Kerosene and defence equipment and spares from the erstwhile Soviet Union. Other items imported from the USSR were ferrous and non-ferrous metals, newsprint, fertilizers and chemical products.

India's exports consisted of processed foods, spices, jute and coir goods, hosiery, leather goods, paints, chemicals, cosmetics, tea, coffee, pepper, tobacco, drugs and pharmaceuticals, detergents and toiletries. India's dependence on the Soviet Union was substantial. What is more, there was a high degree of instability in the Soviet demand. Nevertheless, Indo-Soviet trade led to diversification of India's export markets and better terms of trade.

Disintegration of Soviet Union

Disintegration of the Soviet Union led to a disruption for many sectors of India's economy and Indo-Russian trade underwent a dramatic change. There are two channels for India's exports to Russia - the debt route (to repay India's debt to Russia) and the convertible currency route. The latter did not become popular because Indian goods were not able to face international competition. The following table gives an idea of the Indo-Russian Trade since 1992-93:

Indo-Russian Trade (Rs. Crores)

Year	*Export*	*Percentage share of India's Exports*	*Imports*	*Percentage share of India's Imports*	*Balance of Trade*
1992-93	1,759	3.3	737	1.2	1,022
1993-94	2,037	2.9	807	1.1	1,230
1994-95	2,534	3.1	1,584	1.8	950
1995-96	3,496	3.3	2,864	2.3	632
1996-97	2,880	2.4	2,231	1.6	649
1997-98	3,542	2.7	2,521	1.6	1,021
1998-99	3,038	2.1	2,221	1.3	817
1999-00	4,108	2.6	2,700	1.3	1,408
2000-01	4,061	2.0	2,365	1.0	1,696

Indian army became the largest recipient of Soviet arms. Even today, 70 per cent of the Indian army, navy and the air force is of Soviet origin. There was a change in the situation with Gorvachov's perestroica when Soviets demanded international prices and were reluctant to provide any long term credit on easy terms. Indian army is still largely dependent on Russia for upkeep and support in spare parts as Soviets never helped indigenisation. The former Defence Minister Jaswant Singh publicly said India needed to reduce its dependence on Russian arms.

A perusal of the above table shows that Indo-Russian trade has shown an uneven trend and that there is a precipitate decline as compared to the Indo-USSR trade. However, the balance of trade continues to be in India's favour. Another significant fact is that although Russian imports showed decline in 1999, India's exports to Russia showed an increase.

Russia is an open economy now and consumer goods from across the world are available in plenty. Russian consumers are becoming discriminatory. Unfortunately, the impression about Indian goods seems to be one of poor quality. Some Indian exporters have also indulged in fraud. Much of the goodwill and brand awareness that existed for Indian goods seems to have wiped out.

No doubt, Russia provides a large market estimated at about $20 billion. It is growing by 4 to 6 per cent every year especially for foodstuffs, beverages, textiles, leather goods, consumer electronics and cosmetics. The emphasis is on goods satisfying basic needs. Because of easy availability of foreign goods, Russians have learnt to demand the best; Hence quality of goods supplied should never be compromised. Russian inspection is stringent and mistakes are severely punished. Also, prices quoted should be competitive. Russians not only have excellent market intelligence network worldwide but also a system of checks and balance. They also enjoy bargaining and some margin may be provided for this. Unless attention is paid to these aspects, we might lose our market share.

Tea, leather garments and tobacco are just some of the sectors that have been taken over by other countries, including Sri Lanka and China, to a large extent. In fact, were it not for debt repayment arrangement whereby Russia buys Indian goods in return for defence purchases, Indo-Russian trade would have been lower.

Diversification Needed

India's exports need not be confined to a few limited numbers of commodities. India is exporting goods worth $8.5 billion a year to the USA, about $10 billion to the European Union and $4.7 billion to Japan. A good part of these exports is manufactured goods from engineering goods to sophisticated electronic items, textiles and processed foods. Russia should not find it difficult to accept these items. These items have already carved a niche for themselves in the TRAID markets. Of course, we should continue to export products like tea, cotton textiles, pharmaceuticals, yam, readymade garments, fertilizers, etc.

India should continue to benefit from Russian equipment and technology in exploration, extraction and transportation of hydrocarbons, construction of thermo-hydro nuclear power plants and high tension transmission lines, modernizing and widening highways and space exploration. Attempts should also be made to obtain as much crude oil, petroleum derivatives, coking and power generation coals as possible.

One of the important items that could be added to Russian exports is high quality stones. In the past, Indian and Russian diamond industries only worked together via De Beers. With the dismantling of De Beers' global monopoly in diamonds, this could add a new sparkle to Indo-Russian ties. Indian diamond merchant would be able to obtain diamonds at a cheaper rate.

In must be admitted, however, that the shared ground between India and Russian interests is shrinking not expanding. Putin is interested in reviving Russia and in attracting foreign capital and India cannot do much in this respect. Russia would prefer to be a part of Western Economic system. Under the Putin Doctrine, India is just a place to make quick money through arms sale. Pramit Pal Chaudhry, "Why the Indo-Russian Relationship is going nowhere in a hurry", Hindustan Times.com., December 16, 2002.

Another area of Indo-Russian cooperation could be import of Russian gold and joint production and sales of gold jewellery not only for meeting the requirements of the local population of the two countries but also exporting them to third countries.

Collaboration in aircraft manufacture could be another field of Indo-Russian cooperation. Russia is still the only country apart form the USA and the European Union to have capacity to manufacture aircraft. While Boeing (USA) and Airbus Industries (European Union) are the only aircraft manufacturers, Russia has the capacity for manufacturing aircraft for short-haul routes.

Possible Measures for Greater Cooperation

Some possible measures for greater cooperation between India and Russia could be:

1. Exploration of 60 Production Possibilities

Indian and Russian firms could enter into co-production and sales arrangements for the conversion into finished goods of mutually supplied raw and other materials, their packaging and delivery to end users. A beginning has already been made in Russia's light and food industry and in packaging and sales of medicines, tea, office and spices bought in India. Such co-production and marketing can be extended to other India made products.[1]

2. Establishment of Joint Ventures

Russia and India have agreed to set up a joint venture to make the spares necessary to maintain aircrafts of Russian origin in India, Again, India is still heavily dependent on Soviet arms and there have been problems connected with the availability of spare parts. Joint ventures could be established to produce these parts in India for use in India and export to other countries that use Soviet Equipment. Though 256 joint ventures with participation of Indian firms with an investment of $18 million were registered in Russia, they were engaged mainly in short-tenn trade operations and not in setting up industrial ventures in Russia. Indian companies should find it interesting to step into Russia with joint venture arrangements. Companies like Ranbaxy or Cipla in the field of pharmaceuticals, Hindustan Lever in the field of detergents and Britannia in the field of biscuits, could find it interesting to work out joint venture arrangements with suitable Russian private enterprises. Financing of some of these joint ventures could come from the Rupee Debt finds available to the Russian enterprises.[3]

Role of Chambers of Commerce

The Federation of Indian Chambers of Commerce and Industry (FICCI) has been playing a major role to promote cooperation between Indian and Russian businessmen. FICCI has set up a composite agenda for firms and Governments of both the countries to be implemented in the first decade of this century, CII also organised a delegation to Russia in September 2000. It organised another delegation to Russia in September 2001 with the participation of major Indian companies, to examine ways of setting up joint ventures, joint investment, joint marketing of each others' products, etc. To enhance bilateral trade relationships, the Russian Federation, the Confederation of Indian Industry (CII) has opened a representative office in Moscow in October 2001. All these efforts will definitely lead to improvement in Indo-Russian trade and economic relations.

References

1. German Graf, Russo-India Trade and Economic cooperation, The Economic Times, October 2, 2000.
2. Girija Nair, The Enduring Relation, The Economic Times, December 21, 1998.
3. The Economic Times, November 2, 2001.

20

Economic and Trade Relations Between India and Russia

R.K. Wadhwa

Economic and trading relations between India and the Soviet Russia dates back to fifth century when American merchants had established trade relations with the Indian people. In the Seventeenth century a group of Armenians settled in Kokatta and played an important role in the economic life of the country. Indian traders were also active at Astrakhan and in the Volga delta region during the same period. Indian black pepper, ginger, sandalwood, handloom and other commodities were, thus well known in ancient and medieval Russia. After the victory of the Great October Socialist Revolution in Russia, the first Soviet products to enter the Indian market, in 1925, were crude oil, petrol, kerosene and sugar. But trade contacts between the two countries were reduced to nil by the British colonialists. However, the first Soviet trade agency was established in Kolkata in 1943 and her trade ties with India, though very much restricted, revealed the wide potential of expansion once India gained Independence.

In the independent India, the trade relations between the two countries ushered with the conclusion of an agreement in 1950 on regular sea communication followed by a barter agreement in 1951 for the supply of Soviet wheat in exchange for Indian tea and jute. During the period 1951-2001, there have been a number of agreements (usually covering a span of five years to suit the planning process) between the two countries directed at developing and strengthening the trade and economic relations. Since the signing of first agreement in 1950s, the bilateral trading relationship has broadened, deepened and been institutionalized within a framework of special payments arrangements designed to balance exports and imports. These agreements have been based on the principle of equality and mutual benefit.

Indo-Russia trade relations occupy an important place in a comprehensive and diverse complex of politico-economic relations between the two countries. Starting with a modest trade turnover of Rs 1.56 crore in 1950-51, the Indo-Soviet trade registered a phenomenal and impressive growth at Rs 7800 crore in 1990-91. As a result total trade turnover between the two countries increased from 0.12 per cent of India's total trade in 1950-51 to a peak level of 11.63 per cent in 1980-81. While India's exports to USSR grew from 0.22 per cent in 1950-51 to 18.27 per cent during 1980-81, India's imports from USSR rose from 0.034 per cent to 8 per cent during the period. The decade of 80s experienced a decline in India's exports and imports that stood at 17 per cent and 5.9 per cent respectively. The sluggishness in the trade could be attributed to collapsing prices of oil and oil products that created difficulties in Indo-Soviet trade and settlement. The following graph shows the trend in Indo-Russia bilateral trade during 1950-51 to 2001-02 (Data in Table 1)

The phenomenal growth in Indo-Soviet trade during the first four decades could also be attributed to the rupee-rouble clearing -house arrangements- the key to the bilateral balanced trade deals between India and the USSR- which have had several attractions for India development finance , export expansion, guaranteed markets for products that were uncompetitive on world markets, trade diversification, and hard-currency conservation.

Following the break - up of Soviet Union, while Russia's international trade has been growing, India's share has been falling. Indo-Russia trade turnover has drastically declined from US $ 5.5 billion in 1991 to US $ 1.3 billion in 2001. In rupee terms it has slumped from Rs. 7800 crore to Rs. 6337 crore-a fall of 18.76 per cent. A sharp decline in the total trade was witnessed in the year 1992-93 immediately after the disintegration-a fall of 66.53 per cent in exports and 68 per cent in imports Though in absolute terms the trade has recovered in subsequent years, in percentage terms the share has continued to decline. One of the reasons for the decline in Indo-Russia trade could be that the bulk of the trade was being conducted with other republics of the USSR. Secondly, during the days of Soviet Union, public sector was playing an important role in setting up industrial units and it found economic cooperation with the Soviet Union more beneficial. The imports were paid for either in rupee or by exporting a part of the output of units set up with Soviet collaboration. Liberalisation, privatisation, and globalisation are the other important developments, which have been instrumental for both the countries to look towards west and European Union.

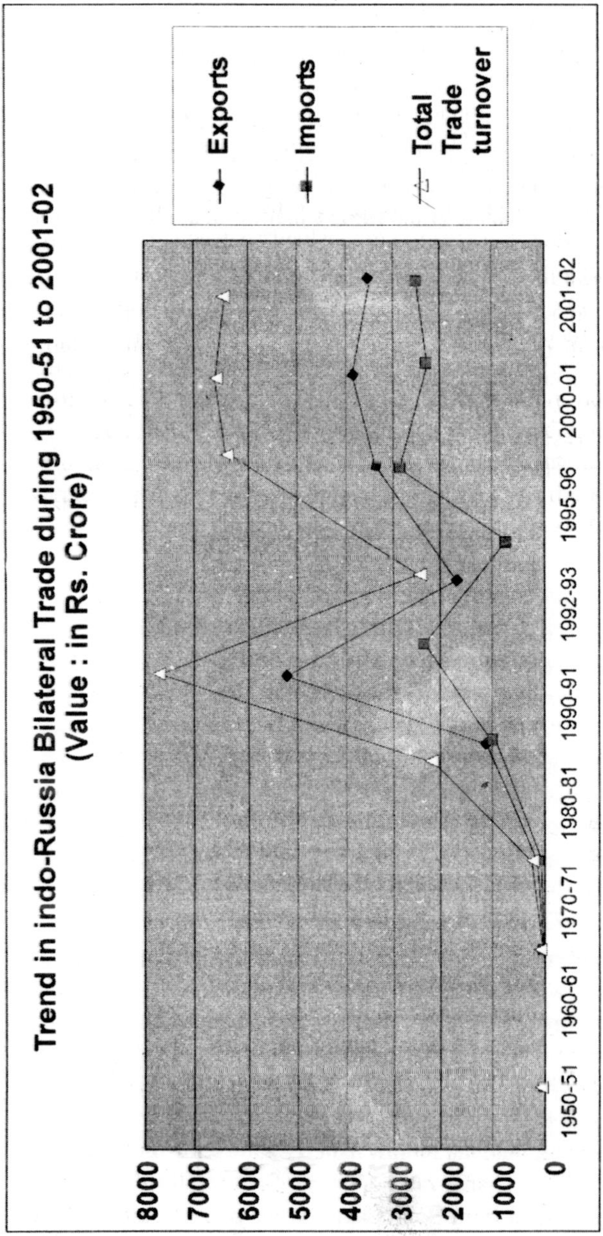
Trend in indo-Russia Bilateral Trade during 1950-51 to 2001-02
(Value : in Rs. Crore)
Exports
Imports
Total Trade turnover
8000
7000
6000
5000
4000
3000
2000
1000
0
1950-51
1960-61
1970-71
1980-81
1990-91
1992-93
1995-96
2000-01
2001-02

In spite of the continued decline in trade turnover, India continues to enjoy a favourable balance of trade with Russia. But the favourable balance of trade is somewhat misleading as the trade figures do not include the purchase of Russian defence equipment by India payment for which are made through Indian exports.

It is worthwhile mentioning here apart from the official trade between the two countries, substantial amount of Indian goods enter Russia either by way of shuttle trade (brought by Russians visiting India in large numbers) or through export of Indian-origin goods to Russia from Singapore, Hong Kong, Thailand, Malaysia and Middle East. Similarly, India purchases industrial raw materials of Russian origin (e.g. metals scraps, fertilisers, paper and paper products) from Canada, USA and Israel due to absence of established Russian international marketing mechanisms.

According to the Russian State Customs Committee, shuttle trade accounts for an estimated import of US $ 10 billion annually into Russia, one-fourth of its regular global imports. Main countries from which such shuttle trade imports arrive are Turkey, Finland, China, Saudi Arabia, and Cyprus. Export figures of such shuttle trade from India is, however, difficult to estimate.

Pattern of Russia's International Trade

The disintegration of the Soviet Union in 1991 into 15 independent republics has had adverse effects on the economic and trade fronts. Firstly, the economy experienced a decline in the output that reached at its low point by early 1997. Secondly, the collapse of rouble in 1998 led to a decline in its foreign trade and slowed down the economic growth. Russia's total foreign trade turnover which witnessed an increase of 83.5 per cent from US $ 75 billion to US $ 137 billion during the period 1992-97 dropped to 16.8 per cent and 25.3 per cent in 1998 and 1999 respectively over the 1997 level. The following graph shows the trend in International Trade of Russia during 1992-2000. (Data in Table 2)

The disruption of payment arrangements with other former Soviet republics (alongwith their ability to pay) and the evident constraints of the autarky attempted under communism made integration with the world economy a priority for reformers. The continued reform process, however, gave a boost to growth in foreign trade that witnessed a rise of 33.2 per cent in 2000 over the previous year. The main spurs for this export growth were weak domestic demand for raw materials and semi-finished goods, an undervalued rouble exchange rate and the profit to be gained from diverting previously subsidized intra-Soviet exports on to hard-currency markets

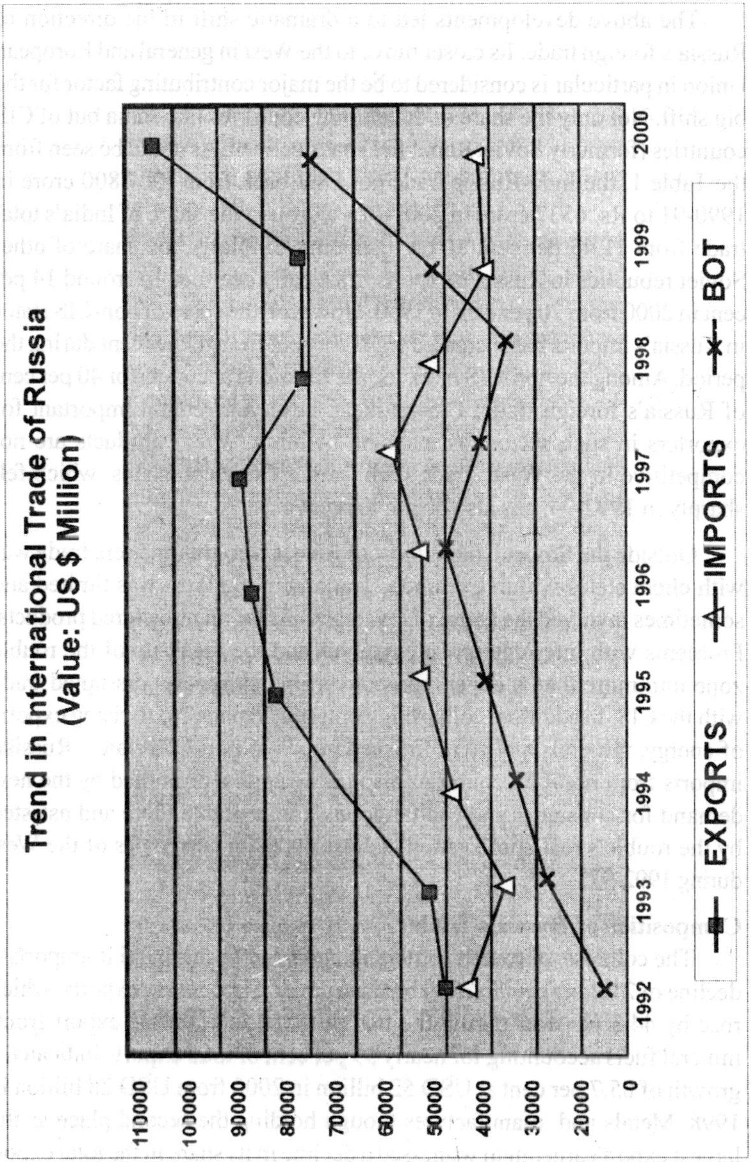
Trend in International Trade of Russia
(Value: US $ Million)
110000
100000
90000
80000
70000
60000
50000
40000
30000
20000
0
1992
1993
1994
1995
1996
1997
1998
1999
2000
EXPORTS
IMPORTS
BOT

where world prices could be charged.

Direction of Trade

The above developments led to a dramatic shift in the direction of Russia's foreign trade. Its closer move to the West in general and European Union in particular is considered to be the major contributing factor for the big shift. Not only the share of developing countries like India but of CIS countries (formerly Soviet Republics) has declined. As could be seen from the Table 1, the Indo-Russia trade got a set back from Rs. 7800 crore in 1990-91 to Rs. 6337 crore in 2001-02 - a drop in the share of India's total trade from 11.45 per cent to 1.15 per cent. Similarly, the share of other Soviet republics in Russia's exports drastically declined to around 14 per cent in 2000 from 70 per cent in 1990. However, the share of non-CIS states in Russia's imports has increased to 70 per cent from 47 per cent during the period. Among the non-CIS markets, the EU alone accounts for 40 per cent of Russia's foreign trade. CIS markets, however, remain important for exporters in such sectors as machine building, where products are not competitive in the West. Trade with former Comecon states, which fell sharply in 1992-94, has also begun to recover.

Outside the Soviet Union, most of Russia's communist-era trade was with client states within Common. Trade with the West was limited and sometimes involved the barter of raw materials for manufactured products. Problems with inter-enterprise payments and the break-up of the rouble zone into more than a dozen non-convertible currencies disrupted trade with the CIS. In addition, collapsing domestic demand led to rising exports of energy, minerals and semi finished goods to non-CIS states. Russian imports from non-CIS countries also grew rapidly, prompted by the new demand for consumer and capital goods not available there and assisted by the rouble's real appreciation against the main currencies of the West during 1992-97.

Composition of Russia's Trade

The collapse of rouble in 1998 not only led to sharp fall in imports-a decline of 21.2 per cent in 2000 but also gave a big boost to exports, which rose by 44.3 per cent during the two years period. On the export front, mineral fuels accounting for nearly 59 per cent of total exports indicated a growth of 85.7 per cent at USD 52 billion in 2000 from USD 28 billion in 1998. Metals and manufactures though holding the second place as the largest export earner item witnessed a decline in its share in the total export earnings from 24.5 per cent in 1998 to 18.9 per cent in 2000. In absolute terms, however, it grew by 12.7 per cent. Share of other principal items in the export basket namely, machinery and transport equipment, chemicals, and pulp, paper, wood and manufactures also dropped during the period.

The import bill is mainly dominated by the import of machinery and transport equipment, and metals and manufactures which together consitute more than one-third of total imports. While the share of machinery and transport equipment has dropped to 27.2 per cent in 2000 from 31.5 per cent in 1998 that of metals and manufactures has risen to 8.3 per cent from 6.9 per cent. However, in absolute terms import of machinery and transport equipment dropped by 33.5 per cent in 2000 at USD 8.1 billion from USD 12.2 billion in 1998, and that of metals and manufactures by 7.1 per cent at USD 2.5 billion from USD 2.7 billion during the period. The only item, which has grown in, imports both in absolute terms and the percentage share during the period is the textiles and clothing. In absolute terms it indicated an increase of 18.1 per cent in 2000 at USD 1.3 billion from USD 1.1 billion in 1998 while in terms of percentage share it has gone up from 2.9 per cent to 4.5 per cent. Food, beverages and tobacco constituting 20.6 per cent of total import is the second largest item in the import basket followed by chemicals having a share of 16.9 per cent.

Composition of Indo-Russia Trade

There has been a major shift in the composition of India's exports to Russia. As supplier of traditional and low value items like black pepper, tea, ginger, jute, sandalwood, handloom, etc. to the ancient and medieval Russia, India has now emerged as supplier of non-traditional and valued added items to Russia. During the year 2001-02 readymade garments as a group accounting for 39 per cent of India's exports to Russia has witnessed a five times increase over 1995-96 which reflects that the Indian garments have wide acceptance among Russian consumers and is continuously growing. As against this export of cotton yarn, fabrics and made ups having witnessed a steady growth till 2000-01 suddenly dropped by 66.2 per cent. Tea, which was occupying the top position in the export basket till 1998-99, registered a fall of 57.6 per cent in 2001-02. The drastic fall in exports of tea could be attributed to stiff competition from other global suppliers like Sri Lanka. Export of drugs and pharmaceuticals has shown an upward trend over the last few years. Other potential items in the India's export basket to Russia include coffee, tobacco unmanufactured, electronic goods, machinery and instruments, plastic and linoleum products, and castor oil.

As regards imports, though fertilizers constitute one-fourth of India's total imports from Russia, its demand over the years has dropped by 32.8 per cent. Similarly import demand of iron and steel and non-ferrous metals have dropped by 16.4 per cent and 3.3 per cent respectively. As against this demand for synthetic and reclaimed rubber rose by nearly eight times during 1995-96 to 2001-02. Other principal items of import from Russia include non-electrical machinery, and coal and coke briquettes.

Prospects of Trade and Economic Cooperation

India and Russia continue to sustain the close and cordial political relations in the post Soviet era. In recent years both the countries have been pursuing the course for establishing a strategic partnership that is regarded as the ultimate form of relationship between the two independent states. This goal indeed demands that the present relationship be enhanced to a qualitatively new level, particularly in the trade and economic spheres. This is reflected in the exchange of visits between the two countries at the levels of heads of state and prime ministers, besides other political levels, exchange of trade delegations, etc. Several agreements and Memorandum of Understandings have been signed during these exchanges to further strengthen the economic relations. These agreements covering bilateral cooperation have been in the areas of telecommunications, air services, business, cultural, tourism, industrial, financial, and scientific fields.

Several initiatives have also been taken by the Government of India to get Russian regions interested in India. In order to promote cooperation with the regions a Working Group has been set up under the Inter-governmental Joint Commission, the apex decision body for shaping bilateral ties. To encourage bilateral ties in the education field, the Government of India announced a grant of ten million roubles for opening a Centre for Indian Studies in the local universities of Russia.

Under the 1993 agreement, India makes an annual debt repayment of about Rs. 3000 crore to Russia. These repayment funds are maintained in a Central account in the RBI which is used for purchase of goods and trade related services from India. Russia is free to import all goods and trade related services from India permissible under Indian Export Import Policy utilising Rupee Repayment Funds. The mechanism of the debt repayment was that the Russian Government would allocate the Rupee Repayment Funds to various state bodies, regions, ministries, and Russian firms for utilising the same for importing from India. However, the above mechanism did not find favour in promoting exports from India, as the organisations that were allocated funds were neither interested to import from India nor used it for genuine imports.

The Russian Government, therefore, took a decision that effective from I January 1998, it would not allocate funds to various organisations but dispose of the funds through weekly auctions to be conducted through the BFEA. The auction system proved to be transparent and helped a number of Indian companies in promoting their exports. However, following the financial crisis in August 1998, the Government again decided to revert back to the allocation system in favour of various State organisations and the auction system was, therefore, stopped in October 1998. It is reported that the allocation system is more transparent and finds favour with both Russian imports and Indian exports.

Another area where both the countries can strengthen the bilateral ties is the rough diamonds, gems and jewellery sector. Russia being one of the largest producers of the diamonds in the world has an estimated production of 14 million carats, 80 per cent of which goes to the world market for sale through various channels. As against this India has the largest diamond processing capacity in the world and processes more than 100 million carats of rough diamonds out of the total estimated world annual production of 120 million carats. Having its strength in the processing, cutting and polishing of rough diamonds, India accounts for 80 per cent of the total annual trade of the polished diamonds.

Besides, Russia with an estimated production capacity of around 150 tons of gold per annum can find India a ready market because of its large consumption of gold, which is supplemented by the import to the tune of US $ 7 billion.

Besides, Russia with an estimated production capacity of around 150 tons of gold per annual can find India a ready market because of its large consumption of gold, which is supplemented by the import to the tune of US $ 7 billion.

Conclusion

In view of the long-standing cordial, political, and economic relations between India and Russia, the prospects of strengthening Indo-Russia trade ties are bright. The recent visit (third in 26 months) of the Russian President Putin to India is a testimony to strengthen the Indo-Russian ties. Several agreements, including a joint declaration on strengthening and enhancing cooperation in the economic, science and technology, telecom and IPR spheres were signed. The Delhi Declaration consolidated existing strategic partnership and charted out a broad agenda for cooperation in areas considered strategically important for both countries, and reiterated their commitment to tackling international terrorism. Taking a stock of the earlier agreements, leaders of both the states have recognized that there was a need to boost bilateral economic relations that have stagnated and even gone down over the last few years, and finally to take forward the long-standing defence cooperation between the two countries. It is believed that the current Putin visit will provide the much-needed direction in the economic and investment fields, the results of which may be apparent in a year's time. However, from the Indian side there is a need to broaden its narrow vision of a US-centric worldview and establish itself as a formidable global player.

As regards trade relations, some blame can be put on to the attitude of our businessmen who have tended to take close relations with Russia for granted and did not pay much attention on the quality of their goods. This type of attitude has paved the way for other countries; especially China and Sri Lanka, to make inroads into sectors like tea and leather garments that were earlier dominated by Indian businessmen. It would be pertinent to mention that had the debt repayment mechanism not been there where Russia buys Indian goods in return for defence purchases, the Indo-Russia trade would have been much lower. It is, therefore, high time that the Indian exporters should lay more emphasis on improving the quality of their goods and make them more competitive to make a mark in the now competitive Russian market. Concerted efforts may also be made on fostering joint ventures to enhance cooperation in hi-tech, scientific and energy related areas.

Table 1

Trend in Indo-Russia Trade during 1950-51 to 2001-02

(Value in Rs. Crore)

Year	*Exports*	*% Share*	*Imports*	*% Share*	*Total Trade*	*% Share*
1950-51	1.34	0.22	0.22	0.034	1.56	0.12
1960-61	29	4.36	16	1.39	45	2.48
1970-71	210	13.66	105	6.40	315	9.92
1980-81	1226	18.27	1014	8.08	2240	11.63
1990-91	5255	17.00	2548	5.9	7800	11.45
1992-93	1759	3.30	737	1.20	2496	2.25
1995-96	3496	3.30	2864	2.30	6360	2.80
2000-01	4061	2.00	2365	1.00	6426	1.50
2001-02	3787	1.82	2550	1.05	6337	1.15

Note. Figures from 1950-51 to 1990-91 relate to Indo-USSR Trade and from 1992-93 Onwards with Indo-Russia Trade.

Source. DGCIandS Kolkata.

Table 2

Trends in International Trade of Russia

(Value us $ million)

Years	*Exports*	*% Change*	*Imports*	*% Change*	*BOT*	*% Change*
1992	39931	-	34981	-	4950	-
1993	44047	10.3	26751	-23.5	17296	249.4
1994	63078	43.2	38600	44.3	24478	41.5
1995	77595	23.0	46399	20.2	31196	27.4
1996	83979	8.2	44504	-4.1	39475	26.5
1997	85077	1.3	52400	17.7	32676	-17.2
1998	71389	-16.1	42939	-18.1	28450	-12.9
1999	72453	1.5	30286	-29.5	42167	48.2
2000	102998	42.2	33853	11.8	69145	64.0

Source. Direction of Trade Statistics, IMF 2001.

References

1. Direction of Trade Statistics, IMF, 2001.
2. EIU Reports.
3. Centre for Monitoring Indian Economy.
4. DGCIandS, Kolkata.
5. Financial Express, December 8, 2002.
6. Indo-Soviet and India's Economic Development.
7. Soviet relation with India and Vietnam.

21

Indo-Russian Trade : Trends and Prospects

Shri Prakash

The present Research Paper is being produced inorder to answer a few precise questions which have a bearing both on a comparative analysis of Indo-Soviet and Indo-Russian trade and future prospects for the latter.

It is not very logical to compare Indo-Soviet with Indo-Russia trade unless one also takes into account the fact that in terms of size as well as population U.S.S.R. was several times larger than the present Russian Federation. One should not only compare like with like but also note the differences when changes take place in either of the entities being compared. The overall value of USSR's trade was about 152 billion US dollars (USD) in 1981 and 192 billion USD in 1985 (c.f. Table I) compared to this total the value of the overall trade of the Russian Federation was about 150 billion US Dollars (ISD) in 1996 and 149 billion USD in 2000, which respectively was about 99 per cent of the value of USSR's trade in and per cent of the 5 total trade value (Table IV). It is obvious that compared to the days of the Soviet Union Russia is trading on a much bigger scale since in the Soviet era Russia was not paid separately for her exports and also could not regulate imports according to its own national requirements but had to cater to the needs of a much larger social entity. As the data in Table I shows the Soviet Union in the 1980s had usually a small surplus in its balance of trade the value of its exports being move than its imports. However, this did not take into account the values of its inter-provincial trade which are now included in the profile of Russia's trade as 'trade with other countries'. The extent to which this could affect our view of the trade of now individual and independent countries can be seen when we compare countries Indo-Soviet trade with Indo-Russian trade.

On the face of it the overall value of Indo-Soviet trade was much larger than those of Indo-Russia trade today. When one considers the data in Table I and Table III, it is evident that India's annual trade with the Soviet Union was worth 3.3 billion USD in 1981 and 4.2 billion in 1985. India's trade with Russia was worth 1.4 billion USD in 1996 and 1.6 billion in 2000. It ranged from 48 per cent to 33 per cent of the value of Indo-Soviet trade. This is perhaps no commensurate with the size of the Russia market as compared to the Soviet market. The principal reason for India not being able to retain its share of the Soviet or the Russian markets is the greater competition it faces from global players. Where as Soviet Union's principal trade partners where mainly communist countries or newly independent ex-colonial nations. USA's share of Soviet trade in 1981 was just 1.7 per cent and that of U.K. 1.4 per cent. In the same year Cuba's share of Soviet trade was 4.4. per cent and German Democratic Republic had 9.7 per cent. India's share at 1.7 per cent was the same in 1981 as that of USA's and at 2.2 per cent in 1985 was more than that of USA's which was 1.9 per cent.

The situation in relation to Russia's trade partners has changed United Germany in 1996 had 15 per cent of Russia's trade. (cf. Table II) Ukraine at 9.2 per cent was the second largest trading partner USA had 5.3 per cent of Russia's trade in 1996 and China 3.8 per cent which was more than that of India and China. The vastly different trade profile of Russia could be explained by the new loans and credits it could get from new trading partners as well as the exchange agreements selling military equipment and buying commodities as with China. Price and quality accounted for the fact that Tea and Coffee were bought not only against Rupee holdings in India, but also in hard currency from other sources. Between 1996 and 2000 Indo-Russian trade except for one year increased from 1397 million USD in 1996 to 1638 million in 2000 or by 17 per cent, when Russia's total trade value (Table IV) not only fluctuated but was approximately the same in 2000 as in 1996. (Table III) when we compare the commodity composition of Soviet trade in the 1980s with that of Russia in the 1990's the biggest change is in the diminished share of Petroleum products in Russia's exports. It hovered around an average of 30 per cent compared to the 51 per cent in Soviet days. An increase in the share of pharmaceuticals in Russia's trade is another feature of the post Soviet period. The share of food items remains more or less the same.

When the commodity composition of India's trade with Russia is considered along with that of Russia's overall trade one can see that India's share of pharmaceuticals, tea, textiles etc. imports is a small one. AE 1 billion USD India had 20 per cent of the 5 billion worth of pharma products imported into Russia in 1997-1999 period. The 1.9 billion USD worth of Tea and Coffee India exported to Russia in 1999 was much less than half of the total value of Tea and Coffee imported by Russia. Similarly, the 1.3 billion USD worth of textile exports from India was less than 20 per cent of the overall textile imports into Russia. India was exporting far fewer cars and computer software, sugar preparations, milk products than it actually could. (Cf. Table IV and V). Thus, Indian business has to work hard to become competitive in the Russian markets. Its handicapped by higher transport costs which must be countered by setting up joint ventures to manufacture these items in Russia and by extending provide bank credits to facilitate imports from India no longer against government guarantees but on the strength of its price and quality

It is well known that the better part of Russia's Rupee holdings will be used up by 2005. The new military agreements signed between Russia and India are being paid for a Dollars so they will not generate new rupee reserves. However, India's exports are growing precisely to the Developed markets like USA, Europe, Japan, ASEAN, China etc. So with proper arrangements for transport and payments and better quality their prospects in Russia too should be optimistic. This is borne out by existing trends. The most recent economic Report on Russia by Mckinsey after a thorough analyses predicts an annual growth rate of 8 per cent for Russia's GDP during the decade (2000-2010) (cf. Mckinsey's plan for Russia, Economic and Political Weekly Nov.10, 2001, pp. 4300). With Russia accumulating international currency reserves due to its trade surplus it can both pay off its debts and finance the needed imports. Both with China and India, military purchases from Russia compensate it for short falls in commodity trade. Given the likely strategic situation in Asia, where a balance of power is needed to keep the peace, Russia is likely to retain its number two place in the arms exports field. This too will help to boost its foreign exchange reserves and sustain its external trade as will to prevailing high prices for petroleum products and natural gas. Given the mark up in the value of its natural resources Russia looks to be a growing market for which India should compete keenly.

Table I : Union of Soviet Socialist Republics, Direction and value of Trade

(in million of US Dollars)

Country	*Year 1981 Imports*	*Exports*	*Total*	*Year 1982 Imports*	*Exports*	*Total*	*Year 1983 Imports*	*Exports*	*Total*
World	72824	79176	152000	77652	87107	164759	80410	91340	171750
German Democratic Republic	7132	7662	14794	7951	8853	16804	8901	9146	18047
Czechoslovakia	5680	6074	11754	6514	6961	13475	7315	7900	15215
Poland	4457	6837	11294	5640	6637	12277	6460	7091	13551
Hungary	4566	4585	9151	5157	5112	10269	5407	5460	10867
FRG	3740	5040	8780	4010	5606	9616	4535	5471	10004
Cuba	2840	3819	6659	3729	4318	8047	3634	4574	8209

Country	*Year 1981 Imports*	*Exports*	*Total*	*Year 1982 Imports*	*Exports*	*Total*	*Year 1983 Imports*	*Exports*	*Total*
Finland	3768	3175	6943	3851	3304	7155	3630	3341	6971
Japan	3062	1132	4194	4028	1043	5071	2936	1115	4051
USA	2300	254	2554	2875	213	3083	2119	444	2563
France	2304	3500	5804	1745	3160	4905	2331	3259	5590
India	1846	1475	3321	2029	1434	3463	1418	1711	3129
Canada	1905	N.A.	1905	1874	N.A.	1874	1724	N.A.	1724
Italy	1386	3444	4830	1682	3949	5631	1938	4034	5972
U.K.	1188	895	2083	1036	1121	2157	853	1594	2447

Country	*Year 1981 Imports*	*Exports*	*Total*	*Year 1982 Imports*	*Exports*	*Total*	*Year 1983 Imports*	*Exports*	*Total*
Australia	745	N.A	745	701	N.A	701	546	N.A	546
Switzerland	699	460	1159	575	764	1339	487	688	1175
China	130	115	245	142	166	308	314	344	658
Egypt	370	338	708	416	302	718	481	343	824
Afghanistan	439	470	909	383	569	952	370	540	910
Spain	519	380	899	229	219	448	337	430	767
Iran	649	567	1216	259	796	1055	509	752	1261
Iraq	5	1255	1260	25	1346	1371	516	500	1016
Vietnam	231	1004	1235	284	1109	1393	317	1216	1533
Malaysia	242	N.A	242	323	N.A	323	333	N.A	333
Singapore	94	N.A	94	56	N.A	56	88	N.A	88
Pakistan	67	106	173	97	98	195	91	105	196

Country	*Year 1984 Imports*	*Exports*	*Total*	*Year 1985 Imports*	*Exports*	*Total*
World	80623	91650	172273	93475	98023	191498
German Democratic Republic	9092	9218	18310	10218	10351	20569
Czechoslovakia	7426	8121	15547	8911	9217	18128
Poland	6537	7478	14015	7474	8815	16289
Hungary	5472	5324	10796	6560	6168	12728
FRG	4166	5589	9755	4387	5750	10137
Cuba	4275	4623	8898	5600	5207	10807
Finland	2847	2983	5830	3634	3110	6244
Japan	2535	1035	3570	3094	1253	4347
USA	3491	377	3868	3215	441	3656
France	2193	3015	5208	2169	2941	5110
India	1570	1894	3464	2028	2128	4156
Canada	1731	N.A.	1731	1283	N.A.	1283
Italy	1635	3889	5524	1792	3338	5130
U.K.	1011	1716	2727	938	1648	2586

Country	*Year 1984 Imports*	*Exports*	*Total*	*Year 1985 Imports*	*Exports*	*Total*
Australia	,593	N.A.	593	720	N.A.	720
Switzerland	537	668	1205	777	520	1297
China	692	577	1269	1118	1035	2153
Egypt	333	341	674	409	382	791
Afghanistan	375	733	1108	437	744	1181
Spain	378	410	788	478	317	795
Iran	298	299	597	194	276	470
Iraq	826	336	1162	753	362	1115
Vietnam	318	1237	1555	379	1576	1955
Malaysia	265	N.A.	265	244	N.A.	244
Singapore	250	N.A.	250	108	N.A.	108
Pakistan	56	94	150	79	79	158

Source U.N., International Trade Statistics.

TABLE II : Commodity Composition of Soviet Union's Trade (in 1981)

(Value in Millions of Dollars)

	Value of Imports	*% Share of total Imports*	*Exports*	*Value of Exports*	*% Share of total Exports*
All Commodities	72823	100%	All Commodities	79176	100%
Meat and Preparations	1639	2.3%	Wood and Crude Minerals	9894	12.5%
Cereals and Preparations	7866	11%	Metal ores	3266	4.1%
Fruits Nuts/ Poultry/Butter	1557	2.1%	Petroleum + Gas and Products	39957	50.5%
Sugar and honey	3927	5.4%	Pig Iron	1087	1.4%
Alcoholic Beverage and Wine	1334	2%	Steel	3077	3.9%
Textile Fibers + Raw Cotton	836	1.2%	Paper	395	0.5%
Textile Yarn + Cotton Fabrics	902	1.3%	Basic Manuf. Fertilizers	6028	7.6%
Pharmaceuticals + Cosmetics	1814	3%	Motor parts	2225	2.8%
Wool + Floor Coverings	912	1.3%	Constr. Machinery Civil	2074	2.6%
Paper	283	0.9%	Other Spl. Machinery	2309	2.9%
Leather +Travel goods	819	1.2%	Road Vehicles	3564	4.5%

	Value of Imports	*% Share of total Imports*	*Exports*	*Value of Exports*	*% Share of total Exports*
Footwear +Misc. Wear	3831	5.2%	Aircrafts + Helicopters	836	1.1%
General Machinery + Iron+Steel	5348	7.3%			
Special sed Machinery	7635	10.5%			
Flour of Wheat	557	0.8%			
Raw beet and Cane Sugar	419	0.6%			
Pestailes	337	0.5%			
Oil fats + Soya beans	1835	3%			
Rolling Mills $ Calculators	1722	2.5%			
Fork Lift and Road Vehicles	2076	3%			

Source U N. International Trade Statistics.

Table III
Imports and Exports of the Russian Federation
Value in millions of U.S. Dollars

	1996			*1997*			*1998*		
	Imports	*Exports*	*Total*	*Imports*	*Exports*	*Total*	*Imports*	*Exports*	*Total*
World	61147	88703	149850	67619	37368	154987	58996	74160	133156
Germany	15584	7080	22664	14797	6531	21328	15285	5721	21006
Ukraine	6295	7555	13850	3982	7240	11222	3282	5563	8845
Belarus	2908	3357	6265	4626	4631	9257	4555	4623	9178
United States	2922	5069	7991	4060	4486	8546	4123	5138	9267
Kazakhstan	3042	2552	5594	2744	2472	5216	1885	1967	3852
Italy	2342	2823	5165	2640	3564	6204	1821	3222	5043
Finland	1676	2638	4314	1874	2774	4648	1447	2076	3523
China	1004	4751	5755	1261	3981	5242	1160	3200	4360
Netherlands	1020	3328	4348	1206	4553	5759	917	3994	4911
Japan	999	3367	4366	985	2935	3920	819	2194	3013
Republic of Korea	836	1340	2176	837	835	1672	1009	508	1517

(1)	(2)	(3)	(4)	(5)	(6)	(7)	(8)	(9)	(10)
Uzbekistan	656	N.A.	656	1015	N.A.	1015	537	N.A.	537
India	603	794	1397	801	918	1719	669	585	1254
Hungary	658	1978	2636	921	1854	2775	608	1486	2094
Turkey	589	1686	2275	795	1983	2778	519	1937	2456
Brazil	205	N.A.	205	467	N.A.	467	654	N.A.	1121
Czech Republic	535	1939	2474	586	1822	2408	531	1397	1928
U.K.	1146	3544	4690	1505	3055	4560	1229	3025	4254
Cuba	406	N.A.	406	352	N.A.	352	430	N.A.	782
Ireland	323	2907	3230	409	2499	2908	297	644	941

	1999 Imports	Exports	Total	2000 Import	Export	Total
World	40429	74663	115092	45453	103008	148461
Germany	10137	6202	16339	11531	9231	20762
Ukraine	2528	4792	7320	3650	5025	8675
Belarus	3236	3259	6995	3764	5535	9299
United States	2389	4714	7103	2703	4648	7351
Kazakhstan	1398	1226	2624	2200	2247	4447
Italy	1160	3755	4915	1211	7255	8466
Finland	948	2414	3362	958	3105	4063
China	894	3759	4653	949	5535	6484
Netherlands	689	3673	4362	739	4341	5088
Japan	456	2125	2581	572	2763	3335
Republic of Korea	317	826	1143	359	972	1337
Uzbekistan	468	N.A.	1005	663	N.A.	1668
India	677	1177	1854	556	1082	1638
Hungary	313	1549	1862	404	2406	2810
Turkey	313	1631	1944	349	3098	3447
Brazil	717	N.A.	717	388	N.A.	1105
Czech Republic	344	1325	1669	366	1745	2111
U.K.	676	2886	3562	820	4669	5489
Cuba	366	N.A.	366	305	N.A.	305
Ireland	190	658	848	106	288	394

Source : U.N.Trade Statistics.

Table IV

Commodity Composition of Russia's Trade 1997 and 2000

(Value in millions of U.S. Dollars).

1997						2000				
Commodities	*Imports*	*% of*	*Commodities*	*Exports*	*% of*	*Commodities*	*Imports*	*Commodities*	*Exports*	*% of*
All Commodities	67619	100%	All Commodities	87368	100%	All Commodities	45453	All Commodities	103008	100%
Food and live animals for food	9928	15%	Food and live animals	940	1.1%	Food and live animals for food	5287	Food and live animals	933	1%
Vegetables and fruits	1842	2.7%	Cork and wood	1728	2.0%	Vegetables	1212	Cork and wood and fruits	2113	2%
Sugar and Preprations	1320	2.0%	Metal ores	1812	2.1%	Sugar and Preprations	895	Metal ores	984	1%
Tea	281	0.4%	Minerals fuels and Lubricants coal	40002	46%	Tea	226	Minerals fuels and Lubricants coal	52846	51%
Beverages and Tobacco	2049	3%	Inedible eg. Crude Urea Materials	5322	6.1%	Beverages and Tobacco	1129	Inedible eg. Crude Urea Materials	4671	4.6%
Inedible Crude eg. Materials Urea	2408	3.6%	Petroleum Products	22699	26%	Inedible Crude Materials	2452	Petroleum products	34500	34%
Petroleum/ Products	1798	2.7%	Manufactured good	17428	20%	Petroleum Products	823	Manufactured goods	18367	18%
Aluminum	899	1.3%				Aluminum	997			

1997						2000				
Commodities	*Imports*	*% of*	*Commodities*	*Exports*	*% of*	*Commodities*	*Imports*	*Commodities*	*Exports*	*% of*
Vegetables oils	526	0.8%				Vegetable Oils	381			
Chemicals and related products incld. Drugs/ medicines	4952	7.3%				Chemicals and related products incld Drugs/ medicines	3716			
Manufactured goods like Rubber Manufactured Textiles paper products	6385	9.4%				Manufactured goods like Rubber Manufactured Textiles paper product	4779			
Iron and steel	1841	2.7%				Iron and steel	1424			
Machinery and transport equipment	14777	22%				Machinery and transport equipment	7698			

N.B. Petroleum products are also included in Mineral fuels Hence not separately.

Source U.N. Trade Statistic.

Table V : Commodity Composition of Indo-Russian Trade Value in Indian Rupees in Lakhs.

Commodities	*India's 1999-2000 imports from Russia*	*% of Imports*	*Commodities Exports to Russia*	*India's Exports to Russia*	*% of Exports*
All Commodities	270043		All Commodities	410723	100%
Vegetables oils	47	.02%	Tea	70145	17%
Synthetic Rubber	7401	2.8%	Coffee	24572	6%
Waste paper	416	0.2%	Tobacco	20170	5%
Raw Hides and spines	534	0.2%	Castor oil	5007	1.2%
Raw Cotton	6643	2.5%	Drugs and pharmaceutical	53187	13%
Salphur	1686	0.7%	Jewellary	234	0.06%
Other Crude Minerals	2473	1%	Plastic Products	11028	2.7%
Metal ores	9485	3.5%	Machinery	10506	2.6%
Coal	18789	7%	Computer Software	14556	3.6%
Organic Chemicals	6634	2.5%	Cotton Yarn Fabrics	29943	7.3%
Inorganic chemicals	1383	0.5%	Cotton	65945	16%
Pharmaceuticals	2199	0.8%	Accessories	65945	4.7%

Fertilizers	86977	32%	Synthetic Fibres	19285	4%
Newsprint	22942	8.5%	Wool	16506	
Pig Iron	26363	9.7%			
Iron and Steel	26271	9.8%			
Machirery not Electronic	13333	4.9%			
Electrical and Electronics	3984	1.5%			
Transport Equipment + Project goods	10931	4%			

Commodities	*2000-2001 India's from Russia Imports*	*% of Imports*	*Commodities Exports to Russia*	*2000-2001 India's Exports to Russia*	*% of Exports*
All Commodities	234447	100%	All Commodities	405465	100%
Vegetables oils	0	0%	Tea	54233	13.4%
Synthetic Rubber	1582	3.2%	Coffee	28632	7%
Waste paper	492	2.1%	Tobacco	12512	3.1%
Raw Hides and spines	30	0.1%	Castor oil	4978	1.3%
Raw Cotton	4311	19%	Drugs and pharmaceutical	49679	12.2%
Salphur	187	0.8%	Jewellary	807	0.2%
Other Crude Minerals	3113	1.8%	Plastic Products	9757	2.4%
Metal ores	3265	1.4%	Machinery	6430	1.6%
Coal	2860	1.2%	Computer Software	7108	1.8%
Organic Chemicals	1954	0.8%	Cotton Yarn Fabrics	30512	7.5%
Inorganic chemicals	4697	2%	Cotton	94945	23.4%

Commodities	*2000-2001 India's from Russia Imports*	*% of Imports*	*Commodities Exports to Russia*	*2000-2001 India's Exports to Russia*	*% of Exports*
Pharmaceuticals	2286	1%	Accessories	94945	23.4%
Fertilizers	39344	17%	Synthetic Fibres	20503	5%
Newsprint	29053	12.4%	Wool	16448	4%
Pig Iron	46167	20%			
Iron and Steel	26981	12%			
Machinery not Electronic	7440	3.2%			
Electrical and Electronics	5295	2.3%			
Transport Equipment + Project goods	15634	6.7%			

Source : Foreign Trade Statistics of India DG CIS, Calcutta.

22
Indo-Russian Trade

Girish Mishra

If one looks back at India's progress since Independence, the important role played by Indo-Soviet relations in general and trade and economic cooperation in particular will become obvious. It is no exaggeration to say that, without them, India would not have been able to withstand the machinations of Western powers and international financial institutions that tried hard to convert it into a neo-colony. Thanks to wide-ranging relations with Soviet Union, India could protect its national integrity, political freedom and embark on the path of building an independent economy.

It was demonstrated, by bringing in the rupee trading system, that the availability of foreign exchange could not be a limiting factor in India's economic development. India could import capital goods and technology from the Soviet Union to set up modern industrial enterprises and pay for them in the rupee. In other words, an ever-expanding market was created for its traditional exports as well as for the goods produced in the factories set tip with Soviet assistance. Not only this, but India's military needs were also met by the Soviet Union for which the payment was made in the Indian currency. The implications of this arrangement for India's security and foreign policy could never be overstated.

During the period 1955-90 India could devote its foreign exchange earnings to import from elsewhere and realize better per unit price for its traditional exports as a result of finding an alternative ever-expanding market i in the Soviet Union.

The situation has, however, radically changed since 1991 when the Soviet Union collapsed and disintegrated. Its successor state-Russia-no longer remained ideologically committed to socialist ideology. India also strayed away from the Nehruvian model of economic development wherein emphasis was placed on domestic demand-led development.

The changed world situation and the growing attempts to thrust the Washington Consensus-based globalisation on both the countries have brought a sea-change in the strategies of economic development pursued by them. Russian economy is still not on an even keel and over the years has suffered from pains of restructuring and financial crisis. In this situation both economic relations in general and bilateral trade in particular have suffered a great deal. The rupee payment arrangement and production cooperation has been given up. During the 1990s the financial crisis and the pains of restructuring had an adverse impact on bilateral trade.

If one looks at the figures, it becomes obvious. In 1960-61, 4.5 per cent of India's exports went to the Soviet Union, this share rose to 13.7 per cent in 19707 1, and 18.3 per cent in 1980-8 1. Even in the last year of the Soviet Union it came to 16.1 per cent. The slump took place after that and the share of Russia in India's exports came to 3.3 per cent in 1995-96 and to just 2.1 and 2.6 per cent in 1998-99 and 1999-2000 respectively. In 2000-01 it was lower at merely 2 per cent. Thus so far as Russia is concerned, it is no longer the desired destination for Indian exports. For this many reasons are indicated. They include the weak and unreliable financial institutions, increasing crime rate in Russia posing grave risks to life and property of Indian businessmen, various kinds of fraudulent practices adopted by the Russian mafiya posing as genuine traders and the greater attraction of other sources of supply.

India's imports from Russia have declined more sharply. During the Soviet days they went up from 1.4 per cent in 1960-61 to 8.1 per cent in 1980-81 and then the downhill journey began. In 2000-01 Russia accounted for just 1 per cent of India's total imports.

There are several reasons for the declining share of Russia in India's total imports. With liberalisation, privatisation and globalisation in ascendancy, India has been looking to the West for foreign direct investment and technology and this is bound to affect India's imports from Russia. There is a feeling, I do not know how far correct, that Russian technology is outdated and more expensive. Since in new production units being set up in India both capital and technical know-how employed are of Western orientation, there is little prospect for imports from Russia. Earlier during the days of the Soviet Union public sector was playing the key role in setting up industrial units and it found economic cooperation with the Soviet Union more beneficial. The imports were paid for either in rupee or by exporting a part of the output of units set up with Soviet collaboration. Oil and natural gas sector in India could come up largely as a result of cooperation with the Soviet Union and Romania.

India purchased military hardware from the Soviet Union on the basis of rupee payment. Now, it has started diversifying its purchases and there is a clear cut preference for Western sources.

In Russia too with dismantling of the state sector the orientation has shifted to Western markets. It wants to sell and shop there as much as possible. It is evident from the figures that, while the international trade of Russia have been growing; India's share has been falling. Between 1992, Russia's total exports went up from $39931 million to $69730 million, India's share declined. During the same period Russia's imports increased from $4950 million to $27254 million, yet India's exports to Russia went down.

Obviously, there has been a big shift in the direction of Russia's foreign trade. Not only the share of developing countries like India but of former Soviet republics (or CIS) in Russia's foreign trade too has declined. The move on the part of Russia to move close to the West in general and European Union in particular has also been a major contributing factor. It is not surprising that European Union now accounts for 40 per cent of Russia's foreign trade.

In 1999-2000 there was some growth in bilateral trade though it could not -be sustained in the following year. This growth was mainly due to increased import of rice, fruit products, potatoes, tea and coffee, besides medicines, from India. It is said, in addition to direct bilateral trade, there is trading through third country. This goes by the name of bilateral trade. It is not easy to estimate the extent of such trade relations between India and Russia.

The major items figuring in India's exports to Russia consist of readymade garments (both woollen and cotton), tea, coffee, spices, electronic goods, leather goods, tobacco, rice, drugs and pharmaceutical products. So far as imports from Russia are concerned major items are fertilizers, iron and steel, non-ferrous metals and newsprint. Military hardware and spare parts too are imported in significant amount.

In the years to come India will have to do a number of things to increase its trade turnover with Russia. Its business houses will have to have an effective presence in Russia to explore and Study the possibilities of widening trade relations as well as taking them to a new high. It will face competition from countries like China, South Korea and others. In the fields like information technology, it can do better. There is no dearth of Russian speaking trained engineers in India who are familiar with the environment and prevailing needs in Russia. Meantime, financial sector seems to be more organised and stabilised. Besides, there are great possibilities in areas like tourism and scientific and technological collaboration. The two countries take steps to modernise and technologically update enterprises set up during pre-1991 era.

Indian entrepreneurs can collaborate with their Russian counterparts in infrastructure sector like building metro railways, setting up power plants, constructing and operating hotels, etc. There is a great possibility of translating and publishing literary and scientific works written by Indian and Russian scholars in their respective languages. Moreover in the sphere of science and technology there are tremendous possibilities for collaboration and trade.

In the oil sector the scope for collaboration can be explored. This will benefit both the countries. Besides, Indian entrepreneurs can collaborate by importing gold, rough diamonds and gems from Russia and refining and converting them into ornaments for export to world market. Indian craftsmanship has already established its reputation. While Russia is among the largest producers of diamonds, India possesses largest diamond processing capacity and excellent skills. The same may be said about gold.

In the end, it is high time that both the countries setup a number of teams of experts to explore the possibilities of increasing trade relations and economic cooperation not only in traditional and familiar areas but in new fields. They should study all aspects such as technical, financial, infrastructural, etc. and establish a monitoring group to look into and solve whatever problems and difficulties arise.

The two countries have a long history of close ties that should be further strengthened and diversified to benefit their people.

23

India-Russia Cultural Relations

Manohar Singh Batra

India and Russia have a long history of mutual cultural influences. Russian travellers and representatives have been showing profound respect and goodwill for the Indian people. These influences took concrete form when Russian scholars started taking interest in Indology. Pioneering work was done by Gerasim Lebedev, who successfully established close cultural contacts between India and Russia. Russian scholars started evincing keen interest in Sanskritology and linguistics and Indians got an opportunity to learn about the European drama and theatre. Lebedev, who lived in India from 1785 to 1797, became a catalyst in the studies of Indian religion culture and customs in Russia. He wrote a book on the grammar of the Calcutta dialect of Hindustani. His second book was *on India's economy* and religious and moral traditions of its people. In cooperation with a few Bengali intellectuals he was successful in creating as Indian theatre, which combined the Indian and European traditions.

Bhagavadgita was translated into Russian in 1788 and Shakuntala in 1792. The Russian translator of Shakuntala spoke very highly of Kalidasa and described him as a great poet of the stature of Homer. The Russian scholars embarked on the studies of Indian languages like Sanskrit, Bengali, Marathi, Gujarati and Telugu at various centres like Astrakhan, Irkutsk, Kazan, Nizhni Novgorod and Tobolsk. Indian studies became very popular and a chair of Sanskrit was set up at Moscow University in 1851 and another at the St. Petersburg University in 1855 sanskritology became a favourite subject of study with some scholars at some most important centres of Russia and a Russian school of Sanskritologists emerged comprising among others K. Kossovich, I. Minayev and P. Petrov.

The first war of Independence of 1857 in India evoked deep sympathy for the Indian cause among the Russians. A probing article by N. Dobrolyubov castigated the colonial rule in India and touched a sympathetic chord for political aspirations of the Indian people- By about the middle of the 19th century studies of the contemporary situation got underway alongwith further development of Sanskritology. The difficulties faced by the Indian people were ably reflected by Russian artists. The works of Vereshchagin depict vividly the vicissitudes of the Indian people, who were groaning under the foreign rule. He managed to display his drawings about India in various cities of Europe and America. During the early 20th century, vignettes of Indian classics continued to be translated into century, exemplified by the translations of excerpts from Ramayana and Mahabharata. The commonality of interests in democracy and freedom between the authors and artists of both the countries became a source of strength to each other. Maxim Gorky and Leo Tolstoy became household names among the Indian intelligentsia. The correspondence between Leo Tolstoy and Mahatma Gandhi served as a most important link in crystalisation of thought processes between the two countries. It was amazing the way Tolstoy could so clearly understand the problems of Indian people.

After the Great October Revolution the understanding and cooperation between the peoples of India and Russia became closer and deeper. Their mutual cultural ties were also strengthened. As Indians were engaged wholeheartedly in their own freedom struggle they greatly admired the Soviet people for speedy reforms in economy, education and culture which they were able to bring about in such a short time. Though the colonial rulers of India were circumspect about such sentiments in Indian intellectuals, the latter would not lose any opportunity of acquainting themselves with the advances being made in Soviet Russia in various fields including sciences, literature and culture. Rabindranath Tagore's visit to the USSR in 1930 was a milestone in the development of Indo-Russian cultural bonds. In his Letters from Russia he told about the life in the Soviet Union, the endeavors of its people, their joys and sorrows and the stupendances tasks before them. He admired their earnestness and solicitude, their sense of purpose, their mission of eradicating illiteracy from their midst and their drive to achieve higher goals. He deeply appreciated the single-minded devotion of the Russians to strive to come out of the deep degradation to which they had been pushed and to achieve equality in social life.

Like the prerevolution days, the Russians pursued their interest in indology and continued to explore the Indian cultural heritage, philosophy, art and literature. Literary giants like Gorky, Tolstoy and somewhat later Chekhov contributed such a literature, which influenced the literary effort in this country. Some progressive Indian writers learnt from the literary trends in Russia and some Russian writers were also swayed by the writings of Indian men of literature.

Ever since India became free from the colonial domination in August 1947 the relations between the Socialist Soviet Union and an independent, democratic Indian become closer based as these have been on mutual respect and equality with concern for each others integrity and well being. The event of India's independence provided a fillip to the development of cultural relations between the two sovereign states. The writers, artists and performers from both the countries have been taking special interest in cultural development of each other and in the exchange of their views and works to our mutual advantage. There have been frequent visits of cultural troupes, scientists, literatures, the younger people and women to each other's country with a fund of goodwill and genuine desier to learn and benefit from each other's experience. Some top Indian musicians dancers, composers and painters have been visiting Russia with a more than enthusiastic response from the other side. Folk dancers, puppeteers, theatre personalities and film artists have been exchanging frequent visits, whereas Russian circuses and ballet troupes have been making their presence felt in the Indian cities.

The Russian people have been taking keen interest in the modern impressions for wider disseminations among their own people. Their productions of Indian classics on stage like Mrichchhkatika, Shakuntala and Ramayana, among others speaks of their deep-rooted and genuine interest in delving into various segments of Indian culture. The Indian theatre has not lagged behind in understanding the art of Russian, drama. Innumerable productions of Chekhov's and Gorky's plays have been tried in this country. The Stanislavsky system is very well studied and followed in productions of drama by highly eminent Indian producers.

Quite frequently the Indian and Russian film festivals are held in each other's country, which attract wide audiences. Whenever there in such an occasion either in India ANA or Russia people throng the theatres with avid interest. Similarly exhibitions of *handicrafts, sculpture* and paintings draw heavy crowds, Books are translated and distributed in large numbers. Interestingly most valuable Russian literary works have been available in India at affordable prices.

A large number of Indian students have studied in a wide range of universities in Russia and Russian students have been coming in quest of knowledge to the Indian educational institutions The School of International Studies and the Russian language Department of the Jawaharlal Nehru University have been offering courses and research work about Russia to a considerable extent. Extensive educational contacts were forged under cultural agreement between the two countries in the 1960s. Bilateral exchanges between the universities of the two countries and exchange of textbooks etc. have been a common feature. Cooperation in the medical field has benefited both the countries. The sponsorship of cultural troupes by the Indian council of Cultural Relations to the Russian Federation has been of great help in furthering the common bonds between the two nations.

Apart from delegations, speakers, intellectuals, artists and indologists, a regular traffic of tourists to India and Russia has been of great significance is the promotion of cultural ties. Way back in 1963 Pandit Jawaharlal Nehru had written to the National Council of the Indo – Soviet Cultural Society that our contacts and relations should be close, friendly and cooperative. He had added that from the larger point of view of international affairs, this was necessary. Mrs. Indira Gandhi, Mr. Rajiv Gandhi, Mr. P.V. Narasimhar Rao, Mr. H.K. Deve Gowda, Mr. I.K.Gujral and Mr. Atal Behari Vajpayee all Prime Ministers have been attacking great importance to the mutual cultural relations between the two nations. In almost all the newspapers and periodicals published in India, the cultural bonds between India and Russia have been. Frequently commented upon. Very rarely indeed a dissident voice has been raised as far as the relations between India and Russia are concerned.

According to V. V. Balabushevich and A. H. Wafa, Indology in Russia has been a complex affair, as it has embraced history, economics, literature, arts, linguistics and culture in its fold. The research work in these fields has been carried out with the support of state bodies and has been well, coordinated. Important work in Indology has been done in research institutes of state departments and the institutes of the academies of sciences. Indology met the mounting interest of the Russian people in the life and struggle of the *Indian people*. Many of their publications have dealt with philosophical and social outlook and the culture of India. Those have also tried to establish that the Indian history has been an integral part of the world historical process. Though Indian civilization in the remote past has always been a area of attraction for Indologistay the problems of political history, religion and culture in the recent periods have been a source of inquiry for the *Russian* researchers. Some Indological publications have devoted their attention to an analysis of the problems concerned with the Indian national bourgeoisie. The fundamental analysis made by Russian *indologists* has enabled them to focus their attention on the study of the culture of the Indian people. An objective Outline of the development of Indian national culture has been given, which leads one to the underlying features of some aspects of spiritual life of this country. The Russian classical Indo-studies have continued discovering new fields. Russians have published books on the ideological heritage of B.G.Tilak, Rabindranath Tagore, R.M. Roy, Aurobindo Ghosh, Bankimchandra Chatterji, Swami Vivekananda and Mahatma Gandhi. A.D. Litman's monograph 'Philosophical Treads in Independent ladia 'throws copious light on India's spiritual life and L.R.Gordon-Polonskaya's book 'Noslem Treads in the Social Outlook of India and Pakistan' has dealt with social thought of India.

Translating Indian literature has been another passion with the Russian scholars. Literary works of the Middle Ages, of contemporary and modern times have been translated into Russian. They have been studying and analysing the development of literature in various national languages and establishing a common thread among these works. They have also been trying to fathom the depth of connections between the literary trends and the strivings of the Indian people. They have been trying to discern the ideological and aesthetic trends of writers to discover the influence of philosophical, religious and ethical doctrines on their writings. Many Soviet scholars have been working on various aspects of Indian literature, including V. A. Novikovat E. P. Chelyshevt A. S. Suhochov and many others.

A number of Russian Indologists have been devoting their attention to the Indian art of all ages. A composite book entitled 'The Culture of Modern India[2] authored by a group of writers has attempted to examine the main problems in the spiritual life of the post-Independence India. Books by writers like S. I. Tuliaevap N.R. Babkina, N.R. Guseval and a host of others evince their keen interest in Indian art like paintings, theatre, choreography and architecture etc.

Studies in 'Indian languages have expanded considerably. Many a research paper has been published in the various languages which includes studies in grammar syntax and vocabulary. Phonetics and dialects have also not escaped their attention apart from phonology and morphology Russian Indologists have found this field very useful in understandin Indian history, literature and social norms. Contacts between Indian an

Russian scholars have been close and intimate. The works of Indian authors are very much in demand in. Russia and countless people in this country have been enjoying Russian literature. This has given insight n the history, struggles, social developments and cultural trends in both the countries . But this does not mean that in India there are as many Russianoligists as are Indologists in the Russian Federation.

Some advanced countries like have spearheaded studies on the Soviet Union and now Russia on a wide scale. But India has been lagging behind in this field inspire of its traditional friendship with the erstwhile USSR and now Russia. Its one reason can be traced to the mindset of the British rulers in India, who had created deep distrust of Russia in the Indian people. Britain did not want Indians to forge close personal contacts with the Russians. Indians were also fed with the anti Bolshevist propaganda. Their minds were more oriented towards the English literature and other things English than any other identity. As a result Indian universities started churning out graduates with a narrow outlook. They learnt a great deal about the British history and very little of the history and culture of other countries including arguably of their own.

Since the knowledge of the Russian language among the Indian scholars before Independence was almost nil, whatever they came to understand of the Russian literature even after Independence was from the English translations of the great Russian masters viz. Pushkin, Dostoevsky, Tolstoy, Chekhov, Gorky, Gogol and others. In philosophy the knowledge of Indians was mainly confined to the anarchist doctrine of Mikhail Bakunin and Prince Kropotkin. Of course there was greater awareness of Marx and Lenin. Nehru was particularly critical of the lack of interest among Indian intellectuals about the Soviet Union and encouraged Indian institutions to send professors and students to learn about the nation which had launched a great experiment in history.

Nehru's advice was resisted by some Indian universities, who were still under the hypnotic influence of things British. The speed of initiating either course of study or research programmes on the USSR was rather tardy. But as the demand for translators and interpreters in Russian picked up, Russian language courses were started in the Delhi University Allahabad University and the IIT Mumbai. Later, the Russian language courses were introduced in Aligarh, Kolkata, Lucknow, Varanasi, Mumbai, Bangalore and many institutions like the Bharatiya Vidya Bhawan, the School of Foreign languages, Ministry of Defence and the Indo-Soviet Cultural Society. The Jawaharlal Nehru University offers a Master's course in Russian. A numbers of Indian researchers have written Doctoral theses on subjects related to Russia, especially its relations with the United Nations and some foreign countries. Scores of books and journals dealing with Russia are now available in libraries across the country.

During the last few decades a large number of books on USSR/ Russia have been published in India in English, Hindi and various regional languages. Greater interest than ever before is being evinced about the Russian way of life, their literature, music~ drama, sports, science, arts, folklore, sartorial diversity and cuisine. Broadcasts in Indian languages are beamed from Moscow and regular programmes in Russian have been a part of the external services of All India Radio.

The two countries have been progressively getting closer. Political exigencies, cooperation in defence and geo-political matters, the emergence of the USA as a solitary super power, the China factor and other reasons have been the main catalysts in bringing our two countries nearer each other. Though cultural relations are not an offshoot of these considerations, these are an essential ingredient to cement the ties between the two peoples. Russia has been contributing a larger share of goodwill in achieving greater proximity between India and Russia. That country has stood by India in thick and thin in the international arena and has helped us in the hour of need. There is scope indeed for extending the cultural bonds at least to ensure an enduring relationship. The following pages would show the extent of endeavor to which our leaders have gone to strengthen our bonds and the initiative of cultural bodies to explore and discover the minds of the people in both the countries to transform our relations into closer and lasting ties.

The Russian Schools of Ballet have been functioning in New Delhi and Chennai, where regular training in ballet is imparted by trained teachers to Indian students. The Russian language courses are also run. In Kolkata, the Cultural Centre is a living beacon of arty culture and literature. "Gorky Sadan" is considered as an abode of amity and understanding between the Indian and Russian peoples in the field of culture. The cultural centre at Mumbai is a favourite haunt of academic, public figures and celebrities. Film shows draw huge crowds. There is an ever-growing demand for Russian language courses. Seminars and exhibitions are often organised at the centre. A monument to the memory of Afanasi Nikitin, a Russian traveller in India has been built at the Mumbai centre.

At Thiruvananathapuram, the Gorky Bhavanam was reopened on the 11th October, 2000 after a gap of nine years, an earlier it had been closed due to the difficulties arising out of the fall of the Soviet Union. Ever since it's reopening the Russian language institute has been working in full measure. The Chess Club, the Music School, Film Circle, Russian Speakers' Forum, the Library and the Drama Club have been revived. Cultural programmes, film shows, discussions and theatre related activities are being regularly organised. Birth anniversaries of Pushkin and Dostovsky have been celebrated, the commemoration functions on the national days of India and Russia have been organised and musical programmes dedicated to Tchaikovsky and Rahmaninov have been held. Russian film festivals in December 2000 and February 2002 were big draws. The Gorky Bhavanam is also a source of information on educational institutions in Russia. It caters to the needs of genuine candidates seeking admission to the higher educational establishments in Russia. At the Russian Cultural centre, special courses for the Russian language piano / guitar crash courses, painting and cartoon camps and special training programme for chess players are organised.

India's Prime Minister, Mr. Atal Behari Vajpayee has characterised the Indo-Russian interaction as civilisational, which means the meeting, blending and mutual enrichment of the two great civilisations.

Russia's President, Mr. Vladimir Putin was delighted to visit the Taj Mahal at Agra during his Indian tour of 2000, after which he remarked that people of Russia are proud of having friends like the Indians. He reiterated that he would come to this country again.

In an exhibition organised in New Delhi on the 26th September, 2000, the Russian Ambassador, Mr. Alexander Kadakin lauded the major landmarks in the development of ties between Russia and India. The credit of trust and mutual understanding accumulated by our country during several centuries of relations with India, he said, is viewed by us as one of the greatest treasures of the Russian foreign policy. Inaugurating the exhibition, the former Indian Prime Minister, Mr. I.K.Gujral said that the relationship between India and Russia is unique. People of India, he observed, would understand and appreciate Russia in a better manner.

The cultural and spiritual significance of the precious work undertaken by Yuri Roerich in India were remembered at a meeting in New Delhi to mark the 100th birth anniversary of the eminent scholar and orientalist. His contributions went a long way in links between India and Russia meant to strengthen the cultural relations between the two countries. The valuable research and translation work carried out by Yuri -Roerich were described an worth emulating for generations to come. His contribution towards promotion of Sanskrit is really remarkable. Yuri Nikolayevich Roerich was the elder son of the famous Russian artist Nikolai Roerich and Svyatoslav Roerich was his younger son who became a prominent artist. Yuri was attracted to Buddhism and in 1923 he received a Master's degree in Indian philosophy in the Sorbonne, from where he alongwith his family came to Mumbai. In India he began to learn local languages and saw this country being ruled by spiritual ecstasy.

The family, after a brief trip to Europe and . 'America returned to the Himalayas. They went into Tibet, from where, after some vicissitudes, they came to the Kulu valley near the Baas river, where in December 1928 they built a house. Yuri Roerich worked as the Director of the Institute of the Himalayan Studies and head of the ethno-linguistic department. Yuri returned to Moscow where he started to work at the Institute of Oriental Studies. He wished to publish the Indian epic story Dhammapadu, but suddenly breathed his last on the 21st May, 1960.

An exhibition of paintings "Glimpses of Mountain" by contemporary Indian artists, dedicated to the 128th birth anniversary of Nikolai Roerich was inaugurated on the 8th October, 2000 in New Delhi. On the occasion a sentiment was expressed that this reflected the living spirit of Roerich among Recalling the functioning of the Russian-Indian Roerich Trust in India under the patronage of the Prime Minister Mr. Atal Behari Vajpayee, Mr. Sorokin, Head of the Cultural Department of the Russian Embassy remarked that the Indian government was paying special attention to renovate the Roerich Museum.

During the 33rd International Film Festival in India, the Russian film "Letters to Elsa" was given the Golden Peacock for the artistic reflection, of a woman's inner world through her beauty character and freedom. On the 29th November, 2002 a spectacular performance of Kuban Cossack Quartet "Kumovia" was held in New Delhi which enthralled the audience of art lovers, critics and others.

According to Tatyana Shaumyan, Head of the Centre of Indian Research of the Institute of Oriental Studies, Russian Academy of Sciences, the Russian study of India has a two-hundred year history. The founder of Russian Indology, the talented musician Gerasim Lebedev travelled to Madras in 1789 and after two years moved to Kolkata, where he performed music, gave lessons and studied Sanskrit Hindi and Bengali. He founded Kolkata's first drama theatre. After returning from India he published Bengali texts in the Devnagari script. After Lebedev, Indian culture was studied by prominent scholars like K.A. Kossovich, I. P. Minayev, S. F. Oldenburg,

P. I. Shcherbatskoy and others. All of the them held India and its culture in high esteem.

The first translations of Indian classical literary works appeared in the latter half of the 18th century. Whereas excerpts from 'Panchatantra' and 'Hitopadesa' came into print in 1762, 'The Bhagavad Gita and 'Shakuntala' were published in 1792. These works were translated from the *English texts and the* direct translations were done in the early 1840s. The first Indological centre in Russia was set up at St. Petersburg University. In the following yearly Indological centers came up at the Moscow University, the Institute of Oriental Studies of the Russian Academy of Sciences and two more in Kazan and Tashkent. Later similar centres were established in provincial towns like Lipetsk, Ryasan, Tomsk, Penza, Samara, Ufa and Ulan-Ude. A score of seminars were conducted under the aegis of the Institute of Oriental Studies of the Russian Academy of Sciences and the 'Indian Embassy in Russia during 2000-2002. That goes to prove that interest in Indian culture was not centered only in Moscow and Petersburg, but the currents of inquiry in the Indian ethos have been spreading to various region of Russia. These activities have been coordinated by the Institute of Oriental Studies of the Russian, Academy of Sciences and its major subsidiary, the Centre of Indian Research.

The Russian Institute of Oriental Studies founded in 1818 has from the very beginning been occupied with Indology. The contemporary generation of Indologists was raised by prominent scientists like I. M. Reisner, A. M. Dyakov, B. B. Balabushevich, N. M. Goldberg, A. M. Osipov and others. They were complemented by V. O. Pavlov, A. I. Levkovsky, L. I. Reisner, A. D. Litman, K.Z. Ashrafyan and many others. Ye. P. Chelyshev has to his credit a number of research papers dealing with Indian literature and culture. G.M.Bougard-Levin has authored many books on history and culture of India and in a winner of the Nehru Prize.

In 1987, the Indian and South Russian Department of the Institute of Oriental Studies of the Russian Academy of Sciences was turned into a Centre of Indian research headed by Prof. A. A. Kutseakov who has brought out works on social problems and the caste system of India. In November 2001, India and Russia signed a Memorandum on Development of Indological Research in Russia to be supported by the Indian Embassy in Moscow The scientists conducting research in Indology include G. K. Shirokov, R.B. Rybakov, V.G. Rastyannikov, F. N. Yurlov, A.A. Suvorov and many others. Apart from a number of researchers at this centre, many other units are engaged in research in *Indology.* The top level Russian

Indologists have been assigned the task of teaching Indology. The main educational *centre* teaching oriental studies in Moscow University's Institute of Asia and Africa, various other Russian universities, the Philosophical Institute, the Institute of World Literature, the Institute of Ethnology and Asthropology, the Russian Academy of Sciences and other institutions are the centres of elaborate lectures on indology. An outstanding Sanskritologist Professor T. Ya. Yelisarenkova has accomplished the task of translating the Rig Veda in the Russian language.

Research in Hinduism and classical Indian literature in continuing in Russia. A series of publications entitled "Indian Social Thought" were brought out. Works dedicated to Raja Ram Mohan Roy, Swami Vivekananada, Aurobindo Ghosh and other illustrious personalities were published under the *name* of "The Tree of Hinduism" in 1999. A compendium of articles was published under the title "Inter-Religious Relations on South Asia - The Past and Present." The eminent Indologist I.P. Glushkova has published a monograph "Indian Pilgrimage; the Metaphor of Movement and the Movement of Metaphor." A work on India's prominent women of the 20th century has been completed by Ye.S. Yurlova and O.A. Shaumyan. It contains articles on Sarada Devi, Sarojini Naidu, Vijaya Lakshmi Pandit, Indira Gandhi, Kasturba Gandhi, Aruna Asaf Ali and others. "Russian View on Indian History" is another outstanding work. The Yasnaya Polyana Museum of the Russian thinker and writer Lev Tolstoi houses extensive material on India, Baddhism and Hinduism. It also has correspondence between Tolstoi on the one hand and Baba Bbarati, Gopal Chetti, U.K. Dutt, Mahatma Gandhi, A. Ramaseshan etc. on the other.

According to Nikolai Zherebtsov, President Putin has recently spoken of Buddhism an one of the four religious that are traditional for Russia. Buddhism appeared in Russia in its Northern branch known as the 'Mahayana chariot' among the Siberian nations; in the European, part of Russia, it is professed by the Kalmysks inhabiting the Caspian Republic, which is a part of the Russian Federation. Buddhism attracts people because of its renunciation of destructive struggle for power with emphasis on peace and tranquility, where compassion in a guiding force. Buddhism influenced entirely the Buryat people. In the regions of Baryatia, Tuva and Kalmykia, a number of new Buddhist temples and ministries have been built since 1990.

1987 saw the publication of a book "India through the Eyes of Soviet Poets". In it modern Poets like Robert Rozhdestvensky, Rimma Kazakova, Alexander Mezirov, Valentin Sidorov, Rasul Gamzatov, Lev Oshanin and others have published their poems on various themes relating to India. An effort had been made to bring out image of this country as a mysterious land of wealth and wisdom. Most of these poets have visited India and travelled here widely. Their works exhibit originality of vision and poetic depth. A book in Hindi published in India entitled 'Volga ke Darpan me Ganga ka Chitr' makes a compulsive reading.

A festival of India was inaugurated jointly by Mr. Mikhail Gorbachev and Mr. Rajiv Gandhi in Moscow on the 3rd July, 1987. It travelled to Leningrad and Tashkent, returning back to Moscow. It was a breathtaking event with the participation of over 1800 performing artists. The festival was a year long holiday of friendship, as it attracted millions of people. It proved to be a vehicle of a great discovery and enrichment.

The Russian festival in India was inaugurated on the 21st November, 1987. Mr. Nikolai Ryzhkov came to participate in the opening ceremonies in New Delhi. Rajiv Gandhi described the festival as the offering of a flower of friendship and love. The event flowed towards Mumbai, Bangalore and Kolkata. It was described as a unique event in the cultural life of the two countries.

Both the festivals revealed the fundamental unity which underlined the cultures of the two friendly countries. These symbolised a confluence of two multi-ethnic societies, 'where a massive exchange of cultural values took place.

A large bronze statue of the great Russian poet Alexander Pushkin was unveiled at the Rabindra Bhavan in New Delhi on the 20th November, 1988. Pushkin, an intellectual giant, dominated his era. Both Pushkin and Tagore had fought against tyranny and oppression. The setting up of the statue was described as a testimony of friendship between the peoples of the two countries.

A two-day mela was held in New Delhi on the 8th and 9th October, 1988. Twenty-one folk troupes of singers and dancers took part and circus and puppet shows were held. A planeload of wooden structures and 360 artists were flown in.

During his second visit to India on the 18th November, 1988, Mr. Gorbachev, apart from in other dignitaries, brought his Minister of Culture Rafiq, Nishanov in his entourage. Mrs. Raisa, Gorbacheva had a meeting with the editorial board of the Indo-Soviet women's magazine Hamari Goshthi, with the editorial board of the indo – Soviet women's magazine Hamari Goshthi, published in English and Russian. It was suggested that contacts between the women of the two countries should be expanded through the magazine, through exchanges of journalists and children groups, through exhibitions and sales of handicrafts. Proposals were also made for the exchanges of visits by teenagers, who could stay with families in both the countries.

Russian leaders have described 2002 as among the best years for an further development of Indo-Russian relations. They have reiterated their desire to strengthen the relations of mutual understanding and cooperation between the two countries in all spheres. As India is the most populous democracy of the present times, Russia is keen to have a long friendship, mutual understanding and partnership with this country.

In an effort to further enrich Delhi's ties with Moscow, Delhi's Mayor, Ms. Shakuntala Arys inaugurated on the 8th September, 1997 an unique exhibition to mark the 850th anniversary of the ancient city, in New Delhi. The Exhibition picturising Moscow in all its scenic cultural and architectural splendour was a special tribute to the Russian capital, which celebrated its 850th anniversary in September that year.

On the Indian Republic Day in 1998, Russian artists mounted a massive exhibition of their paintings of India as a tribute to the cultural relations between the two countries. The paintings were landscapes, graphics, oil painting and applied art exhibits depicting the serene natural beauty of the Himalayan foothills, religious rituals on the banks of the Ganga at Varanasi, the streets of Kolkata, the exotic Indian bazars, the simplicity of rural life and majestic palaces. Portraits of prominent leaders like 'Mahatma Gandhi, Jawaharlal Nehru and Indira Gandhi were a special source of attration.

'Day of Moscow in Delhi' were held from 23rd to 27th September, 1998. Ballet, jazz, circus, classical music, folk music, film shows were held and a literary meeting on Pushkin was arranged. This initiative was taken to foster greater understanding between the people of Moscow and New Delhi. Similarly 'Days of Delhi' were held in Moscow to which thousands of people thronged to have glimpses of Indian culture. The fest included classical dances, Indian pop music, folk dances, art exhibitions, film shows and literary seminars. Among the folk dances were included garb, dandia, chhau and gidda. Gurdas Mann, popular Punjabi folk artist was a big draw. An exhibition of paintings and handicrafts, where some of India's eminent artist and craftsmen displayed their techniques were welcomed by the Russian people. They had a chance to see the work of M. F. Hussain, Satish Gujral, Anjolie Ela Menon and many others.

Leading Russian book dealers and publishers took part in, the Delhi

Book Fair in February 2000. It was the biggest exhibition of Russian books and periodicals since the end of communism and censorship in Russia. On the 27th March, 2000 an exhibition on 'Indology in Russia and Publication of Books on Indology in India was inaugurated. It was a joint venture of the Russian Centre of Science and Culture, Bnaratiya Vidya Bhawan and the Indian Council of Historical Research.

On the 5th November, 2001 Prime Minister, Atal Behari Vajpayee inaugurated an exhibition in St. Petersburg of paintings by prince Soltikov, a member of the Romanov family that ruled Russia till the Revolution of 1917. The Prince, a romantic wanderer had travelled to India twice in the 1840s and painted graphic pictures of his travels. Mr. Vajpayee also interacted with academics and intellectual, many of them being Indologists, who had flown from Moscow, Kazan and even Vladivostok. Mr. Vajpayee was presented a book of translations of his speeches. The Indian government has set up several chairs in Indology in some universities in Russia. Indology is attracting young students.

On the lst April, 2001, the world's coldest region, Yakutia became the seventh Russian province to have an Indian cultural centre. The centre, set up in the region's capital Yakutsk was inaugurated by the Indian Ambassador to Russia, S.K.Lambah. During the visit of the Russian President, Mr. Putin in 2000 to India, a working group on regional cooperation under the inter-governmental joint commission had been set up. They had signed a bilateral agreement on regional cooperation, the first such accord that either side had with any foreign country. The agreement allows the States in India and Russian regions to directly enter into various economic, cultural and educational ventures within the framework of their constitutional powers.

On the 8th March, 2002, former Prime Minister, Mr. I.K.Gujral inaugurated an exhibition of paintings, sculptures, graphics and drawings by contemporary Indian and Russian Artists in New Delhi. The exhibition comprising works of 57 artists presented a panoramic view of the art of the two countries.

A group of Russian children and teachers visited Delhi as a Part of a students exchange programme. India is a land of their dreams, they said, and went round a number of historical monuments in the Capital.

The saga of Svetoslav Roerich in India has been more fascinating than any other Phenomenon. Though his father, Nicholas Roerich focussed more on landscapes, the junior Roerich was enamouredby the incredible beauty of the earth and its smells. As per O.T. Bopanna, the father-son duo have left behind a rich cultural legacy to their adopted land of India. Roerich, who had-married, the beauty queen of the Hindi silver screen, Devika Rani painted with passion. Her beauty has been immortalised by her painter husband on canvas. Some of his Paintings are masterpieces. A total of 117 paintings, including 81 by Svetoslav and 36 by his father Nicholas were on display in Bangalore in February 2002. In fact Nicholas was reputed to have painted a staggering seven thousand pieces. Svetoslav was a worshipper of beauty and had made pursuit of the Beautiful his daily prayer.

While in India, Nikolai Roerich published a number of books and articles on Russian art and wrote his memoirs. Among those who held him in high esteem and paid tribute included Rabindranath Tagore, Jawaharlal Nehru and Indira Gandhi. His books published in India are widely known. Nehru once commented that Roerich's Himalayan landscapes captured the spirit of those mountains. His paintings, according to S.V. Nairs captured the spirit of those mountains. These told of the Indian people's history, philosophy, cultural and spiritual heritage. Nehru was of the view that Roerich expressed that spirit in his superb pictures.

Many a Russian artist, musician and scholar has made India his or her destination in the recent years. In that chain a fourteen year old piano prodigy Assya Korepanova arrived in New Delhi in March 2000 to enthral audiences in packed houses. Her first concert tour was two years earlier to Kolkata, where she had performed to capacity halls. Another pilgrim from Russia to the hoary land of India the same month was a painter, Natalia E. Surina. She confessed that India fascinated her no end and she loved to capture the spirit of the Himalayas on her canvas. She travelled through this country quite a bit and loved the Indian ambience.

Dr. Eugenia Vanina, Head of the History and Cultural Section of the Oriental Studies in Moscow, who came on a visit to Delhi had many interesting things to say about the crave for Indology in Russia. According to her the first translation of the Bhagwad Gita from English to Russian was published as far back as in 1788. Vallathol, Subramania Bharati, Munshi Prem Chand and Tagore - have all been translated into Russian. The translated versions of the Rig-Veda, Ramayana and Mahabharata are also immensely popular in Russia. Interestingly, the founding father of Russian indology, Lebedev, lived among the people in Kolkata in the late 18th century, which gave him an insight into the Indian culture and traditions. According to B. Kannan, he learnt Sanskrit under the tutelage of Indian families and in return taught them how to play the cello. Amir Khusroj

Ghalib, Faiz all of them are available in Russian translations. Even "The God of Small Things' by Arundhati Roy has been translated into Russian. Dr. Vanina has completed an anthology of 'Voices from Medieval India' featuring Somadev, Namdev, Tuka Ram and Mira Bai among others.

A young Russian painter, Ekaterina Smirnova on her long cherished visit to India described it a dream come true. She visited Kolkata, Puri, Konark, Bhubaneswar, Jaipur, Agra, Khajuraho and Delhi. Another young Russian artist, Sasha came to India in the following month to put up an exhibition.

India's Minister for Human Resource Development, Dr. Murli Manohar Joshi was elected Honorary Member of the Russian Academy of Natural Sciences, St. Petersburg in July 2001. He joined a galaxy of international Scientists including 24 Nobel Prize winners, who made up the membership of that prestigious institute. A year earlier he had delivered a talk at the Moscow University.

A Moscow trio of violinists Vladimir Ivanov and Elena Chvertok and pianist Natalia Gavrilova enthralled a packed house at Bombay in October 2001. In April 2002, a Russian film festival depicting films paying tribute to the Russian cinematographer Andrei Tarkovsky was held at India International Centre, New Delhi.

It may not be a very well known fact in India, but the truth is that Indian cuisine is very much in demand in Russia. The two Indian restaurants in Moscow Jaltarang and Bombay are highly popular. As per Vladimir Shreter, who returned to Russia after a decade long stay in India, he is highly appreciative of Indian food. There are many other restaurants which cater to the taste of many a gourmet of a large variety of Indian dishes.

To mark the 55 years of Indo-Russian diplomatic relations, a performance by the musicians of the Bolshoi theatre was held in New Delhi. Almost at the same time Alexander Kalashkov and Valentina Igoshina were regaling an audience with their violin and piano performance. Kalashkov said that the age of Raj Kapoor and his films is past and though Indian films generate interest, it is nothing compared to the yesteryears.

A Moscow dance troupe - the Russian Soul - gave a delightful performance in New Delhi on the 29th November, 2002. They came here under a bilateral cultural exchange programme. Liudmila Nikolaeval the lead singer set the tone with a reflection that she known India as the home of Raj Kapoor and fondly remembers Mera Joota hai Japani. A quartet from Russia a part of the gala 'From Russia with Love' performed for a week in

India's and capital, as also at Kolkata and Hyderabad.

The opening of an Indian cinema club in Moscow added a new chapter in the onward march of the Indo-Russian cultural commonality. This club was inaugurated in the Film Museum in Moscow with an avowed purpose of popularizing Indian art films among Russians. In the early years of India's independence, Satyajit Ray had launched a cinema club named after the great Soviet film director Sergei Aijenstine in Kolkata to popularise Soviet films in India. Though the Indian art films are not as popular as the commercial films in this country, the object of the Indian cinema club in Moscow was to give the maximum space to the art films. The screening of each film in the club is followed by a discussion with the participation of film critics specialists and fans. During the golden jubilee year of India's independence, film festivals across Russia were organised, in which Richard Attenborough's momentous saga of Mahatma Gandhi's life and nonviolence was the centerpiece. According to India Abroad News Service, the festival travelled to cities like St. Petersburg, Krasnoyarsk, Voronezh, Tver and Ufa.

Russian folk-dancers performed at a cultural programme at Faridkot on the 23rd September, 1998 on the occasion of the Birth anniversary of the sufi saint, Baba Farid. A Russian dancer Michael Krevchak performed 'Shiv Tandav in New Delhi on the 15th October, 1998. The great grandson of Leo Tolstoy, Vladimir delivered a lecture on Leo Tolstoy and Gandhiji at a function organised by the Sarvoday International Trust in New Delhi on the 19th October, 1908 in which he pointed out similarities in the character of the two great men. Both of them understood the privations of the underprivileged and downtrodden. Tolstoy's anti-war feelings got consolidated and translated into his philosophy of non-replication of force, which was very close to Gandhiji's philosophy of non-violence, Vladımir said.

Some post -modernist Artists like Vishnyah Vishnyak, Eugeny Kuznetsov, Valery Bokhin and others appeared in New Delhi on the 12th March, 1999. They brought a basket of their painting to put them on show. Some young artists from took part in the -painting contest organised by the Nehru Bal Samiti and the Indo – Russian Council the for child Development on the 5th May, 1999 in India's capital. As a part of an understanding between the two countries, the Russian International Children's Defence. Day was celebrated here with a dance competition.

A Russian Sufi dance teacher, Lyudmila Tavana Of chiniki came to India twice - in 1998 and 2001. She produced n movie which took her to the backwaters of Karala, the Taj Mahal at Agra, Mumbai and Hardwar. She found spiritual solace in Rishikesh and is in quest for learning Buddhism at Bodh Gaya.

A group or Russians travelled to Punjab and Chandigarh, to learn more about the Sikh faith. A Russian artist played the Guslio, a rare instrument in front of a painting of -the tenth guru, Guru Gobind Singh. In November 2001 a young Russian girl from Kazan, a small town on the Volga with the name of Svetlana, Gatina, and joined the Gandharva Mahavidyalaya. Having got immersed in Hindustani vocal music, she plans to do Ph.D. in the same.

The kaleidoscope of Indo-Russian cultural relation is throbbing with currents of brightness. Many hues are being added to it with the passage of time. With a genuine desire on the part of the people in both the countries to add more substance and meaning to their mutual bonds, cultural kinship would be the best guarantee of forging Listing relationships.

References

1. India and the Soviet Unions Cooperation and Development edited by Rasheeduddin Khan, D.D.Narula, Z.Zuberi Sudipta Kaviraj; Soviet-Indian Cultural Relations by M.P. Babkina, S.L.Potabenko, Allied Publishers 1975.
2. Rabindranath Tagore, Letters from Russia, Visva-Bharati, Calcutta, 1960.
3. Collected Works of Mahatma Gandhi, Vol. V, Delhi.
4- Modern Review, 1918, June.
5. The Political Future of India, 1921, p. 20.
6. The Discovery of India, London, 1956.
7- India and the Soviet Union: Indology in USSR, V.V. Balabushevich, A.H.Wafa, 1975.
8. The Great Indian Mutiny, A.M. Osipov, 1857-59, Moscow.
9. Selected Works by Russian Indologists (Philology), Moscow, 1962.
10. Modern Indian Culture, Edited by M.P. Babkin, A.D. Litman, E.P. Chelyshev, Moscow, 1966.
11. Soviet Russia, Jawaharlal Nehru, Bombay, 1929.
12. The Russian Review, Vol. 25, 1966.

13. The Rlussian Panorama, K. P. S. Menon, Bombay, 1962.
14. Russian Revolution, R.S. Avasthy, Kanpur, 1920.
15. The Rebirth of Russia, S.D. Vidyalankar, Banaras, 1921.
16. Mera Rusi Safarnama, Nagendra Pal Singh, Ludhiana.
17. India and the Soviet Union - a symposium, Ed. By V. V. Babushevich, Bimla Prasad, People's Publishing House, 1969.
18. Festival of USSR in India 1987/88, Delhi diary.
19. India's Relations with Russia and China - A New Phase, Ed. by M. Rasgotra, V.D.Chopra Gyan Publishing House, 1997.
20. New Theme Vol V. Issue No. 3 July-September 2002.
21. Druzhba - Dosti, The Festivals, Allied Publishers Ltd. p. 1987.
22. Novaya Vesna - The New Spring, Issue 1, Vol 1, October 2002.
23. New Theme Vol V Issue No. 1 January-March 2002.
24. News from Russia Vol. VI, No. 4, 24 January, 2003.
25. New Theme Vol. V. Issue No. 4 October-December 2002.
26. The Asian Age, 21st October 1998.
27. The Sunday Statesman, 27 December 1998.
28. The Hindustan Times, From Russia with Love, Pankaj Tuli, 12 March 1999.
29. The Hindu, 6 May, 1999.
30. The Statesman, 10 September, 1999.
31. The Hindu, 24 February, 2001.
32. The Hindustan Times, From Moscow, with a Sufi Spin, Asmita Aggarwal, 23 April, 2001.
33. The Hindu, Depicting the Spirit of India, 24 October, 2001.
34. The Asian Age, Windows, 9 November, 2001.
35. HT City, Sight & Sound, 10 November, 2001.
36. The Hindu, The life and times of Nikolai. Roerich, 6 October, 2002.
37. The Pioneer, Master as the Muse, Sudhakaran, 15 October, 2002.
38. The Times of India, 4 March, 1999.

39. The Statement, 23 August, 1998.
40. The Hindu, 9 September, 1997.
41. The Statement, 26 January, 1998.
42. The Indian Express, 24 September, 1998.
43. The Hindu, 6 February, 2000.
44. The Hindu, 28 March, 2000.
45. The Pioneer, PK savours creativity in the city of Czars, Chandan Mitra, 6th November, 2001.
46. The Hindu, Indian Cultural Centre Opens in Russia, Vladimir Radyuhin, 2 April, 2001.
47. HT City, 9 March, 2002.
48. The Asian Age, 5 May, 1999.
49. The Asian Age, 2 March, 2000.
50. The Asian Age, 16 March, 2000.
51. The Pioneer, A pirouette with sparkling life, 5 February, 1998.
52. The Asian Age, 30 January, 1999.
53. The Hindustan Times, 21 March, 1998.
54. The Pioneer, Roerich's Legacy, P.T.Bopanna, 10 February, 2002.
55. The Hindustan Times, The Passion of Rhythm about the Russian Soul, -30 November, 2002.
56. The Hindu, A rich Indology in Russia, K.Kannan, 27 May, 2000.
57. The Pioneer, 3 September, 2000.
58. The Asian Age, 28 May, 2001
59. The Hindustan Times, 29 July, 2001
60. The Hindustan Times, 4 October, 2001
61. The Asian Age, 13 April, 2002
62. The Pioneer, 8 June, 2002
63. The Hindustan Times, 30 November, 2002.
64. The Hindustan Times, 19 February, 1999.
65. The *Hindu,* 24 September, 1998.

66. The Hindustan Times, 8 August, 1999.

67- The Asian Age, 16 January, 1998.

68. The Hindu, 29 January, *1998.*

69. Studies in Indo-Soviet Relations, Ed. by V. D. Chopra, Patriot Publishers, New Delhi, 1986.

70. India Through the eyes of Soviet Poets, V. M. Ashitkov, 1987.

24

India's Relations with Russia Rooted in History

V. D. Chopra

India in the early 21st century has become a focus of international attention more than ever before. Last over five decades and a half, since India became politically independent, have witnessed tremendous changes in the socio-economic base of the country and there upon in its political structure – political system and political parties. In fact, the last over 55 years will go down in the history of India as an era of change – change hitherto unprecedented in scale and depth. This has altered the entire course of the history of the Indian people because they have not only become masters of their destiny but have already begun to play a significant role, influencing world events and moulding world-situation. It is, therefore, but natural that every major power in the world should have started watching India from close quarters.

India is the seventh largest country in the world and next to China has the highest population on our planet. It is well marked off from the rest of Asia by mountains and seas which give the country a distinct geographical identity. Bounded by the great Himalayas in the north, it stretches southwards and at the Tropic of Cancer, shrinks off into the Indian Ocean.

Such a vast country and that too being so densely populated and lying entirely in the northern hemisphere, obviously has a strategic position in the geopolity of the present-day world. A casual look at India's geographical location on the world map immediately brings home the fact of her enviable importance. The Himalayas and other lofty mountain ranges of Muztagh Ata, Aghil and Kunlun to the north of Kashmir and south-eastern portion of Zaskar mountains to the east of Himachal Pradesh form India's northern boundary. She is adjoined in the north by China, Nepal and Bhutan. A series of mountain ranges in the east separate India from Burma. Also in the east, lies Bangladesh, bounded by the Indian States of West Bengal, Assam, Meghalaya, Tripura and Mizoram. In the north-west, Afghanistan and Pakistan border on India. South of the Tropic of Cancer, the country tapers off into the Indian Ocean between the Arabian Sea on the West and the Bay of Bengal on the East. The Gulf of Manner and the Palk Strait separate India from Sri Lanka. The Andaman and Nicobar Islands in the Bay of Bengal and Lakshadweep in the Arabian Sea are parts of the territory of India.

Geopolitical location and its population apart, one thing that stands out clearly and unmistakably is that long before most parts of the world had embarked upon the path of civilisation, India could already boast of culture and progress with millennia of human endeavour behind it. Perhaps these civilisations flourished in the third millennium before Christ. The mystery of the ancient Indian culture remains a mystery even today because the distinction between 'history' and 'pre-history' is peculiarly elusive in her case. None can fully reconstruct the story of the culture that once thrived in this great country. Though writing was known and employed in India in the third and second millennia B.C., the exclusive script has yet to be deciphered in a meaningful way. It is recognised fact, however, that along with Persia, Mesopotamia, and Egypt, India was one of the most important centres on the globe where the civilisation-processes were initiated and matured.

No wonder then, India and its cultural achievements has started shaping the evolution of human thought, even during the unrecorded periods of history, by forging contacts with other areas and people.

Mohenjo-Daro and Harappa are outstanding examples of what was once Indus Valley Civilisation. That this civilisation takes its rank with the great ages of the Valleys of the Nile, the Tigris and the Euphrates, and had witnessed the rise of the ancient civilisations of Egypt, Assyria and Babylonia are indisputable facts. Its people knew the art of laying out towns and claimed a highly developed culture. Cotton and woollen fabrics were in common use; ornaments were worn both by men and women; polished pottery was produced; the sculptor's technique was fashioned. The carpenter, mason, blacksmith, goldsmith, jeweller, stone-cutter and the ivory worker had flourishing trade and religion with its system of rituals prevailed. The Indus Valley Civilisation is believed to be older than the culture of the Vedic age. While the Vedic Aryans were rural, the people of this valley possessed the amenities of developed town-life. Some hold that they were the same as the Sumerians, while others opine that they were in fact the Dravidians who at one time inhabited the whole of India, including the modern Punjab, the Sind and Baluchistan and had even migrated to Mesopotamia. The Dravidian language is still spoken by the Brahui people of Baluchistan and this further lends support to the original view. But Mohenjo-Daro and Harappa maintain a serene silence, like the inscrutable Sphinx, at the labours of the scholars. Darkness envelopes several succeeding centuries.

The most remarkable of the epic poems of ancient India are the Ramayana and Mahabharata which were written down far later, between the fourth century B.C. and the fourth century A.D. However, the main subject matter of these poems and many of the stories that went into their making undoubtedly stem from the first half of the first millennium B.C.

Both the Ramayana and the Mahabharata are extremely well integrated works, no mosaics consisting of a variety of texts, but unified works, each being a compositional whole. The authorship of the Mahabharata is traditionally ascribed to Vyasa and that of the Ramayana to the poet Valmiki but nothing definite is known about these poets or seers (*rishis*).

These poems are veritable encyclopedias of ancient India. They contain most interesting and informative material on various aspects of social and cultural life, political organisation and philosophical systems of the ancient Indians. It would be no exaggeration to say that these poems have been unrivalled in popularity in India. But what is most significant is that in olden times and in the middle ages they were famed far beyond India's frontiers – in Eastern and Southern Asia and in the Far and Middle East. Translations of the Mahabharata and the Ramayana into a number of European languages were widely acclaimed. Many outstanding figures in the history of Western and Oriental culture, like Beethovan, Heine, Rodin, Gandhi, Tagore and Nehru drew inspiration from them.

It would be true to say that even in the earlier periods, India maintained close links with neighbouring and distant countries. These contacts were developed and consolidated over the centuries and Indian culture penetrated other ethno-cultural zones and a process of mutual cultural enrichment ensued.

The earliest and deepest of these cultural ties were those linking India and Iran, for they can be traced as far back as the Neolithic times. The ancient Indians and Iranians were closely related people, ethnically as well as linguistically. The period of particularly close Indo-Iranian ties began after the formation of the Achaemenid Empire when certain areas of North-Western India were integrated with that empire. Achaemenid-culture (architecture and sculpture) made a great impact on the development of

Indian art during the Mauryan age. Buddhism spread to Iran from India and many Indian scientific achievements and works of art became known there.

Recent excavations made by Soviet archaeologists in Central Asia show that there existed direct links between the southern parts of Central Asia and India as early as the Harappan age and these became particularly deeper in the Kushana period. Central Asian influence took birth in India as the Kushana and the Shakas extended their sway while Buddhism and other aspects of India's religion, culture and philosophy spread to Central Asia in turn.

Judging by the inscription found in Central Asia, a large number of monasteries had been built during the Kushana and Gupta periods. The most striking demonstration of this is provided by the Buddhist monasteries at Kara-Tepeh (near Termez, in the first century A.D.) and in Ajina – Tepeh (Southern Tajikistan, seventh century A.D.).

In the earlier centuries A.D., trade links between India and China grew apace; these were established by way of the Great Silk Route and also by sea. Indian embassies and Buddhist missions were sent to China. In the third century A. D., Buddhist monasteries appeared in China and translations of Buddhist writings into Chinese were undertaken.

Indian culture exercised a strong influence on literature, architecture and religion of a large number of countries. At a very early stage, India began trading with many countries of South-East Asia and later Indian settlements appeared in some of them. The settlers popularised the Sanskrit language in these regions and enriched them with the many achievements of Indian culture.

At the time of the Harappan civilisation, trade and cultural ties were established with the Sumerians. Later, the Indians engaged in overseas trade with Arabia and Africa and consolidated links with countries bordering the Mediterranean, particularly with Egypt.

A new era in relations between India and the west began after the campaign of Alexander the Great, when the Greeks came to acquire first-hand knowledge of India and her culture. During the Kushana period ties between India and Rome grew stronger; Indian embassies bearing rich gifts were sent to Rome and the Romans set up trading centers in Southern India.

The influence of ancient Greece and Rome made itself felt particularly deep when Indo-Greek states were established in North-Western India, and then later in the Kushana period. It was reflected in the art of the period (Gandhara Sculpture), in science and philosophy. Certain Indian astronomical treatises dating from the early centuries A.D. indicate that Indian scholars were acquainted with the work of Alexandrian astronomers and one of the siddhantas (astronomical treatises) actually came to be known as the Romakasiddhanta (the Roman siddhanta).

It would be relevant to stress that many crucial questions concerning the universe, man and Nature were posed and solved through mutual exchange by Indian and classical thinkers. This interplay points to the underlying pattern of cultural advance shaped by the processes of historical development in the ancient period. While maintaining and consolidation trade and cultural links with other lands and people over the centuries, India did not fail to preserve her own essential and distinctive culture, philosophy, traditions and social and political institutions. At the same time, she gave to the world freely and generously. The contribution of ancient India to the common heritage of mankind is truly immense.

"A blind reverence for the past is bad so also is a contempt for it, no future can be founded on either of these. The present and the future inevitably grow out of the past and bear its stamp, and to forget this is to build without foundations and to cut off the roots of national growth."

Jawaharlal Nehru

Jawaharlal Nehru underlined this in his book, "*Discovery of India*" in the context of role of nationalism. But he also said that "*group memory* of *past achievements, traditions and experiences*" is one of the most powerful forces that influence people. Thus when we say that India's relations with the other countries, particularly with Russia are rooted in history, one obviously recalls memory of past relations to mind. Though one need not go into details here, there is sufficient proof that cultural and economic relations between India and Russia and with Central Asia go back to thousands of years. A large number of Buddhist architectural complexes, worship places and monasteries dating back to the period ranging from the first centuries A.D. to the Islamic Middle Ages have been discovered in the Central Asian Rupublics – Uzbekistan, Tajikistan, Turkmenia and Kirghizia. This evidence also shows that the Kushan empire extended to the southern regions of what is now Central Asia. At the time of famous Kushan King Kanishka and his successors, Buddhism spilled over from Hindustan to the north of Hindu-Kush.

This would mean that as neighbours, people of Russia and Central Asia have not been only known to each other but have long been making cultural and economic exchanges. A thirteenth century book in Russian is aptly entitled "*The Story of India, the Richi*". In the last quarter of the eighteenth century Gerasim Stepanovich Lebedev, a Russian musician and dramatist made his way to India. He not only learnt Sanskrit and Bengali but also wrote plays in Bengali.

In fact, there are historians who contend that the Aryan tribes were originally inhabiting the region that comprises the present Tajik, Krigizian and Uzbek Republics. They gradually moved across to present Iran, India and Europe. Alexander's route of conquests lay across Uzbekistan. Later, the Kushans too came from the same region of Central Asia. Kanishka's empire covered a good part of North India, Pakistan, Afghanistan and extended well into Tajikistan, Kirghizia and Uzbekistan.

The sweep of Changez Khan and massive Arab invasions followed by Timur's conquests destroyed the Buddhist culture in these parts. Buddhisam had also spread to some tribes residing in Siberia. They received it from Tibet, Ladakh and Mongolia. Ulan-Ude, the capital of Buriat, is a small 'autonomous region' situated on the bank of Baykal lake, on the border of Mongolia. Even today the people there are mostly Buddhists and have much in common with their co-religionists in the Ladakh area.

The whirlwind of Changez Khan swept through many a land. His thrust covered a vast area including Northern India which suffered calamities of plunder and loot alongwith the people of Central Asia. Timur made Samarkand his seat of power and was buried there after his death. His mausoleum is a beautiful piece of architecture and Humayun's tomb and Shah Jahan's Taj Mahal were probably inspired by this design.

From the fifteenth century, European imperialism was spreading its tentacles in many directions. While India was subjugated finally by the British, the Czar's empire extended to Turkestan. From then on inter-relations between India and Russia were excluded to a large degree by European politics. The mighty powers of Europe had their own wars and peace treaties in a series of changing fortunes. But by the middle of the 19th century, the British Empire had consolidated itself and incorporated the Punjab, extending its rule right up to Khyber. This brought Russia and Britain face to face in open hostility which continued till the First World War.

This notwithstanding, it appears that from the middle of the 18th century onward, interest of Russian scholars in Indian literature in most of the languages, apart from Sanskrit, kept on steadily increasing. As early as in 1851, a chair of Oriental languages was created in Moscow University and in 1855 a chair of Sanskrit was established at St. Petersburg. Progressive intellectuals and political leaders must have watched with interest India's first War of Independence in 1857. More significantly, a Russian scholar, Ivan Pavlovich Minaev, came to visit India a number of times.

Similarly trade between India and Russia has a history going back to many centuries. In the Middle Ages, Indian pepper, ginger, products of sandalwood and handloom were known well to the Russians. It is likely that for centuries, the overland trade between India, Central Asia, Russia and beyond used to be largely in Indian hands. In the capital of Azerbaijan, Baku the great oil city on the Caspian Sea – a historical monument, a temple of fire worshippers was established hundreds of years ago by Indian merchants who had gone there to develop commerce between the two countries. Again in this city, particularly on the banks of the Caspian Sea, at least two "Sarais" – inns built by Indian traders – exist even now and one of these sarais is still known as the "Multani Sarai". Fortunately, the original architecture and the interior decoration of these sarais has been kept intact. One of them is in use as a tourist resort.

It is against this historical background that the real impact of the October Revolution on India's freedom struggle should be analysed.

25

Conclusion : Indo-Russian Relations-A New Phase

V.D. Chopra

Any one who has objectively examined the recent trends in Indo-Russian relations, Indo-Russian summit in New Delhi in the beginning of December 2002, Delhi and Economic Declarations in particular issued on this occasion, would agree that the relations between the two countries are being elevated to a new height. That in a period of uni-polar world, bilateral and multilateral relations among various nations are being restructure reflect a new trend in international relations, which may pave the way for a multi-polar world order. The real significance of the outcome of Russian President Vladimir Putin's visit to India and of the Delhi Indo-Russian summit should be seen in this context. There is something more to it. The Centre of gravity of world's economy and politics have already shifted to the Asia-Pacific region. In this sense Indo-Russian relations and the growing trend of trilateral cooperation among the three major countries of the region-Russia, China and India are developments of far reaching importance, though these relationships should not be seen as a new emerging military alliance. Its real significance is rooted in convergence of their larger national interests.

The harsh reality is that in the beginning of the present century organised terrorism and religious fundamentalism are threatening the stability of a large number of countries and in this sense it is the most dangerous development in world politics. President A.P.J. Abdul Kalam in his banquet speech on the occasion of President Putin's visit recalled how the Russian President Putin on his previous visit to India had referred to the "arc of instability" stretching from the Caucasus to Southeast Asia. The Indian President pointedly mention that "the epicenter of this arc is of course in our common neighbourhood". President Putin was equally forthright when in a strong and clear message, he asked Pakistan to put a stop to infiltration across the Line of Control in Jammu and Kashmir and liquidate terror infrastructure within its boundaries. He further said "Islamabad should cut all routes of infiltration across the Line of Control and increase its efforts to dismantle terror infrastructure in the region" at a press conference in New Delhi. This assertion by the Russian President has deeper implications because even in the assessment of American experts terrorists outfits of Al-Queda are still intact and are operating from Afghanistan-N.W.F.P. province of Pakistan. Mr. Putin further said the international community should be sensitized on the dangers spread of weapons of mass destruction and it's falling into the hands of terrorists. He obviously had in mind the American intelligence reports that some Pakistani nuclear experts had contact with Bin Laden. That perhaps is the reason that President Putin expressed the fear that Pakistan's weapons of mass destruction could fall into the hands of "bandits and terrorists". The assurances of the Pakistani President Pervez Musharraf on the safety of his country's nuclear weapons did not satisfy him. "We take note of the statements made by President Musharraf that the military potential of his country is safely protected strictly under control. But to be frank, our concerns our anxiety, still persist", he underlined.

Prime Minister Vajpayee went out of his way on this occasion to highlight that India and Russia had agreed to intensify their wider level bilateral cooperation against terrorism in multilateral fora. He said the recent terrorist attacks in various parts of India, Bali (Indonesia), Russia and Mombassa (Kenya) had shown that terrorism was seeking ever newer targets and this was a cause for concern. This brings into focus how convergence of understanding about terrorism between the two countries had further deepened.

Another significant achievement of this summit was that the concept of "strategic partnership" between India and Russia was not only reiterated but given a concrete content. This has to be seen in the context of the fact that there are no areas of conflict or interests between the two countries.

"Fundamental and lasting importance of the treaty of friendship and cooperation between India and Russian of 28 January 1993" is as relevant today as before. This strategic partnership has been elevated step by step and in the New Delhi summit, it marked a new watershed. The basic concept of this strategic partnership is based on holding of "annual summit level meetings' regular bilateral political an foreign office consultations on issues of mutual concern; closer cooperation at the United Nations, including its specialised agencies and institutions, at other international and regional fora; further intensifying their efforts aimed at strengthening international peace and security, general and complete disarmament, systematic and progressive efforts to reduce nuclear weapons globally, with the ultimate goal of eliminating these weapons, nuclear non-proliferation and the peaceful settlement of disputes; joint initiatives on key international and regional issues; informing each other of planned foreign policy initiatives in the international arena". Above all, it lays down "non-participation in any military-political or other alliances or associations or armed conflict directed against" each other. The outcome of the New Delhi summit should be examined in the background of this commonality of understanding between India and Russia.

It is also pertinent to mention here that Russia during this summit supported India's candidature for a permanent seat in the United Nations Security Council. Russia reaffirmed "its support to India as a deserving and strong candidate for the permanent membership in an expanded UN Security Council".

A constant factor in Indo-Russian relationship has been the defence cooperation and supply of defence equipment critical for India's defence needs. Some problems arose in the arrangements for supply of defence equipment in the aftermath of the break up of the Soviet Union but these were rapidly overcome. Mr. Putin's visit in the first week of October 2000 finally reopened the way for supply of critical defence items and weaponry to India. The contracts signed with India in the past for licensed production of T 90 C tanks amounted to $ 700 million and $ 1.5 billion for SU-30 MKK fighter for instance. It was expected that the deal on Admiral Gorshkow would be finalised during this summit. Russia has offered this aircraft carrier free of charge, but major differences persist over the cost of retrofitting the vessel.

The bilateral defence relationship included joint research and development, scientist to scientist interaction and service to service contacts between the two countries have begun to take a concrete shape. President Dr. Kalam, for instance, pointed out at a banquet that "the joint supersonic cruise missile is a unique example for the partnership between our two countries in critical areas of research and development". This shows Indo-Russian cooperation in this strategic area is growing. This is further confirmed by the fact India and Russia have signed a protocol under which exports of armament system manufactured in India under license from Russia to third countries will be considered on a case by case basis. Hindustan Aeronautics Limited (HAL) had already exported MiG-21 spares to 17 countries under various agreements this protocol would enable future exports of missiles and spares of advanced fighter jets.

Nevertheless the weakest link in Indo-Russian relations is in the area of economic cooperation. However, Russia is once again emerging as an economic power with its vast natural resources, crude oil, diamonds and its defence manufacturing industries on one hand and expanding internal market on the other. This opens new potentialities for Indo-Russian economic cooperation.

A five-year trade agreement was signed between India and Russia in May 1992 which marked the end of Rupee trade from January 1993 and ushered a new phase of convertible currency trade. India also extended a line of credit of Rs.250 crore for the purpose of financing India's exports of tea, coffee and tobacco to Russia. Indian debt to Russia was to be repaid to the extent of Rs. 3,000 crore annually through exports of goods and services. The Indian debt was evaluated at Rs. 31,377 crore out of this, Rs. 11,733 crore carrying an average rate of interest of 2.4 per cent was to be repaid in 12 years. The remaining Rs. 19,044 crore carrying a nil rate of interest was to be repaid in 45 years beginning April 1993. This another measure laid the basis for restructuring the economic relations between India and Russia in the new conditions. Indo-Russian trade however has not registered a marked change and there are various reasons for this, including tuff competition from Western countries and poor image, which India has created in the minds of Russian consumers. Now fresh attempts are being made to rebuild Indo-Russian economic relations and some of the Indian private sector companies have again begun to tap the Russian market. In a bid to boost flagging bilateral trade, India and Russia have now agreed to explore joint possibilities of regional trade and economic cooperation agreements with other countries. The moral of the situation is that the two countries should evolve a concrete policy to boost trade and economic cooperation because in the final analysis, this will provide long-term basis for strengthening the bilateral relations.

Index

N

P

S

T